The Wordsworth Book of the
Kings & Queens of Britain

Beth.

Happy Birthday

love from

RJb

(Just in case you
had forgotten — a
little reminder!)

The Wordsworth Book of the
Kings & Queens of Britain

—

G. S. P. Freeman-Grenville

Wordsworth Reference

The edition published 1997 by Wordsworth Editions Ltd
Cumberland House, Crib, Street, Ware, Hertfordshire SG12 9ET

Text copyright © G. S. P. Freeman-Grenville 1997
All other material copyright © Wordsworth Editions Ltd 1997

ISBN 1 85326 395 8

Typeset by Antony Gray
Printed and bound in Great Britain by
Mackays of Chatham plc, Chatham, Kent

In affectionate memory of

REX COLLINGS

publisher

1925–1996

CONTENTS

THE WORDSWORTH BOOK OF
THE KINGS & QUEENS OF BRITAIN

PREFACE

At the the time of the Queen's Silver Jubilee the late Rex Collings suggested that I should write an account of the *Queen's Lineage*. The present book expands this with accounts of individual rulers, at his request and that of Michael Trayler of Wordsworth Editions.

After an Introduction it contains an account of the Saxon kings, mostly shadowy figures, tracing their line from Cerdic, first King of Wessex. The Danish kings and the House of Godwin follow. The lineage of the Dukes of Normandy is included, because of the relationship they developed with the French nobility and the Saxon kings. From then on are thumbnail sketches of the life of every king and queen-regnant from William the Conqueror until George VI.

There are three appendices: the rulers of Ireland, and then of Wales; the Kings of Scotland from Kenneth MacAlpin up to James VI of Scotland, I of England. He had inherited both crowns, without uniting them. Under him, and the following Stuart kings of England, the sovereign ruled with a separate Privy Council and Parliament for Scotland, until the Act of Union, 1707, which united Scotland and England as Great Britain. Some maps have been included where wars are more easily illustrated by their movements, based on my *Atlas of British History, from Prehistoric Times until 1978*, 1979. The genealogical tables are shown dynasty by dynasty from Cerdic until the grandchildren of Her present Majesty.

The work is not primarily concerned with politics, but rather with the character and actions of the sovereigns, so far as we can perceive them. An extraordinarily stable institution emerges, defying innumerable changes of fashion and political thinking. Cerdic, in fact a successful tribal chieftain, would hardly recognise the red boxes carried daily to one or other royal palace or their purpose. The institution has undergone change after change, with remarkable adaptability. Isolated by their office, Cerdic's successors have been men and women of special character, some intelligent, some pedestrian, some imprudent and rash, others sophisticated and steady. Few can be said not to have possessed, to use a greatly overworked word, *charisma*. Many came to the throne before they reached maturity. A curious and understandable feature is that so many were at odds with their predecessors. Almost all have shown great qualities of courage and endurance. Often they have reflected the vices as well as the virtues of their age. Isolated, mostly subjected from their earliest years to the adulation of courtiers, trapped in dynastic marriages, it is hardly surprising that so many have fallen for other allurements. There is still a fundamental, rocklike stability, of devotion to duty and of purpose. It is strange that, in little over two centuries, of some forty American presidents, one in ten has been assassinated; of a total of forty-six sovereigns in a period of nearly one thousand years, only one has been executed, only two have abdicated, only four have been deposed, only four have been murdered, and only one has fled.

I must express my gratitude to Alec Hornsby for his patience in setting the work on computer.

G. S. P. F-G.
Sheriff Hutton

INTRODUCTION

This book celebrates nearly a millennium and a half of English rulers since AD 495. In all that time there has been an almost unbroken family succession. Only five rulers – Sweyn, Canute I, Harold I, Harold II, and William I the Conqueror – have not descended from Cerdic, who led the West Saxons into England in 495. In 519, in the words of the *Anglo-Saxon Chronicle*, 'he undertook the government of the West Saxons . . . From that day forth there have reigned the children of the West Saxon kings.'

As King of Wessex Cerdic had a sacred character, claiming to be ninth in descent from Woden (or Wotan, or Odin), the German High God of the Sky. A similar descent was claimed by the six other Kings in England, whose descendants the Kings of Wessex overcame, thus uniting the country. This was achieved in 828, when Cerdic's successor Egbert received homage as King of All England. At some period before this the sovereign had been given a sacred Christian character by a solemn blessing and coronation. The earliest known ritual to survive is the mid-eighth-century Pontifical of Archbishop Egbert of York. We do not know when the practice first originated. Nor do we know when a solemn anointing with oil first preceded the act of crowning, where David's anointing by the prophet Samuel was recalled, and that of Solomon by Zadok the priest and Nathan the prophet. Substantially the same words were said at the coronation of Queen Elizabeth II in 1953:

> As Solomon was anointed king by Zadok the priest and Nathan the prophet, so be thou anointed, blessed and consecrated Queen over the Peoples, whom the Lord thy God hath given thee to rule and govern.

These words thus span a millennium and a half of monarchy. No other western country has so stable a record; no other monarchy is so venerable or has proved so adaptable to changing conditions.

The tale of the history of the eighty-one sovereigns since Cerdic, from the small beginnings in Wessex to the present Headship of the Commonwealth, is longer and more complex than any person is likely to bear in mind. The object of this book is simply to present the backbone of the story, the lineage of the Kings and Queens who have ruled England, and the Scottish line of Kings which, in the person of James VI of Scotland, I of England, united the thrones. As the story unfolds, there are also brief sections on the lineage of the Dukes of Normandy, a thousand-year-old title still borne by the Queen when she visits the Channel Islands, the last of the original Norman possessions.

There are eleven tables, the first ten for the English royal lineage from the King of Wessex to the House of Windsor, including their marriages and those of their sons and daughters, but thereafter only those of their descendants who have affected the fortunes of the throne. In all cases they have been given the names by which they are generally known. It has not been thought necessary to include the lineage of members of the peerage who are of royal descent, nor the numerous descendants of Queen Victoria who married into many of the royal houses of Europe. Both these have been briefly indicated when their earliest royal ancestor is mentioned. In Table 10, however, some exceptions have been made to show the more immediate heirs to the throne.

Table 11 shows the lineage of the Kings of Scotland, who, after Malcolm III's marriage to Saint Margaret, granddaughter of Edmund II Ironside, were all descended from Cerdic.

Since the Act of Settlement of 12 June 1701 the royal succession has been regulated by strict primogeniture. The monarch's male heirs succeed in order of birth, and, failing them, the female heirs: a woman can succeed only in default of male heirs to her father. This has not always been so, and different rules have prevailed at different times. Not infrequently the rules of custom have been far from clear. It is necessary to say something about them if the tables are to be understood.

All the tables show first the sons in order of their birth, and then the daughters in their order. The principles of succession of the Kings of Wessex are unclear (Table 1), the more so because we do not know the relationship of five of the eighteen rulers to the rest. Among the Saxon kings (Table 2) there appears a succession of four brothers in the third generation, albeit Edward had a son who was passed over. Saint Edward the Confessor came to the throne not only as his father's son, but at the request of the Witanagemot, or Council of Wise Men: it might seem that there was a process of election. The Witanagemot did the same after Harold II's death at Hastings in 1066, when they summoned Edgar Atheling, grandson of Edmund II Ironside. The choice was abortive because William the Conqueror steadily won over members of the Witanagemot to himself. In his succession other principles emerge. He claimed the throne by designation of Edward the Confessor in 1051: in right of this the future Harold II is shown by the Bayeux Tapestry kneeling in homage to William in 1064. William's wife, Matilda, was a remote descendant of Alfred the Great; and, by blood only, for he was born illegitimate, William was the great-nephew of Ethelred the Unready by virtue of his marriage with Emma of Normandy in 1002. Edward the Confessor was their son. Thus both William and his wife were cousins. Harold's only claim was the allegation that Edward the Confessor had devised the crown to him on his deathbed. It was this wish which at first the Witanagemot had accepted.

William's succession to Normandy was by his father's designation and by the acceptance of the Norman nobility: they had passed over the possible claims of the heirs of surviving legitimate male heirs of the third son of Richard I, 3rd Duke of Normandy in favour of the illegitimate William. This was fully in accord with Norman feudal custom. Subsequently William was legitimated by the Pope; his title to the throne of England was accepted fully when he was crowned in Westminster Abbey on 25 December 1066, by right of conquest. This itself established a precedent.

On his deathbed William I appointed his eldest son, Robert, as Duke of Normandy, and designated his next surviving son, William II, as King of England. On William II's death Robert was heir presumptive to England, but the throne was seized successfully by the youngest brother, Henry I. He had lost no time in seizing the Treasury.

At this stage the possibility of a woman succeeding to the throne became an actuality, for Henry I left only a female heir, Matilda. The nearest surviving heir of the line was a grandson of the Conqueror, Stephen. A sporadic conflict ensued between her supporters and his from 1135 until 1152, when she resigned the Crown to Stephen for life, but with the provision that her son, Henry II, should succeed him. Thus, failing a direct male heir, a male heir through a woman might succeed. The problem did not arise until 300 years later, in Tudor times.

Henry II's Plantagenet successors followed by male primogeniture from 1154 until 1399. The heir presumptive was Edmund, 5th Earl of March (see Table 4), whose grandmother, Philippa, Countess of Ulster, had been recognised during her lifetime as heir presumptive of Richard II. On 30 May 1399 Henry IV, a grandson of Edward III in the direct male line, usurped the throne from Richard II. It was the first of a series of actions that led to the Wars of the Roses, a struggle too complex even to outline here.

There were three monarchs of the House of Lancaster (Table 5), and three of the House of York (Table 6). The two houses were ultimately united by Henry VII, a scion of the House of Lancaster. His claim by right of conquest was indisputable even if it was otherwise tenuous. His succession was buttressed in 1486 by his marriage to Elizabeth of York, whose claim to be heir of her brother, Edward V, was beyond dispute. Henry's own claim was by descent from John of Gaunt and Katherine Swynford, whose children were born in adultery. They were legitimatised by statute in 1397 after their parents' marriage, but allegedly were debarred from the throne. However this may be, there were heirs of John of Gaunt senior in line to Henry VII in the royal line of Portugal. The right of conquest was not disputed.

Henry VIII's failure to provide an heir other than Edward VI led to his six marriages. Although Mary I and Elizabeth I were declared bastards when the marriages of their mothers were declared null, they were nevertheless recognised as heirs to the throne in that order, failing Edward VI, in 1543. Four years later, when Henry VIII died, his Will passed them over in favour of his younger sister Mary, Queen Dowager of France and Duchess of Suffolk. He passed over his elder sister Margaret, and her descendants, because she had married James IV of Scotland. It was thought unfitting that the throne should pass to a foreigner, nor was there any suggestion of uniting the Crowns.

Mary's granddaughter and heir was Lady Jane Grey, who reigned for eleven days in 1553; it was in accordance also with Edward VI's appointment of her as his heir by Letters Patent. She had too little public support to make good her claim. In the event, following Elizabeth I's death in 1603, James VI of Scotland ascended the throne as heir to Margaret, Henry VII's elder daughter.

The seventeenth century witnessed the struggle between King and Parliament, which Parliament decisively won: it was Parliament which recognised James VI and I's claim by statute, for all his belief in the Divine Right of Kings. It was Parliament, by rebellion, that fought the war that led to Charles I's deposition and compassed his execution. It was Parliament that, when the Protectorate failed, restored Charles II with the support of an army. It was Parliament that proclaimed William III and Mary II as joint rulers on 13 February 1689, after presuming James II's abdication, denying the throne to his son and the subsequent Stuarts of his line, it regulated the succession in the House of Hanover in 1701, following Queen Anne's failure to produce an heir, her many children all having died in infancy.

Since then statute has ordered the succession to the throne by strict primogeniture, prescribing the succession of females in default of male heirs. This has occurred on two occasions. It was Parliament also that in 1936 accepted Edward VIII's abdication after his determination to contract a marriage which did not commend itself to the nation. His last act as Sovereign was to sign the Act himself.

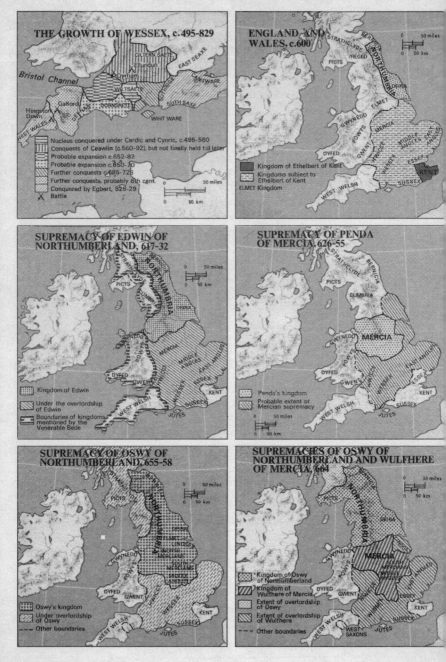

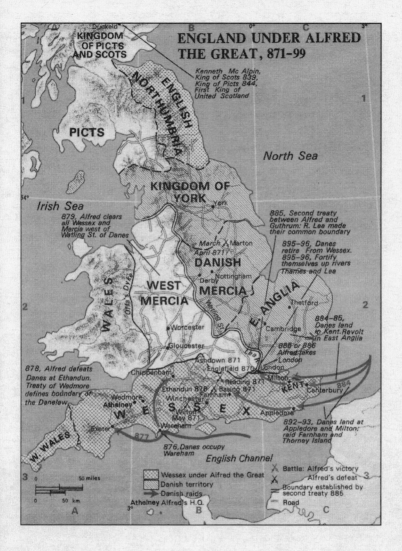

ENGLAND UNDER ALFRED THE GREAT, 871–99

KINGDOM OF PICTS AND SCOTS

Dunkeld

Kenneth Mc Alpin, King of Scots 839, King of Picts 844, First King of United Scotland

ENGLISH NORTHUMBRIA

PICTS

North Sea

Irish Sea

KINGDOM OF YORK

York

879, Alfred clears all Wessex and Mercia west of Watling St. of Danes

885, Second treaty between Alfred and Guthrum: R. Lea made their common boundary

March ✕ Marton April 871

895–96, Danes retire From Wessex. 895–96, Fortify themselves up rivers Thames and Lea

DANISH

Nottingham

WEST MERCIA

Derby

MERCIA

E. ANGLIA

Thetford

WALES

Offa's Dyke

Worcester

Watling St.

Cambridge

884–85, Danes land in Kent. Revolt in East Anglia

Gloucester

885 or 886 Alfred takes London

Ashdown 871 Englefield 870

London

878, Alfred defeats Danes at Ethandun. Treaty of Wedmore defines boundary of the Danelaw

Chippenham

Reading 871

Milton

KENT

884

Ethandun 878 ✕ Basing 871

Canterbury

Wedmore

Farnham

Athelney

Winchester

W E S S E X

Wilton May 871

Appledore

Exeter

877

Wareham

892–93, Danes land at Appledore and Milton; raid Farnham and Thorney Island

W. WALES

876, Danes occupy Wareham

English Channel

50 miles

0   50 km

▨ Wessex under Alfred the Great
▨ Danish territory
➤ Danish raids
Athelney Alfred's H.Q.

✕ Battle: Alfred's victory
✕ Alfred's defeat
═ Boundary established by second treaty 885
═ Road

1   Kings of Wessex

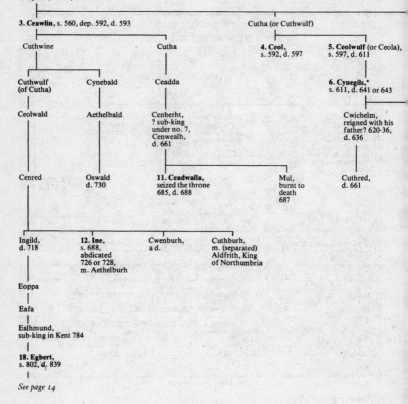

1. Cerdic,
came into Britain 495,
King of the West Saxons 519, d. 534

[? Creoda]

2. Cynric, s. 534, d. 560

3. Ceawlin, s. 560, dep. 592, d. 593   Cutha (or Cuthwulf)

Cuthwine   Cutha   **4. Ceol,**   **5. Ceolwulf** (or Ceola),
                                 s. 592, d. 597   s. 597, d. 611

Cuthwulf   Cynebald   Ceadda   **6. Cynegils,***
(of Cutha)   s. 611, d. 641 or 643

Ceolwald   Aethelbald   Cenberht,   Cwichelm,
                                      ? sub-king   reigned with his
                                      under no. 7,   father? 620-36,
                                      Cenwealh,   d. 636
                                      d. 661

Cenred   Oswald   **11. Ceadwalla,**   Mul,   Cuthred,
                d. 730   seized the throne   burnt to   d. 661
                                685, d. 688   death
                                                           687

Ingild,   **12. Ine,**   Cwenburh,   Cuthburh,
d. 718   s. 688,   a d.   m. (separated)
                 abdicated   Aldfrith, King
                 726 or 728,   of Northumbria
                 m. Aethelburh

Eoppa

Eafa

Ealhmund,
sub-king in Kent 784

18. Egbert,
s. 802, d. 839

See page 14

Ceolwulf
|
Cuthgils
|
Cenferth
|
Cenfus

7. Cenwealh,
s. 641 or 643,
d. 672, m.l, a
sister of Penda,
King of Mercia;
m. 2, no. **8. Queen
Seaxburgh,** s. 672,
dep. 674

10, Centwine,
s. 676, abdicated
and retired to a
monastery 685
|
1 d.

1 d., m. Oswald,
King of
Northumbria

9. Aescwine,
s. 674, d. 676

Cerdic was claimed to be
descended from the god
Woden as follows:
Woden m. Frigga
|
Baeldaeg
|
Brand
|
Frithugar
|
Freawine
|
Wig
|
Gewis (?)
|
Esla
|
Elesa
|
Cerdic

The following kings claimed descent from
Cerdic, but their kinship to the rest is not known:

13. Ethelheard, s. 726 or 728, d. 740, brother of Queen Aethelburh

14. Cuthred, s. 740, d. 756; kinsman of no. 13

15. Sigeberht, s. 756, dep. 757; kinsman of no. 14

16. Cynewulf, s. 757, murdered 786

17. Brihtric, s. 786, d. 802, m. 787 or 789 Eadburh, d. of
Offa of Mercia

*First king to be baptised

2 *Saxon Kings*

Continued from page 12

1. Egbert, King of Wessex 802, King of England 828, d. 4 Feb. 839

2. Ethelwulf, s. 4 Feb. 839, d. 13 Jan. 855,
m.1, Osburgh (d. 852), d. of Oslac, his Cup Bearer; m.2, 1 Oct. 853, Judith, d. of Charles II, King of France, Holy Roman Emperor

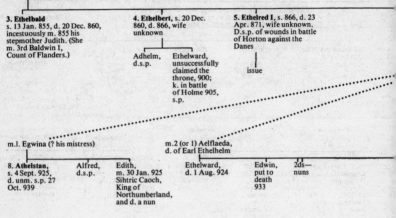

3. Ethelbald
s. 13 Jan. 855, d. 20 Dec. 860,
incestuously m. 855 his
stepmother Judith. (She
m. 3rd Baldwin I,
Count of Flanders.)

4. Ethelbert, s. 20 Dec.
860, d. 866, wife
unknown

Adhelm,
d.s.p.

Ethelward,
unsuccessfully
claimed the
throne, 900;
k. in battle
of Holme 905,
s.p.

5. Ethelred I, s. 866, d. 23
Apr. 871, wife unknown.
D.s.p. of wounds in battle
of Horton against the
Danes

issue

m.1. Egwina (? his mistress)

m.2 (or 1) Aelflaeda,
d. of Earl Ethelhelm

8. Athelstan,
s. 4 Sept. 925,
d. unm. s.p. 27
Oct. 939

Alfred,
d.s.p.

Edith,
m. 30 Jan. 925
Sihtric Caoch,
King of
Northumberland,
and d. a nun

Ethelward,
d. 1 Aug. 924

Edwin,
put to
death
933

2ds—
nuns

Continued from previous page

6. Alfred the Great, b.c. 848, s. 23 Apr. 871, d. 25 Oct. 899, m. 868 Ealswith (d. a nun 904), d. of Ethelred Mucel, Ealdorman of Gaini, and Eadburh, of Mercia

Aethelswith m. Burgred, King of Mercia

7. Edward the Elder, s. 25 Oct. 899, d. 17 July 925

Ethelward, b.c. 880, d. 26 Oct. 922

3 s.

Elfleda, m. 886 Ethelred, Earl of Mercia

Ethelswithe, m. Baldwin II, Count of Flanders (d. 917), d. 7 June 829

issue—from whom descended Matilda, wife of **22. William I the Conqueror**

Ethelgiva, Abbess of Shaftesbury

m. 3 (or 2) Eadgifu, d. of Sigehelm, ealdorman of Kent

Ogiva, m. 917 Charles III the Simple of France (d. 929), having issue; m. 2, c. 951, Herbert III, Count of Vermandois and Troyes (d. 993), and had issue

Eadhilda, m.c. 927 Hugh, Duke of France, d.s.p. *ante* 938

Edith, m. 930 Otto the Great, Duke of Saxony, Holy Roman Emperor, (d. 973), d. 947 leaving issue

Edgiva, m. Eberhard Count of Nordgau (d.c. 960)

9. Edmund I (the Magnificent) b. 921, s. 27 Oct. 940, murdered 26 May 946, m. 940 Edgira

10. Edred, s. 26 May 946, d. 23 Nov. 955

Edgive, m. (?) Conrad, King of Transjuranian Burgundy

issue

Edburga, a nun

11. Edwy the Fair, b. 941, s. 23 Nov. 955, d. 1 Oct. 959, m. (annulled) a cousin, Elgifa, d.s.p.

12. Edgar the Pacific, b.c. 944, usurped Kingdom of Mercia 957, s. 1 Oct. 959, d. 8 July 975

d., name unknown, m. Baldwin, Count of Hesdin

m.1, 961, Ethelfleda, parentage unknown (d. 962)

m. 2 Wulfthryth

m. 3, 964, Elfrida (d. a nun), widow of Earl Ethelwald and d. of Ordgar, ealdorman of Devon

13. Saint Edward II Martyr, b.c. 963, s. 8 July 975, murdered by his stepmother Queen Elfrida 18 March 979 near Corfe Castle s.p.

Edith, Abbess of Wilton

Edmund, Atheling, d.s.p.c. 972

14. Ethelred II

See next page

Continued from previous page

14. Ethelred II the Redeless[1]
b.c. 966, s. 18 March 979, fled to
Normandy 1013, restored 1014,
murdered 23 Apr. 1016

m.1, 984, Elgiva (d. 1002),   m. 2. 1002, Emma, d. of Richard I, 3rd
d. of Earl Thorold of Northumbria   Duke of Normandy (see Table 3); she m.
                                           2, **Canute I** (see 2A)

Athelstan,	Egbert	**16. Edmund II Ironside,**	Eadred	Edwy, 3d.	**20. Saint Edward the**	Alfred,	Goda,
b. 986, k.		b.c. 989, s. 23 Apr.		murdered	**Confessor,** elected	blinded	m.1, Drog
in battle		1016, murdered		1017	King of England by	by Earl	Count of
against		30 Nov. 1016, m.			the Witanagemot	Godwin,	Amiens
the Danes		1015 Algitha,			1042, d.s.p. 5 Jan.	d. in	and Vexin
1011, unm.		widow of Sigfrid,			1066, having left	prison	and had
		a Danish nobleman			as his heir William,	1035	issue, m.
					7th Duke of Normandy,		2, Eustace
					his cousin by blood,		Count of
Edmund, b. 1016,		Edward the Exile, b.			m. 23 Jan. 1045 Edith		Boulogne
m. Agatha, d. of		posthumously 1017, d.			(or Eadgyth), d. of		(d. 1093),
Saint Stephen		1057, m. Agatha, d.			Godwin, Earl of		without
I of Hungary,		of Conrad II of			Wessex (see 2B)		further
d.s.p.		Franconia, Holy Roman					issue
		Emperor					

Edgar Atheling,	Saint Margaret, m. 1068	Christina,
b. 1053, d. unm.	as his 2nd wife Malcolm	Abbess of Romsey,
post 1125,	III, King of Scotland	d. unm.
chosen King	(see Table 11, no. 19)	
of England by	and d. 16 Nov. 1093	
the Witanagemot	leaving issue	
on the death of		
Harold II		

1. Commonly known as 'The Unready'. His nickname
'The Redeless' in fact means that he attempted
to rule without the advice of his council.

2A Kings of the House of Denmark

15. Sweyn, King of Denmark and Norway from 985,
usurper, proclaimed King of England by right
of conquest 1013, d. 3 Feb. 1014, m. Gunhilda,
(d.c. 1015) d. of Mieszko, Duke of Poland

Harold III, King of Denmark 1014, deposed by his brother Canute 1016, d. 1017	**17. Canute I,** b.c. 995, King of Denmark and England, contested the throne of England on the death of his father 1014, received Mercia, E. Anglia and Northumbria by treaty, seized the throne of England 1016, King of Norway by right of conquest 1030-35, d. 12 Nov. 1035,	Thyra, b. 994, m. as his first wife Godwin, Earl of Wessex (see below 2B), and d.c. 1018, leaving issue

m.1, Aelgifu
(whom he repudiated)
(d. 31 Dec. 1044),
d. of Elfhelm,
Earl of
Northampton

m. 2, 1017, Emma, widow of **Ethelred II**
(see above, no. 14)

Sweyn, King of Norway, d. 1036	**18. Harold I Harefoot,** King of England, s. 12 Nov. 1035, d. unm. s.p. 17 March 1040 (cf. 18)	**19. Canute II Hardicanute,** b. 1018, King of Denmark 1035, s. as King of England 17 March 1040, d. unm. s.p. 8 June 1042	Cunigunda, m. 10 June 1036 Henry III of Franconia, Holy Roman Emperor, d. 18 July 1038, leaving issue

2B King of the House of Godwin

Godwin, Earl of Wessex (d. 15 Apr. 1053), son of Wulfnoth, descent unknown,
m. 2, Gythe, a relative of King Canute I, at whose court he was an influential
nobleman

21. Harold II, b.c. 1022, Earl of Wessex 1053, usurped the throne 7 Jan. 1066, k. at Hastings 14 Oct. 1066, leaving 4s. 2d.	Edith (or Eadgyth), d. 19 Dec. 1075, m. 23 Jan. 1045 **Saint Edward the Confessor**

THE SAXON KINGS

The Emergence of the English Monarchy

In AD 410 the Roman Emperor Honorius informed the Britons that they would no longer enjoy the protection of Rome. The legions, which had controlled the country since the conquest in AD 43 now withdrew and left only chaos. There were no government structures left. The Britons were exposed to enemies whom the Romans could no longer afford the troops to contain. Picts raided from the north, and the Scots from Ireland, while Jutes and Saxons attacked the eastern coasts. Shortly the Jutes conquered Kent, while two bands of Saxons took Sussex and then Wessex, while Angles seized the land from Suffolk to the Humber, later East Anglia. Throughout the fifth and sixth centuries the Britons were slowly driven back, into the mountain areas of Cumbria and Wales, and the fastnessess of Cornwall. So Celtic peoples were replaced by Germanic-speaking tribes, who repopulated the country, and absorbed only fragments of the previous population.

Tacitus' *Agricola* describes the peoples of England in the first century AD; and his *Germania* those of Germany. As the facts emerge slowly from the shadows in the sixth and seventh centuries AD much of what he had said about the German tribes remains true. They prided themselves on their freedom and independence. They governed themselves by assemblies, folk-moots, coming together only as convenience or necessity might dictate. In these, leaders were elected, grave matters decided, and peace or war agreed. There were no hereditary rulers or kings. No man dictated; a man could persuade, but not command. If the assembly agreed, the men shook their spears or clashed them on their shields, or disapproved with loud shouts. Their women followed them into battle, urging them on.

In England such assemblies emerge into divisions, shires with shire-moots and courts, and below them hundreds and townships, forerunners of county, district, town and parish councils of today. As kingship emerged, so too did Witanagemots, assemblies of 'wise men' summoned by the king. These were men whose advice and consent the king could not afford to be without. There was no thought of popular representation. With the coming of Christianity bishops also were summoned, while clergy, clerks (*clerici*) came to form a rudimentary civil service. As nonrepresentative the Witans are not to be thought of as forerunners of Parliament, but rather perhaps of what evolved later as the Privy Council.

In the early twentieth century and before historians spoke of these as the 'Dark Ages'. Just as the world war was about to begin in 1939, at Sutton Hoo in Suffolk a mound which proved to be a ship-burial was excavated. It contained the most magnificent assemblage of Anglo-Saxon grave goods. There was golden armour decorated with garnets, a remarkable collection of silver ware and coins, a splendid helmet and face-mask, and a sword of surpassing magnificence. The contents of the tomb were hurriedly evacuated to London, and, because of the outbreak of war, buried in a tunnel off Aldwych underground station. There could be no doubt about the civilised taste and elegance of a sophisticated ruler, whose body had wholly crumbled to dust. Subsequent excavations and study have shown Germanic and Scandinavian connections, as well as with the Mediterranean and Byzantium, and even Coptic Egypt. The ship itself displays a high degree of skill and craftsmanship. It is clear that much remains to be learnt of a pre-literate civilisation. The most recent excavations have revealed the most grisly examples of human sacrifices which are as yet little understood.

Although three British bishops attended the Council of Arles in 314, the Saxon invasions swept away all vestiges of early Celtic Christianity. The Sutton Hoo ship-burial was indubitably pagan. In Wales, Galloway and Iona Celtic missionaries were later at work. In 597 St Augustine was sent to Canterbury, where the king, Ethelbert, was dubious of the new religion, but gave him a ruined church. Then Ethelbert was baptised; and so important was the event reckoned 1250 years later, when the House of Lords was rebuilt after fire, it was commemorated in a wall-painting over the Throne. As to the north, Ethelbert's daughter, Ethelburga, married Edwin,

King of Northumbria, taking with her as chaplain Paulinus to York. The school he founded there in 614 still exists today.

The Celtic missionaries who converted the north followed a different calendar to calculate Easter, and certain practices other than those of the Roman missionaries in the south. The Celtic clergy, intelligibly enough, preferred their ancestral practices. The question of the date of Easter might seem trivial, but fundamentally it was a question of church unity, of whether England was to be at one with a still undivided Eastern and Western Christianity. The king, Oswy of Northumbria, was asked to adjudicate: 'If Peter is the doorkeeper,' he said, 'I will never contradict him, lest when I reach the gates there should be no one to open them.' So England once again became united with Christendom, from which the Saxon invasions had separated her.

By the early sixth century seven kingdoms emerge clearly, known to history as the Heptarchy: Northumbria, divided at times into two, Bernicia, comprising present Northumberland and Lothian, and Deira York and Durham; Kent, Essex, Sussex and Wessex, together with East Anglia and Mercia, making sometimes eight, not seven. It is not known how the idea of a supreme ruler, a Bretwalda, emerged. The meaning of the title is far from clear. The title seems to have passed from kingdom to kingdom, whichever predominated at any given time, but without any defined constitutional significance. All the rulers had elaborate genealogies, and all descended from the Saxon god Woden. Among the names, however, Celtic names appear from time to time, and it has been claimed that the founder of Wessex, Cerdic, was of Celtic stock. There was no crown, but early coins display a jewelled diadem of Roman type. The earliest record of a Christian coronation is in the Pontifical of Egbert, who became Bishop of York in 732. It survives in the Bibliothèque Nationale in Paris. Possibly it was not an innovation, but had been used for earlier Northumbrian monarchs. Save for the difference of language, in every essential it was the same as that used for the coronation of Queen Elizabeth II in 1953. As the monarchy developed, so did the importance of the coronation as the formal recognition of the sovereign by the people and the validation of his legitimacy.

Towards the end of the eighth century a new series of invasions began. Historians have been in the habit of calling them Danes, but preferably they should be called Norsemen. They came from all over northern Germany and Scandinavia as well as Denmark, and all around the coasts of the North Sea. They raided northern France as well as England; they gave their name to the conquest of Normandy. They settled along the Russian rivers, and laid the foundation of the Russian monarchy at Kiev. They settled in southern Italy and Sicily, forming kingdoms; they twice attacked Byzantium, and gave the emperors the Varangian guard. Westward they settled in Ireland, Iceland and Greenland, and reached the north American coasts. Now from 789 until 1017 the history of England is of resistance to the Danes; from 1017–42. Danish kings ruled England; even the Norman conquest was a contest between three Norsemen.

The first Danish raid took place in 789. By mid-century Danes wintered in Sheppey, instead of returning home. By 866 a great army descended on England, landing in East Anglia. Next year it ravaged Northumbria, and then Mercia. In 871 it advanced on Wessex; a series of battles followed, and by 877 all seemed lost. Guthrum, the Danish leader, advanced on Alfred's retreat at Athelney, near Chippenham. There, slowly Alfred gathered men. In 878 he fell on the Danes at Ethandun, drove them in headlong flight, surrounded them and starved them into submission.

Alfred saw beyond the battle, and offered Guthrum peace. The Treaty of Wedmore divided Wessex from the Danelaw along Watling Street, but gave Alfred London and the larger towns. He now reorganised his army, and, for the first time in English history, created a navy of longships. They were twice as long and faster than those of the Danes, some with as many as sixty oars. By 897 the Danes had ceased to invade, and turned to join their brethren in Normandy.

Alfred was more than a soldier. His first concern was for the law, and the 'laws of King Alfred' became proverbial. His concern was also for education, himself translating not only religious works, but books on history and geography. He was the first ruler in Europe to turn his attention to the history of his own country: the *Anglo-Saxon Chronicle* is owed to his initiative. He set up abbeys and religious houses for nuns; and was concerned also for the education of the secular clergy. His best epitaph is in his own words: So long as I have lived I have striven to live worthily.

The part of England ceded to the Danes lacked unity. Under Alfred's son Edward (the Elder) the Danes were slowly brought under control, and in 925 not only the Danes, but the Angles of Bernicia, the Welsh of Strathclyde and even Constantine, King of

Scotland, swore to him as 'father and lord'. In 937 Northumbria rebelled, supported by Danes from Ireland, and were defeated by Athelstan at Brunanburgh. His brother Edmund succeeded him in 940 and once again the Danes revolted. Edmund reduced the rebels, and Malcolm, King of Scots, was given Strathclyde as a 'grant', later claimed by Edward I as grounds for claiming the overlordship of Scotland. Under Edmund's successor and brother Edred the Witan which assembled to confirm him included both Danes and Welshmen as well as Saxons, one further step towards English unity. It was in this reign that the great Dunstan emerges, later to become a reforming Archbishop of Canterbury. It was the time of the reforms initiated by the great abbey of Cluny. In England seventeen new abbeys were set up following its strict observances. Emphasis was placed on clerical celibacy for the secular clergy; it was not yet the universal rule of the west. In Worcester and Winchester monks replaced the secular canons. Diocesan boundaries were reorganised to enable better episcopal control, while the bishops themselves were made independent of the monasteries, where hitherto they had been subject to the abbots. At this time too was the first religious coronation of a King of all England, when Edgar (959–75) was crowned at Bath in 973, fourteen years after he had succeeded his brother Edwy. A picturesque legend relates that he was rowed on the Dee by six vassal kings, a tale told perhaps to emphasise his pre-eminence.

On his death in 975 his son Edward (the Martyr) succeeded him; shortly he was murdered at the instigation of his stepmother, so that her son, Ethelred, could have the throne. This Ethelred is known as the 'Unready', in Anglo-Saxon meaning the 'Man of Ill Counsel'. Selfish, idle and weak, so far from resisting fresh Danish invasions he tried to fob them off by bribery, with what became known as Danegeld; it only encouraged them.

In 1013 Sweyn of Denmark and Norway invaded England, and Ethelred fled to Normandy. Sweyn thus became king, although in London the Witan elected Edmund Ironside (1016–17). When Sweyn died his son Cnut or Canute succeeded, and also as King of Denmark and Norway. It seemed that a Danish Empire was emerging, but it did not survive Canute. From the point of view of commerce, since the Danes were active traders, it was a successful arrangement, and since it brought peace it was a welcome change. Canute's sons, Harold and Hardicanute were unworthy successors. Since Hardicanute spent most of his time in Denmark, Harold was the effective ruler. He died in 1040, and with his brother's death two years later, Danish rule came to an end.

The Witan was now the only effective power left in a kingless land. The nearest candidate for the throne was a grandson of Edmond Ironside who had gone to Hungary. The Witan thus chose Edward (the Confessor), a son of Ethelred, by Emma, daughter of Richard I, Duke of Normandy. When Ethelred had died, she married Canute, giving him a species of legitimacy.

Edward was now thirty-five years old, and wholly Norman in culture. He had no knowledge of England, and spoke only French. All his friends and connections were Normans. It was nevertheless a coup for Earl Godwin, Earl of Wessex, the most powerful man in the Witan and in England. His ancestry and family connections, in an age when such things could be of crucial importance, are wholly unknown. Some years before Edward's elder brother, Alfred, had attempted to seize the throne from Canute's son Harold. Godwin pretended to join Alfred and then took him prisoner with his followers when they were in their beds. Harold had Alfred put to death by goudging out his eyes, brutality that Edward was unlikely to forget.

By 1051 Godwin overplayed his hand. He had acted almost as an independent monarch. His son Sweyn had kidnapped and run off with an abbess. He had refused direct royal orders. The earls of Mercia and Northumbria were ready to take up arms against him. Summoned to a Witan at Gloucester, Godwin arrived with armed followers, only to be deserted by them. Godwin and his sons fled abroad. It was in this year, 1051, that Duke William of Normandy visited his cousin Edward, and received some sort of promise that he should succeed to the English throne.

Edward's Norman court, and pro-Norman policies, whether in Church or State, lacked popularity. In 1052 Godwin returned with his sons Harold and Leofwine; all were reinstated in earldoms. By ill luck a ship in which Harold was sailing was driven on to the coast of Normandy. Harold was taken prisoner, and brought before William. Harold was released only after William had made him swear to recognise William's claim to the throne. The stage was now set, but it was not until 5th January 1066 that Edward the Confessor died.

All was by no means simple.

3   Dukes of Normandy and Norman Kings of England

Halfdan the Old, a Norwegian noble, b.c. 730 (?)

Ivar Uppland

Eystein Glumra

Rögnvald the Mighty, Earl of Möre

Ivar
k. in the
Hebrides

Rollo or Robert, b.c. 850, seized Rouen 876,
1st Duke of Normandy, 911, d.c. 932, m.l, 912,
Giselle (d.s.p. 919), d. of Charles III of
France m. 2, 919 Papie (or Poppet), his
former mistress, d. of Berengar, Earl of
Bessin and Bayeux, abdicated 927

Thorir the Silent,
m. Arbot, d. of Harold,
King of Norway

Gerloc or Gerletta,
bapt. Adela, m. 933
William, Count of
Poitiers, 3rd Duke
of Aquitaine, and d.
963
     issue

William Longsword, 2nd Duke of Normandy,
b.c. 905, s. 927, assassinated 17 Dec.
942, m.l, Espriota, a noblewoman

**Richard I the Fearless, 3rd Duke of
Normandy**, b.c. 933, s. 17 Dec. 942, d. 20
Nov. 996, m.l, 960, Emma, (d.s.p. 968) d. of
Hugh, Duke of Burgundy, Count of Paris,
Duke of France; m. 2, Gonnor or
Gunnora, his former mistress (d. 1031)

m. 2, Luitgarde, d. of
Herbert, Count of
Vermandois, by his wife
Hildebrande, Princess of
France

**Richard II the Good
4th Duke of Normandy**,
s. 20 Nov. 996, d. 1027,
m.l, Judith (d. 1017), d.
of Conan I, Count of
Brittany, and Ermen-
garde, Princess of
Anjou

Robert, Count of
Evreux, Abp of
Rouen, d. 1037

Mauger, Count of
Corbeil *jure uxoris*,
m. Germaine,
Countess of Corbeil

issue—Grânville and
Grenville families

?2s.

Emma, d. 1052,
m. 1002 **Ethelred II** of
England (see Table 2,
no. 14) and had issue;
she m. 2, 1017, **Canute
I** of Denmark, Norway
and England (Table 2A,
no. 17), and had issue

**Richard III, 5th Duke
of Normandy**, s. 1027,
d.s.p. 6 Aug. 1028, m.
Adela, d. of Robert I
of France

**Robert II, 'The Devil'
or 'The Magnificent',
6th Duke of Normandy**,
s. 6 Aug. 1028, d. unm.
2 July 1035. By
his mistress,
Harlette, ? d. of a
tanner of Falaise, he
had   :

William,
a monk,
d. 1025

Adelais, m.
c. 1023
Renaud I,
Count
Palatine
of
Burgundy
   issue

Eleanor, m.
Baldwin IV,
Count of
Flanders, d.s.p.

**22. William, 7th Duke of
Normandy**, b. 1025, made
his heir by his father,
s. as Duke 1035, **King of
England** by right of conquest
1066, d. 1087, m. Matilda, d. of
Baldwin V, Count of Flanders, a descendant of Ethelswithe, d.
                       of **6. Alfred the Great**

See pages 26 and 27

Hawise, m.
Geoffrey I,
Count of
Brittany, d.
1034

issue

Maud (or
Matilda),
m. Eudes,
Count of
Blois,
Chartres
and Troyes,
d.s.p. 1017

Beatrice,
m. Ebles,
Viscount
of
Turenne

Duke **Richard II**, m. 2,
Margaret, d. of **Sweyn**,
King of Denmark, Norway
and England, d.s.p.

Duke **Richard II**, m. 3, Papie,
of unknown parentage

William, Count of
Arques, m. a d. of
Hugh, Count of
Ponthieu. Claimed
Duchy of Normandy
in 1035 as legiti-
mate heir of Duke
Robert II

Mauger, a monk,
Abp of Rouen,
d.c. 1055

Harlette, mistress of Duke **Robert II**, m. later
Harlevin, Seigneur de Conteville

Odo, Bp of
Bayeux, Earl
of Kent,
Regent of
England, d.
1096

Robert,
Count of
Mortain,
d. 1091

Adelaide, m. **Waltheof**,
Earl of Huntingdon

Matilda, Countess of
Huntingdon, m.l, Simon
de Senlis or St Liz; m.
2, c. 1114, David I, King
of Scotland

subsequent Kings of Scotland

See page 226

Robert III, 8th Duke of Normandy, b. 1051, d. 1134, m. Sybilla (d. 1103), d. of Geoffrey, Count of Conversano issue	Richard, Duke of Bernay, b.c. 1054, d. 1081	**23. William II Rufus,** b. 1056, s. 9 Sept. 1087 by designation of his father, d. unm., k. hunting in the New Forest 2 Aug. 1100	**24. Henry I,** b. 1070, usurped the throne from his brother Robert 2 Aug. 1100, d. 1 Dec. 1135; m.1, Matilda (Eadgith) (b. 1079, d. 1 May 1118), d. of Malcolm III of Scotland (see Table 11, no. 19), great-grand-daughter of Edmund II Ironside (see Table 2, no. 16); he m. 2, 2 Feb. 1121, Adela, d. of Godfrey, Duke of Lower Lorraine, d.s.p.	Cecilia, b.c. 1055, d. 1127, Abbess of Caen
William. 10th Duke of Normandy, b. 1101, m. 1119 Isabella, d. of Fulk of Anjou, King of Jerusalem, d.s.p. 26 Nov. 1119, drowned in the *White Ship*	Richard, d. unm., drowned in the *White Ship* 26 Nov. 1119	**26. Matilda,** Queen of England, b. 1103, recognized heir presumptive 1119, d. 1167, m.1, Henry V of Franconia, Holy Roman Emperor (d. 1125); m. 2, 1127, Geoffrey V Plantagenet, Count of Anjou, Duke of Normandy (d. 1150) (see Table 4); proclaimed Queen Apr. 1141, but never crowned; renounced claim in favour of her cousin **25. Stephen** 1152, for his life, with remainder to her son **27. Henry II**		
27. Henry II, King of England 1154-89 *See Table 4: House of Anjou or Plantagenets, on page 45*	Geoffrey VI, Count of Anjou and Nantes, b. 1 June 1134, d. unm. 1157	William, Count of Poitou, b. Aug. 1136, d. unm. 1164	Emma, m. 1173 David (d. 1204), s. of Owen Gwynedd, Prince of North Wales issue	

| Adelaide, formally betrothed to Harold II, King of England (see Table 2B), d. unm. 1065 | Matilda, d. unm. | Constance, b. 1061, m. 1088 Alain V, Count of Brittany, d.s.p. 1090 | Adela, b.c. 1062, d. (a nun) 1137, m. 1080 Stephen (or Henry) Count of Blois and Chartres (k. 1102) | Agatha, d. unm. c. 1080 |

25. Stephen, b.c. 1096, usurped England and Normandy from his cousin **26. Matilda** 1135; lost Normandy 1144; d. 25 Oct. 1154; m.c. 1123 Matilda, Countess of Mortain and Boulogne, d. of Eustace II, Count of Boulogne and his wife Mary, d. of Malcolm III of Scotland (see Table 11, no. 19)

5s. 1d.

| Baldwin, b.c. 1124, d.c. 1135 | Eustace IV, Count of Boulogne, b.c. 1127, d.s.p. 1152, m. Constance, d. of Louis VI, King of France | William II, Count of Mortain and Boulogne, b.c. 1137, d.s.p. 1159, m.c. 1149 Isabel, d. of William de Warenne, Earl of Surrey. K. in battle | Matilda, b. 1134, d.c. 1137 | Mary, Countess of Mortain and Boulogne, b. 1136, d.s.p., a nun, 1182, m. Matthew I, Count of Alsace |

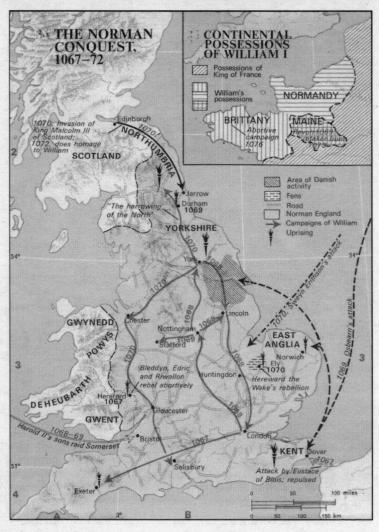

THE NORMAN CONQUEST, 1067-72

CONTINENTAL POSSESSIONS OF WILLIAM I

- Possessions of King of France
- William's possessions

NORMANDY
BRITTANY   MAINE
Abortive campaign 1076
Revolt 1069 retaken from 1073

1070: Invasion of King Malcolm III of Scotland; 1072, does homage to William

SCOTLAND

Edinburgh
NORTHUMBRIA

- Area of Danish activity
- Fens
- Road
- Norman England
- Campaigns of William
- Uprising

"The harrowing of the North"

Jarrow
Durham 1069

YORKSHIRE

York

1070: Sweyn Estrithson's attack

1069 Osbearn's attack

GWYNEDD
POWYS
DEHEUBARTH

Chester
Lincoln
Nottingham
Stafford

EAST ANGLIA
Norwich
Ely 1070
Hereward the Wake's rebellion

Bleddyn, Edric and Riwallon rebel abortively

Huntingdon

Hereford 1067

GWENT

Gloucester

Harold II's sons raid Somerset 1068-69

Bristol

London

KENT   Dover
1067
Attack by Eustace of Blois; repulsed

Salisbury

Exeter

0   50   100 miles
0   50   100   150 km

WILLIAM THE CONQUEROR

1066–1087

England already had some experience of foreign rulers under the Danish kings. The Saxons and Danes had a Germanic community of language and culture, nor had the Danes disrupted the customs and laws of the country. Now with the Normans there came a dynasty French and Latin in culture, which would make profound changes in law, custom, taxation, justice and culture. It was to be strong government, of which the stone castle can be taken as the symbol. Only one existed in the reign of Edward the Confessor; twenty-one years later, when William the Conqueror died, there were twenty-seven royal castles.

The Norsemen who founded the dukedom of Normandy had originated much as the Danes who had harassed and raided England. The founder, Rollo, Hrolf or Robert, was the fifth known of a succession of Norwegian nobles; his brother was married to a daughter of the King of Norway. Rollo seized Rouen in 876; in 912 he married the daughter of Charles III of France, who ceded the dukedom to him in the following year: it was a dukedom the king could no longer keep. Four generations later his successors had become virtually independent monarchs, with a wide range of family relationships. There were close ties with Norway, Denmark and England as well as with the French nobility.

Robert II, sixth Duke of Normandy, had no legitimate issue. His son William was born *c.*1025 or 1027, by his mistress Harlette, a tanner of Falaise. When Robert was setting out on a pilgrimage he designated his son as heir, so that he succeeded when his father's death became known in 1035. Four of William's guardians were assassinated. He was despised for his birth, and his lords were disloyal to him. An attempt was made on his life, and his mother's brother Walter only saved him by concealing him in a peasant cottage.

The young man grew shrewd and brave. The Scandinavian, or western part of the duchy was faithful to him, as against the eastern part nearest the French king. By the time he was twenty he had established his authority throughout the duchy. In 1048 he supported the French king in an expedition against the Count of Anjou, showing such bravery that the king warned him to be less adventurous. In 1059 he married Matilda, daughter of Baldwin V, Count of Flanders, a descendant of Ethelswithe, a daughter of King Alfred the Great.

When Edward the Confessor died William immediately put it in hand to conquer Britain. Apart from his own subjects, the Counts of Brittany and Boulogne joined him, and volunteers from Anjou, Aquitaine, Flanders and even Naples followed. A fleet was assembled; nothing was left to chance.

While this was afoot Harold, who had been recognised by the Witan as King of England, was not idle. He called out an army, but, because William showed no signs of movement until September, his men slowly drifted away. In June, his brother Earl Tostig attacked him in Lindsey, south of the Humber; he was joined by Harold Hardrada, King of Norway. Harold of England rushed his troops north, and fought a decisive battle at Stamford Bridge in Yorkshire, on 25 September 1066.

William moved his fleet of transports from Dives to St Valery on 12 September, but the wind blew from the north, and he could not cross the Channel. On 27 September the wind changed, and he crossed immediately to the low-lying coast near Pevensey, landing the following day. Harold was caught unawares: 'Had I been there,' he said, 'they would never have made good their landing.' He hurried south on 2 October, and marched out of London with his army on 11 October. Two days later he confronted William.

Harold's exhausted army had spears, javelins, throwing axes and other missiles. William had cavalry, and bowmen as well as infantry. At first the battle was even, and William could not pierce the Saxon line. It had been drawn up on a hill. In the afternoon William ordered a feigned rout. The Saxons were deceived, only to be cut down and trampled to death. The end came when Harold was struck by an arrow in the eye; the remaining Saxons retreated into the woods at their rear.

William now had to make good his victory. The Witan chose Edgar Atheling as Harold's successor, but shortly found they could not resist. Edgar himself came to offer the crown to William.

William thus could say that he was rightful King of England, by designation of Edward the Confessor, by right of conquest and by the choice and election of the Witan. Nevertheless he thought it best to make a demonstration, in force. He marched past London as far as Wallingford, and back to Berkhampstead before Edgar's submission. William was duly crowned in Westminster Abbey on 25 December.

He now had to consolidate his power. Rebellions broke out in the southwest, in the Midlands, in Northumbria, and in the Fens near Ely. A first expedition took Exeter, and then harried Gloucester and Worcester. In the north Waltheof, Earl of Huntingdon, took the field with the King of Scotland; Sweyn of Denmark joined in, in the hope of restoring Canute's kingdom. William harried the whole of the Vale of York and beyond. Everything that could be burnt from the Humber to the Tees was destroyed. Those who were not killed either died of starvation or fled. The 'Harrying of the North' may have been an act of great cruelty, but it showed that rebellion would not be endured. In the Fens Hereward the Wake held out for a year, and then broke out and escaped.

By right of conquest William declared all land to be forfeit to the Crown. Under the Saxon rulers there had been a species of feudal system by which the tenants-in-chief of the Crown were able to make grants to sub-tenants at their own will. Thus a kind of pyramid emerged, of free tenants, minor tenants owing them allegiance, and with the king only at the top. In this way smaller men might have any number of allegiances, irrespective of the king. Below the sub-tenants were serfs under different names, with the right only to work on the lord's land and to gather crops for him.

Under William's forfeiture all grantees, tenants-in-chief and minor tenants whosoever owed allegiance to the king, and were answerable for military service if called out. William now distributed the land under barons, scattering their estates, so that blocks could not be formed against him. Only the earldoms of Durham, Kent and Chester were exempt. Durham went to a bishop, Kent to William's half-brother Odo, while Chester, it could be certain, would have his hands fully occupied with the Welsh. Among the barons Robert of Mortain was the largest holder, with 793 manors, but scattered over twenty different counties.

The culminating point of William's reorganisation came in 1085, when, after 'very deep speech' with the Witan, William ordered what is known as the *Domesday* survey. It described all the lands in

England, the holder, and from whom it was held; the number of serfs on each estate, horses, sheep and pigs, oxen, ploughs, mills and fishponds. The detailed knowledge acquired thus gave a firm base for taxation. Twenty years after the 'Harrying of the North' estate after estate was marked 'Waste'.

The last great act of William's reign was the 'Oath at Salisbury' in 1086. Every free tenant of land was summoned to a great *gemot* or meeting at Salisbury. By this oath every tenant, high or low, had as his first duty to obey the king. Thus the great feudal lords had no vassals who owed obedience to themselves alone, as was the case in continental Europe.

Then, in 1087, William went to war with France. While his men sacked and burnt Mantes, his horse was struck by a falling beam. He was thrown against the pommel of his saddle. He never recovered, and died a few weeks later in Rouen. His body was taken to be buried in the Abbaye-aux-Hommes in Caen in front of the High Altar. His tomb was desecrated during the French Revolution, and his bones scattered. A great black marble slab bears his name.

Given the difficulties of his early life, William was a man of remarkable genius, iron will and courage. If at times he showed a cruel streak, it was the custom of the times. He was religious, and generous to the Church. The 'Harrying of the North' and the depopulation of the New Forest to make a hunting park may seem over-harsh. Yet he 'loved the tall deer as though he had been their father', while inflicting blindness on any who should slay them. Disorder had been put down with a strong hand. He knew little English; perhaps now the greatest change had been that there was now a ruling class which did not use the language of the people. It took three centuries to eradicate the difference.

WILLIAM II

1087–1100

As he lay dying, William I designated his eldest son, Robert, Duke of Normandy; William, his second son, was designated King of England 'if Archbishop Lanfranc should think him worthy of coronation'; the youngest son, the future Henry I, got nothing. When he burst into tears, William said, 'Do not cry. You will become king.'

William II has received more abuse than any other monarch. Bishop Stubbs called him 'a foul incarnation of selfishness in its most abhorrent form, the enemy of God and man'. A.L. Poole said that he was 'from a moral standpoint . . . probably the worst king that has occupied the throne of England'. Dr Margaret Murray claimed that he was a practitioner of witchcraft, albeit a 'dutiful son . . . a faithful friend . . . recklessly courageous, lavishly open-handed'. E. A. Freeman remarked that his private life shocked even his younger brother, and suggests that he was given to homosexual vice. No positive evidence for this exists, any more than for his practice of witchcraft. The fact that he never married is wholly inconclusive, and, if it is the case that he took numerous mistresses, no children are known to have been born or to have survived. He could well have been infertile or impotent.

As it was, when he sailed from Normandy he took with him two prisoners whom his dying father had just released, one of them the brother of Harold II. William took them to Winchester and imprisoned them for the rest of their lives. On 26 September 1087 Lanfranc crowned him at Westminster.

Rufus he was called because of his red face. Well-built and strong, he was of middle height. His father was perhaps right in preferring him to his brother Robert, for he was strong-minded and of decisive character. Robert immediately rebelled against him, as he had done against his father. At Easter 1090 a great council held at Westminster assented to war against Normandy, but William has already prudently seized castles in eastern Normandy. Philip of France was thus drawn in, but easily bought off. At Candlemas 1091 William himself went to Normandy, and received such popular support that Robert found it best to agree to a treaty. In William's absence Malcolm III of Scotland, husband of St Margaret, the sister of Edgar Atheling, invaded England. Malcolm was persuaded to do homage, not however for Scotland, but for lands held by him in England.

Lanfranc had died in 1089. William, short of money, seized the opportunity not to apply for a new archbishop, but to take control of the property of the see as feudal superior. This likewise he did to numerous other bishoprics and abbeys in a manner amounting to scandal. In 1093 he fell sick, and the bishops and nobility seized the opportunity to warn him that he might die if he did not mend his ways.

In 1092–3 Anselm had been inveigled into coming to England. He knew that his name was on everyone's lips as successor to Lanfranc. The king thought he was dying, and without further ado offered him the archbishopric. Anselm had no wish for the office, and told the king that he would recover. When the bishops pressed him he said: 'Do you know what you are doing? You plan to place an untamed bull and a feeble old sheep in the same plough under a single yoke. And what will come of it? The untameable ferocity of the bull will drag it through thorns and thickets, and so lacerate it that it will become utterly useless.' Further quarrels now ensued with Robert, with Malcolm of Scotland, and then over the contribution to a campaign in Normandy with Anselm. In 1095 he attempted to refuse Anselm permission to proceed to Rome to receive the *pallium*, the vestment which is the sign of an archbishop's authority and which can be given by the Pope alone.

Now, by a turn in the wheel of fortune, in the spring of 1096 Robert of Normandy determined to take the Cross and go on the crusade. Needing money, he pledged Normandy to William for 10,000 marks, some £6,600 in contemporary money, a trifling sum indeed. Shortly, after a fruitless campaign in Wales, when the defenders withdrew nimbly into the mountains, William acceded to Anselm's demand to proceed to Rome. He now received the homage of Donald Bane, who had succeeded Malcolm III in Scotland, thus securing his rear to attack Maine, the county immediately south of Normandy. In August 1098 he entered Le

Mans in triumph, only to lose it in the following June. War continued intermittently with France, and William once again returned to recover Le Mans.

At Michaelmas 1099 William returned to England. In accordance with custom he held court at Christmas at Gloucester, Easter at Winchester, and Whitsun at Westminster. The Duke of Aquitaine offered him the duchy in pledge while he went on crusade. It would have made William master of all western France from the Channel to the River Garonne. A large fleet was ordered, and an enormous army summonsed to cross the sea. It never did.

On 1 August 1100 at a deer hunt in the New Forest, William's favourite venue for his most-liked sport, he was asked where he would keep Christmas. 'At Poitiers,' he said. The *Anglo-Saxon Chronicle* continues: 'But thereafter on the morrow was the King William shot off with an arrow from his own men in hunting.'

This is all that the chronicler says, and the truth has never been uncovered. Some claim that it was an accident; others that the murderer was Walter Tirel, but Tirel himself denied that he was there nor even saw the king that day. Gerald of Wales names a different bowman, Eader, so that it is disputed how he actually died, whether the arrow struck him, or whether he fell on it by accident. The chronicler goes on without further discussion. 'He was hated by almost all his people and abhorrent to God. This his end testified, for he died in the midst of his sins without repentance or any atonement for his evil deeds'. Inevitably legends clustered round and embroidered accounts of the event. What followed left no doubt of public opinion.

All the hunt followers dispersed, and the body was left to the local peasantry. It was carried on a farm cart to Winchester. Next day it was buried without ceremony, but 'out of respect for the regal dignity, under the cathedral tower'. The Pope had threatened to excommunicate William in 1099, but had been persuaded by Anselm to refrain lest he should further attack the church. There was no requiem, nor funeral. The clergy of Winchester treated him as an excommunicated person, and he had the opprobrium of the people.

Says the chronicler: 'Though I hesitate to say it, he was loathsome to well nigh all his people, and abominable to God, as his end showed, forasmuch as he departed in the midst of his unrighteousness, without repentance and without expiation.'

Seven years later the tower of Winchester Cathedral fell, and men ascribed the event to the divine judgment. Later William's tomb was removed to the Lady Chapel, where it is marked by a marble slab, like that of his father in Caen.

What followed William's death makes it unavoidable to question whether his brother and successor Henry I had anything to do with it. For Henry was following hounds at the time, and immediately turned his horse's head, and galloped to Winchester. There, as king, he seized the royal treasure, in spite of the expostulations of a Norman baron, William de Breteuil, that Henry had an elder brother living. William had died on 2 August. On 6 August Henry was crowned king in Westminster Abbey church. How was it that the clergy were on hand and had made sufficient preparations? How was it that there was a sufficient number of the nobility present for the *collaudatio*, the formal recognition and acclamation of the new monarch? Anselm was still in exile. The Bishop of London officiated at the ceremony. He could have had no doubts of Henry's worthiness as he anointed him and gave him the Sacred Host.

Perhaps Anselm's judgement that William was an untamed bull is the most sensible. People today, as is clear from the popular press, take delight in stories about royalty, and the more salacious the better. William II was certainly blasphemous, grasping and avaricious. He was an obvious target for the exaggeration of depravities. He clearly enjoyed shocking the clergy; there are examples of this in every age. The question is what is to be found good in William's character? It seems clear enough that his contemporaries saw nothing.

HENRY I

1100–1135

William the Conqueror's prediction that his son Henry would also
become king was now fulfilled. Some historians have held that
Henry I cannot be exculpated from complicity in the death of
William II, but direct evidence is lacking. At any rate he lost no
time. Next day he held what today would be called an Accession
Council, at which such members of the Witanagemot and other
leading persons elected him king. William had died on 1 August: on
6 August Henry was crowned in Westminster by the Bishop of
London. Archbishop Anselm was still in exile, and Archbishop
Thomas of York, who had been summoned, came too late. It was
explained that the haste was for the sake of the peace of the
kingdom.

The new king was thirty-two years old. He was stoutly built, and
of middle height. He was of cheerful disposition, and temperate in
eating and drinking. He was however excessively licentious, with a
large number of mistresses by whom he had some twenty sons and
an unknown number of daughters. He was nevertheless systematic
in his habits as an administrator, and his bookishness earned him
the name of Henry Beauclerk. In common with all his family he was
fond of hunting. His mornings were given to hearing cases and to
affairs of state, and the rest of the day to amusements. He was a
constant traveller all over the kingdom, but seldom north of the
Humber.

He had for some time been in love with Eadygyth (Edith) or
Matilda, daughter of Malcolm III of Scotland. Malcolm's wife,
known generally today as Saint Margaret, was the daughter of the
Saxon King Edward the Exile. He lost no time in marrying her
three months after his accession, on 11 November. The marriage
united the throne once again with a descendant of Cerdic, which
delighted the recorder in the *Anglo-Saxon Chronicle* as a wife of

'England's right kingly kin'. Hitherto there had been few marriages between Norman and Saxon, and the Norman nobility at first held the marriage in disrespect. Nevertheless, it now became quite common for the two races to unite, to the extent that he has been called the 'refounder of the English nation'.

At his coronation Henry swore that he would give peace to the church and people, do justice to all men, and would establish good law. On the same day he published a Charter of Liberties, in which he declared that he had been made king by the common consent of the barons, thus dismissing the claim of his elder brother Robert, who in any case was absent on crusade. The church was to be free, and no longer to be abused as it had been in the previous reign. The tenants-in-chief were to be just in their dealings with their tenants and, a statement of profound importance, were all held to owe direct personal allegiance to the king. The law was to be the 'law of King Edward', with such amendments as had been made by William I. Archbishop Anselm was invited to return. The coinage was reformed, and those who made or kept bad money punished. Henry now showed that he was as good as his word.

The accounts, of taxation and expenditure were calculated on a table covered with a cloth woven in squares, the columns representing digits and multiples, like a chessboard, hence the name Exchequer. Its secretary, or Chancellor, so-called because he and his clerks sat behind a *cancellum* or screen, was subject only to the Justiciar, the highest of the court officials. The Chancellor of the Exchequer was Roger, Bishop of Salisbury, whose court officials, the barons of the Exchequer, were sent on circuit throughout the country, to ensure that the royal taxation was collected correctly.

At the same time Henry revived the former Shire and Hundred Courts. This not only enabled men to obtain justice in their locality, but curbed the power of the manorial courts, in which the 'lord of the Manor' or his steward presided. In the Shire and Hundred courts justice was administered by free tenants, with the Sheriff, an officer appointed by the king, in the Shire Courts. These were the seeds of a system which was to be developed further by his grandson, Henry II. In this way the king's power was strengthened and the royal justice made available to all and in every place. In these two ways, the collection of the revenue and the system of courts, were seen to be connected the one with the other.

The Saxon Witanagemot had been a council of wise men, such as the king might choose. The King's Council, the *Magnum Concilium* as it was called, was no longer on the same basis. To the King's Council all the tenants-in-chief came. Since the archbishops, bishops, abbots, court officials and barons were all tenants-in-chief, they were all summoned to the council by virtue of the holding of land, not by 'wisdom'. In this council there was no question of representation, and it should not be regarded as the forerunner of a modern Parliament. In the sense, however, that all were summoned on an equal footing as tenants-in-chief to give counsel and advice, it was the seed of the House of Lords.

No council as large as this could have managed the affairs of the country. It would have been too unwieldy. Thus day-to-day business fell in to the hands of the *Curia Regis*, the King's Council, at which as in the *Magnum Concilium*, the king likewise presided. With him sat the Justiciar, who was Regent whenever the King was absent, the Justiciar's secretary, the Chancellor, the Marshal, and the Constable, the commander of the guard. It was an all-purpose council, a council of state, a law court, and a collector and accountant of revenue. From its function as a law court descended the Court of the King's Bench, and from its attendant lawyers the King's Counsel. From this descends the whole civil service of today.

Apart from the royal government by far the most powerful organisation was the Church. In the compromise that Henry achieved with Archbishop Anselm was an arrangement that was to last until the reign of Henry VIII. In the eleventh century the Church underwent a reformation, in which the most distinguished reformer was Hildebrand, the adviser to two popes, and finally pope himself, as Gregory VII. The Cluniac reforms had the intention of setting up a purer standard of life for the clergy, a spiritual life separate from worldly cares and the acquisition of worldly wealth and power. The monasteries were the sole sources of education in their schools and of welfare in their infirmaries. The Cluniac monks pressed celibacy on the parish clergy to disentangle them from worldly concerns, and fought against simony, the purchase of office or promotion within the church; and, above all, against lay investiture, the appointment to the clerical office by laymen. The livings of the clergy, and more especially of the bishops, depended upon land, the principal source of wealth; bishops and abbots were among the greatest landed proprietors in the country.

Under William I, although he invested – or appointed – his own bishops, and openly declared that he would not accept the publication of any papal bulls or decrees until he had approved them first, there was no quarrel with the papacy. William had, in fact, appointed Lanfranc, Abbot of Bec, as archbishop and had replaced the Saxon bishops by Normans. He had withdrawn the bishops from sitting in the Shire Courts, allowing rather their separate courts for offences against canon law. For graver matters they had their own synods. It would seem that Gregory VII could gain nothing by quarrelling with him.

With William II matters were different. By refusing ecclesiastical appointments he was able to divert their endowments to himself, whence his quarrel with Anselm. For Anselm it was a question of principle, that spiritual appointments should have priority, and that the titles to land were of secondary consideration. Backed by the Pope, Anselm could not give way to the King. Thus Henry I's recall of Anselm was an event of crucial importance. Bishops and abbots were to be chosen by their chapters. From the Church they were to receive the ring and pastoral staff of office; but for their worldly possessions they were required to do homage to the king. A similar contest took place between the papacy and the Holy Roman Empire, with a similar solution. By it Henry I gave the Church independence from lay control in the spiritual sphere, while retaining control in what were now defined as their temporalities.

Henry's conciliatory policy with the Church was not always in keeping with his ruthlessness as a secular ruler. In 1104 his elder brother Duke Robert returned from the crusade, and attempted to overthrow him. It was not difficult for Henry to persuade Robert to relinquish his claim and do homage. This did not satisfy the Norman nobility who had hoped to gain by supporting Robert. Led by Robert of Bellême, Earl of Shrewsbury, they continued in opposition. The final crisis arose in 1106, when Duke Robert, having refused every form of conciliation, fortified the town of Tinchebrai. In September, Henry, having gathered an army, confronted Robert. At first there was stalemate, but Henry's cavalry succeeded in outflanking the duke. The rear, commanded by Robert of Bellême, promptly fled. The Duke and his other principal supporters were taken prisoner. He was kept prisoner in Cardiff Castle until his death in 1134, but the tale that he was blinded is untrue. No other English ruler treated his brother so. Count William of Mortain was both blinded and imprisoned, while many Norman castles were destroyed. Nevertheless, many more years were spent quelling rebellion.

In 1110, when she was only eight years old, Henry's only legitimate daughter, Matilda, was sent to Germany to become the bride of the German Emperor, Henry V. He dismissed all her English attendants, and brought her up as a German. Henry's only legitimate sons, William and Richard, were both drowned in the *White Ship*, when it foundered in 1120, leaving Matilda as the sole legitimate heir to the throne. When her husband died in 1125 Henry brought her back to England, and at Christmas 1126 had the barons swear to her as Lady of England and Normandy if he should die without a male heir. He declared Matilda his heir when he was on his deathbed in 1135, of a fever brought on by lampreys, not the only King of England to die from eating unwisely.

STEPHEN AND MATILDA

1135–1154

When Henry I died, leaving his daughter Matilda as his heir, the barons of England thought otherwise. Matilda had been recognised as Lady of England at Christmas 1126; in the following year she was sent abroad with her half-brother, Duke Robert of Gloucester, with instructions to the Archbishop of Rouen to arrange her marriage to Geoffrey Plantagenet, heir to the Count of Anjou. Her first husband had been thirty years older than her; she was married to a boy of fifteen, ten years younger than herself on 17 June 1128. Not surprisingly they soon quarrelled. The following year he expelled her from Anjou. Nevertheless, shortly the quarrel was patched up.

The barons had good reason. Stephen, as Count of Blois, was a Norman like themselves. Matilda, for all her birth, had been brought up at a German court, as foreign to the Normans as to the English. Her strength lay in the west, the dukedom of her half-brother; and it was there that her first campaign against Stephen began in 1139.

He was, says a chronicler a 'mild man and a good'. The goodness did not turn out to be very apparent, and the mildness nothing but weakness of character. In 1138, when David of Scotland invaded England on behalf of Matilda, he showed himself brave at the battle of the Standards near Northallerton in Yorkshire. He was wholly incapable of exploiting his victory, and turned aside to harry southern Scotland. The chronicler spoke now of 'sixteen long winters' of civil war and chaos between his party and Matilda's. He mistook violence for firmness, and showed himself incapable of conciliating the barons who had been responsible for his election. In 1141 Stephen was taken prisoner and brought to her. On 8 April it seemed for the moment that she had victory in her hands. She offended the barons by her haughty chilliness, and scornfully rejected the petition of the citizens of London for the renewal of the good King Edward's laws. In short, she was no politician, and no queen.

The war rumbled on sporadically until 1148, when she retired to Normandy, now ruled by her husband by right of conquest from Stephen. There apparently she resided until her son succeeded to the English throne in 1154 and her own death in 1167. Stephen's authority was still disputed. Her son, the future Henry II, had been educated in England up to the age of twelve, and was probably the first of his line to speak English. He made attempts on England in 1147, when he was fourteen, and again in 1149. In this year Geoffrey of Anjou handed Normandy over to him. Then in 1152 the Pope annulled the marriage of Eleanor, Duchess of Aquitaine, to Louis VII of France, and Henry promptly married her, thereby becoming *jure uxoris* the ruler of all the lands from Normandy to the Pyrenees and the Mediterranean, a domain far greater than the King of France.

Shortly, Henry renewed his attempt to seize England, but a compromise was procured by the Archbishop of Canterbury. By the Treaty of Wallingford, 6 November 1153, Stephen was to remain king for life, and that after him Henry should succeed him, the actual work of kingship to be carried out by Henry in Stephen's name as his adoptive son. Stephen died on 25 October 1154.

Stephen's reputation has suffered in that he reigned between two men truly great in character and intellect. His chronicler summed him up: 'he was a mild man, soft and good, and did no justice' – in other words he was not strong enough to control the turbulence of his barons, whom both Henry I and Henry II had the greatest difficulty in keeping in check. The almost constant civil wars of his nineteen-year reign prevented the emergence of any policy of a recognisable kind. Most of all, the sad story illustrates that heredity, designation of a successor, and or even election do not necessarily procure an efficient monarch.

4 *The House of Anjou or Plantagenets*

Geoffrey V, 10th Count of Anjou and Count of Maine (1129),
Duke of Normandy 1144-9, when he ceded it to his son, Henry II,
b. 24 Aug. 1113, d. 10 Sept. 1150, m. 3 Apr. 1127 **26. Matilda**, Queen
of England. With other issue (see Table 3, no. 26) they had

27. Henry II, b. 5 March 1133, s. his mother's cousin **25. Stephen** 25 Oct.
1154, Duke of Normandy by cession from his father 1149, Duke of Aquitaine
jure uxoris 1152, d. 6 July 1189, m. Whitsun 1152 Eleanor (d. 26 Jan. 1202),
div. wife of Louis VII, King of France, d. of William, Count of Poitou

William, b. 17 Aug. 1152, d. 1156	Henry, Duke of Normandy and Count of Anjou, b. 25 Feb. 1155, crowned King of England 15 July 1170 during the reign of his father, d.s.p. 11 June 1183, m. 1173 Margaret, d. of Louis VII, King of France. She m. 2 Bela, King of Hungary, and d. 1198	**28. Richard I, Coeur de Lion**, b. 8 Sept. 1157, s. 6 July 1189, d.s.p. 6 Apr. 1199, m. 12 May 1191 Berengaria (b.c. 1163, d.c. 1230), d. of Sancho IV, King of Navarre, and k. at siege of Chalus	Geoffrey, Duke of Brittany, b. 23 Sept. 1158, d. 19 Aug. 1186, m. July 1181 Constance, d. and heir of Conan IV, Duke of Brittany and Earl of Richmond (d. 31 Aug. 1201)

Arthur, Duke of Brittany, b. posthumously 29 March 1187, d. unm., k. 3 Apr. 1203, on whom the right to the throne devolved on the death of his uncle, **Richard I**	Eleanor, b. 1184, d. unm. 10 Aug. 1241

31. Edward I, b. 17 June 1239, s. 16 Nov. 1272, d. 8 July 1307, m. 1, Oct. 1254 Eleanor (d. 28 Nov. 1290), d. of Ferdinand III, King of Castile	Edmund, Earl of Lancaster and Derby (Crouchback), King of Sicily, b. 16 Jan. 1245, d. 5 June 1296, m.1 Aveline (d.s.p. 10 Nov. 1273), d. of William, Count of Aumale; m. 2, *ante* 3 Feb. 1275-6 Blanche (d. 2 May 1302), widow of Henry I, King of Navarre, d. of Robert I, Count of Artois ╎ issue	Richard, b.c. 1247, d. *ante* 1256	John, b.c. 1250, d. *ante* 1256	William, b. and d. c. 1250 Henry, d. young

John, b. 10 July 1266, d. 1 Aug. 1272	Henry, b. 1268, d.c. 14 Oct. 1274	Alphonso, b. 24 Nov. 1273, d. 19 Aug. 1284	**32. Edward II**, b. 25 Apr. 1284, created 1st Prince of Wales 7 Feb. 1301-2, s. 8 July 1307, d. 7 Jan. 1327, m. 28 Jan. 1308 Isabella (d. 22 Aug. 1358), d. of Philip IV, King of France; dep. 7 Jan. 1327 and murdered at Berkeley Castle, 21 Sept. 1327 ╎ issue	Eleanor (1), b. 1264, d. 1298, m.1, 15 Aug. 1282, Alphonso, Prince of Aragon (d. 1282); m. 2, 20 Sept. 1293, Henry III, Count of Bar ╎ issue	Joan, b. 1272, d. 23 Apr. 1307, m. 1, 2 May 1290, Gilbert de Clare, Earl of Gloucester (d. 7 Dec. 1295); m. 2, 1297, Ralph de Monthermer, Lord Monthermer ╎ issue

See page 46

29. John, b. 24 Dec. 1166, s. 6 Apr. 1199, d. 19 Oct. 1216, m.1., 1189, Isabel, d. of William, Earl of Gloucester (annulled 1200); m.2, 24 Aug. 1200, Isabella, d. and heir of Aymer de Valence, Count of Angoulême (d. 31 May 1246)

Maud, b. 1156, d. 8 June 1189, m. Henry the Lion, Duke of Saxony | issue

Eleanor, b. 13 Oct. 1162, d. 31 Oct. 1214, m. Sept. 1177 Alfonso VIII, King of Castile | issue

Joan, b. Oct. 1165, d. a nun 4 Sept. 1199, m.l, 13 Feb. 1177, William II, King of Sicily (d. 18 Nov. 1189), and had issue; she m. 2, Oct. 1196, Raymond, Count of Toulouse (d. 1222), having further issue

30. Henry III, b. 10 Oct. 1206, s. 19 Oct. 1216, d. 16 Nov. 1272, m. 14 Jan. 1236 Eleanor, (d. a nun 24 June 1291), d. of Raymond Berengar IV, Count of Provence

Richard, Earl of Cornwall, b. 5 Jan. 1208, d. 2 Apr. 1272, elected King of the Romans 17 May 1257, m.l, 30 March 1231, Isabel (d. 19 Jan. 1240), d. of William Marshal, Earl of Pembroke, and had issue; he m.2, 23 Nov. 1243, Sanchia, d. of Raymond Berengar IV, Count of Provence and had issue; he m. 3, 1269, Beatrice, d. of Theodoric von Falkestein,. without issue

Joan, b. 22 July 1210, d.s.p. 4 March 1237-8, m. Alexander II of Scotland | *See page 228*

Isabella, b. 1214, d. 1 Dec. 1241, m. 20 July 1235 Frederick II, Holy Roman Emperor | issue

Eleanor, b. 13 Apr. 1275, m.l, 23 Apr. 1224, William Marshal, Earl of Pembroke (d.s.p. 1231); m.2, 7 Jan. 1238-9, Simon de Montfort (k. in battle of Evesham, 4 Aug. 1265) | issue

Margaret, b. 5 Oct. 1240, d. 27 Feb. 1274, m. Alexander III of Scotland | issue *See page 228*

Beatrix, b. 25 June 1242, d. 24 March 1275, m. 22 Jan. 1260 John II de Dreux, Duke of Brittany and Earl of Richmond (d. 18 Nov. 1305) | issue

King Edward I, m.2, 8 Sept. 1299, Margaret (d. 14 Feb. 1317), d. of Philip III, King of France

Margaret, b. 11 Sept. 1275, d. 1318, m. 9 July 1290 John II, Duke of Brabant (d. 27 Oct. 1312) | issue

Mary, b. 22 Apr. 1279, d.a nun c. 1332

Elizabeth, b. Aug. 1282, d.5 May 1316, m.l, 8 Jan. 1296, John I, Count of Holland (d.s.p. 10 Nov. 1299); m.2, Humphrey de Bohun, Earl of Hereford and Essex | issue

Thomas of Brotherton, Earl of Norfolk, b. 1 June 1300, d. Aug. 1338, m.l, Alice, d. of Sir Roger Hayles, and had issue; m.2, Mary de Braose (d. 9 June 1362), widow of Sir Ralph de Cobham, s.p.

Edmund of Woodstock, Earl of Kent, b. 5 Aug. 1301, beheaded 19 March 1330, m. Margaret (d. 29 Sept. 1349), widow of John Comyn of Badenoch, d. of John, Lord Wake of Lyell | issue inc. Joan, the Fair Maid of Kent, who m. Edward the Black Prince

Eleanor (2), b. 1306, d. in infancy

Continued from page 44

33. Edward III, b. 13 Nov. 1312, s. 7 Jan. 1327, d. 22 June 1377, m. 24 Jan. 1329 Philippa (d. 15 Aug. 1369), d. of William III, Count of Holland and Hainault

John, Earl of Cornwall, b. 25 Aug. 1316, d. unm. 14 Sept. 1336

Eleanor, b. 1318, d. 22 Apr. 1355, m. 1332 Reynald II, Duke of Gueldres (d. 12 Oct. 1343) issue

Joan, b. 1321, d.s.p. 7 Sept. 1362, m. 17 July 1328 David II, King of Scotland

Edward, 'The Black Prince', Prince of Wales, b. 15 June 1330, d. 8 June 1376, m. 10 Oct. 1361 his cousin Joan, 'The Fair Maid of Kent', d. of his step great-uncle Edmund, Earl of Kent (see above)

William of Hatfield, b. 1336, d. young

Lionel of Antwerp, Duke of Clarence, b. 29 Nov. 1338, d. 17 Oct. 1368, m.1, Elizabeth de Burgh, Countess of Ulster (d. 1363), d. and heir of William, 3rd Earl of Ulster; he m. 2, 28 May 1368, Violante (d.s.p.c. 1404), d. of Galeazzo II Visconti, Lord of Milan

John of Gaunt, Duke of Lancaster

See the House of Lancaster on page 80

Edward of Angoulême, b. 27 July 1364; d. 1372

34. Richard II, (Richard of Bordeaux), b. 6 Jan. 1366, s. 22 June 1377, dep. 30 Sept. 1399, murdered 14 Feb. 1400 s.p., m.1, Anne (d. 7 June 1394), d. of Charles IV, Holy Roman Emperor; m. 2, 1396, Isabel (d. 13 Sept. 1409) d. of Charles VI, King of France

Philippa, Countess of Ulster, heir presumptive to King Richard II, b. 16 Aug. 1355, d. 5 Jan. 1377-8, m. 1368 Edmund Mortimer, 3rd Earl of March (d. 27 Dec. 1381)

Roger Mortimer, 4th Earl of March, b. 1 Sept. 1373, k. in battle 20 July 1398, declared heir to the throne 1377, m. Eleanor, d. of Thomas Holand, Earl of Kent

1s. 3d.

Edmund, 5th Earl of March, heir presumptive of England, b. 6 Nov. 1391, d.s.p. 19 Jan. 1424-5, m. Anne (d. 20 Sept. 1432), d. of 5th Earl of Stafford

Roger, d.s.p.c. 1412

Anne, b. 27 Jan. 1390, d. Sept. 1411, m.c. May 1406 Richard, Earl of Cambridge —issue

Eleanor, b.c. 1395, m. c. 1408 Edward, Lord Courtenay, d.s.p.

See the House of York on page 96

| Edmund of Langley, Duke of York— *See the House of York on page 96* | Thomas of Woodstock, 1st Duke of Gloucester, b. 7 Jan. 1355-6, murdered at Calais 8 Sept. 1397, m. *post* 1374 Eleanor (d. a nun 2 Oct. 1399), d. of Humphrey de Bohun, Earl of Hereford | Isabel, b. 1332, d. 1382, m. 27 July 1365 1st Earl of Bedford (d. 8 Feb. 1396-7) | issue | Joan, b. 1335, d. 2 Sept. 1348 | Blanche, b. 1342, d. in infancy | Mary, b. 10 Oct. 1344, d.s.p. 1362, m. 1361 John V, Duke of Brittany and Earl of Richmond | Margaret, b. 20 July 1346, d.s.p. 1361, m. 1359 John Hastings, 2nd Earl of Pembroke (d. 16 Apr. 1375) |

issue

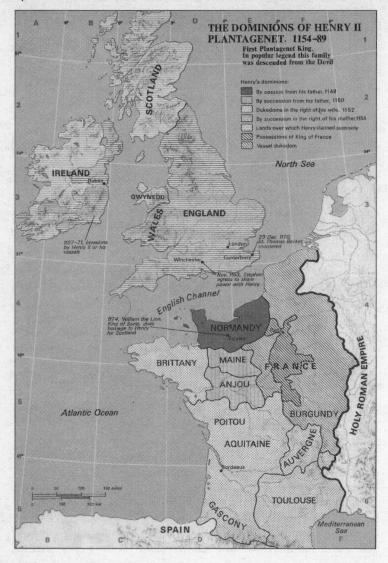

THE DOMINIONS OF HENRY II
PLANTAGENET. 1154–89

First Plantagenet King.
In popular legend this family
was descended from the Devil

Henry's dominions:

By cession from his father, 1149

By succession from his father, 1150

Dukedoms in the right of his wife, 1152

By succession in the right of his mother, 1154

Lands over which Henry claimed suzerainty

Possessions of King of France

Vassal dukedom

SCOTLAND

North Sea

IRELAND

Dublin

GWYNEDD

WALES   ENGLAND

1167–71, Invasions
by Henry II or his
vassals

London

29 Dec. 1170,
St. Thomas Becket
murdered

Winchester   Canterbury

Nov. 1153, Stephen
agrees to share
power with Henry

English Channel

1174, William the Lion,
King of Scots, does
homage to Henry
for Scotland

NORMANDY
Falaise

BRITTANY   MAINE   FRANCE

ANJOU

Atlantic Ocean

POITOU   BURGUNDY

AQUITAINE   AUVERGNE

Bordeaux

HOLY ROMAN EMPIRE

0   50   100   150 miles
0   100   200 km

GASCONY   TOULOUSE

SPAIN   Mediterranean
Sea

HENRY II

1154–1189

Early in the morning of the Feast of the Epiphany, 6 January 1153, Henry stepped ashore on the coast of Hampshire or Dorset and entered a small church just as Mass began. The first words he heard, the *Introit*, or entrance antiphon, were prophetic: *Ecce advenit dominator Dominus, et regnum in manu eius: et potestas, et imperium*: Behold the Lord the Ruler cometh, and the kingdom is in his hand, and power, and government; and even more appropriately continuing: *Deus, iudicium tuum Regi da, et iustitiam tuam Filio Regis*: O God, give thy judgment to the King, and thy justice to the King's Son. For Henry had obtained his right of succession by treaty, and to rule as the king's son, while Stephen was still alive. It was a fitting opening for a formative and innovative reign that would brush away the chaos of Stephen.

Henry now had to make himself supreme. He was to triumph over the barons, but to be defeated by the Church. He restored peace where there had been anarchy; he recovered territory that had been taken by the Scots and made them vassals; he organised a feudal army and a militia; he restored the due collection of the revenue and reformed the coinage; he reorganised the administration of justice, and initiated the representation of the people in the courts and the jury system; he abolished trial by battle and other obsolete practices; he added to his dominions, controlling Ireland as a vassal; he maintained a brilliant and learned court; and died having vowed to go on the crusade. Only in his dealings with the Church did he fail, and this more through inability to reach a compromise than any ill will. After Alfred, and after the Conqueror, Henry I had inaugurated many of Henry II's policies which now gave new life to England, making her among the principal states of Europe.

He was twenty-one, a thick set, sturdy youth, with a lion-like face, but with little regal dignity or conventionality. He was for ever restless, talking and doodling even during Mass, happiest only in the saddle. All folk loved him, says his chronicler, for he did good justice and made peace.

His first act was to issue a charter reasserting all the laws and liberties of the time of his grandfather. A series of measures pacified the baronage, and set the administration of justice in order. In France his vassalage to Louis VII was little more than nominal: he was now the ruler from the Scottish border to the Pyrenees. In 1160 his son Henry was married to Margaret of France, thus securing Normandy. Justice and efficient collection of the revenue, and reform of the coinage replaced the chaotic economy of his predecessor. Most important was his innovation of *scutage*, which substituted a tax on a knight's fee for the obligation of a knight to serve overseas even in person. The knight's fee was a levy upon the tenants of land, and these included the land held by the clergy. It was the beginning of Henry's policy to break down the immunities that the clergy had hitherto enjoyed from the ordinary law in civil matters. The agent of these reforms had been Thomas Becket as Chancellor; it was in the hope that Becket would cooperate over a wider field that Henry raised him to Archbishop of Canterbury.

Becket had hitherto lived the pleasant, lively life of a courtier. He now lived in the most austere fashion, wearing a hair shirt, fasting and giving himself penance. From cooperating as he had previously done, Becket now became the champion of clerical privilege and immunities. By October 1163 the conflict had become so acute that Henry called a great council at Westminster. He required a public acknowledgement of the 'customs of his grandfather', in other words the acknowledgement of the royal supremacy over all persons in both Church and State. To this Becket agreed, adding only 'saving the rights of our order', thus nullifying Henry's intention. It was in this situation that the lay lords wished to depose the archbishop as a traitor. Contrary to law, Becket now fled from the kingdom without royal permission. The fundamental question was that of the investiture of bishops and abbots, and the amenity of all those in the clerical state to the civil law. This included a far wider range of persons than today, sub-deacons, readers, exorcists, and all those in minor orders as well as priests and bishops.

It is probable that Henry had far more sweeping reforms in mind. In his Assize of Clarendon, 1166, he laid down that twelve freemen from every hundred, and four from every township, should denounce all malefactors in the shire court. It was the first occasion that a king had made a law rather than referred to previous 'custom', and the first occasion which acknowledged by law the principle of the representation of the people. It was the first attempt to break down the system of feudal justice, by which a man could obtain justice only from his lord; it now gave every man the right to complain even to the king himself, so reasserting the ancient Teutonic principle that all have the right to self-government. To the historian Maitland it was 'perhaps the greatest event in the history of English law'. At first what was a jury of presentment applied to criminal cases only. By the Assize of Northampton, 1176, this was enlarged to include civil cases. As it developed, it became the germ of our modern jury system.

The departure of Becket into temporary exile made Henry the laughing-stock of Europe, save for the Holy Roman Emperor and the antipope. It was at this moment that the Assize of Clarendon was issued. He made advantageous matrimonial alliances for his daughters, and now was imprudent enough to have his heir, also Henry, crowned as king on 14 June 1170. The action was wholly without English precedent, and an insult, so it was seen to be, to Becket as Archbishop of Canterbury, whose conventional privilege it was to conduct a coronation. It was insulting, too, so it was seen to be, to the French king's daughter, Henry's wife, who was not crowned at the same time. So angry was Henry at these, and other reproaches, that he fell in to a rage, and burst out with words that are variously reported: 'What a parcel of fools and dastards have I nourished in my house that not one of them will avenge me of one upstart clerk.'

Four knights took him at his word in the literal sense: on 29 December 1170 Henry was 'avenged' – by the murder on the altar steps in Canterbury cathedral of Archbishop Thomas Becket.

The pope threatened excommunication, while Henry set off for Ireland. The King of Leinster, who had been driven from his throne, had asked Henry's aid. Henry accepted his homage, and Richard de Clare, and other knights from the Welsh border went to the king's aid, proceeding to set up a feudal state. Henry went swiftly to Ireland with some 4,000 men. This in October. By Christmas, which Henry kept in Dublin, all the Irish princes except the King of Connaught, had done him homage and become his vassals, together with their bishops and clergy. He then returned to Normandy, and received the papal legates, promised expiation and penance: four months later he received public absolution for Becket's murder.

It was not the last of his troubles. For now the French king, and barons in Henry's dominions in Normandy and France, as well as in England, his sons Richard and Geoffrey, and his queen, Eleanor, set out to attack him, in favour of his son. After securing some of his oversea possessions, he crossed to Canterbury. There, on 7 July, he did penance for Becket's murder. Dressed in pilgrim's dress, barefoot, he submitted to be scourged by all the seventy monks of the chapter, and spent the night beside the shrine, at which he presented costly gifts.

Then he quelled rebels in England, and received the homage of the Scottish king. There was a general amnesty and reconciliation, save for one rebel – his queen, whom he kept in captivity for the rest of his life.

In England he again took up his work of reform. The Assize of Northampton, while attending to a number of matters of detail, obtained a partial acknowledgement of the Constitutions of Clarendon from the papal legate, bringing the clergy as well as the laity under the royal power. He further required that every man, 'from earl to rustic', should take an oath of fealty to the king. In 1178 Henry reorganised the Curia Regis in a fashion that enabled it to emerge as the Court of the King's Bench. The Assize of Arms, 1181, required every free man to bear arms in defence of the country, and made taxation incumbent upon a man's annual revenue and movable goods, in lieu of taxes assessed upon the value of land. Its remote descendant is income tax.

The three Welsh campaigns, 1157, 1163 and 1165, made the Welsh princes dependent; 1175 saw the homage of the Scottish king, while, in 1173 the King of Aragon and the Count of Toulouse sought his services in arbitration, as did the kings of Navarre and Castile in 1177. He mediated in France in 1180–2, and in 1185 the Patriarch of Jerusalem implored him to lead a crusade to save the Angevin dynasty in the Holy Land. While clearly these events emphasise his standing in Europe, Henry suffered most from the rebellions of his three sons, Henry, Richard and John. Henry predeceased him in 1183, leaving Richard as heir. In 1187 Jerusalem fell to Saladin, Henry declined to recognise Richard as his heir apparent; and Richard renounced homage to his father, and declared it to Philip of France. On 4 July Henry was forced to acknowledge Richard; he spent two days delirious with fever, murmuring: 'Shame, shame on a conquered king.'

He is buried at Fontevrault, where his funeral effigy lies with that of his queen and his son Richard. Apart from his legitimate offspring, three illegitimate sons are known by name, one of them an Archbishop of York, another a Bishop of Durham. A contemporary said of Henry: 'He left the palm of vice to his grandfather.'

Yet he was a wise and far-sighted ruler, the effects of whose work can still be perceived today.

RICHARD I

1189–1199

It is one of the paradoxes of English history that the most promi-
nent statue in London is that of Richard I Coeur-de-Lion – the
Lionheart – which stands outside the House of Lords beside the
Palace of Westminster. Mounted on a charger, waving on his troops
with drawn sword, his statue by Marochetti was placed there at the
suggestion of Prince Albert. Yet in his ten-year reign Richard spent
a total of only six months in England. He ruled through a succession of Justiciars, all ecclesiastics, who acted as regents in his
absences abroad.

Although born in England, the third son of Henry II, his only
expectation was his mother's inheritance of the Duchy of Aquitaine,
of which he was acknowledged Duke in 1172. It was the largest
province in France, more extensive than the territory under the
control of the French king. The courts of the Counts of Toulouse,
Limoges, Poitiers and Angoulême were distinguished not only for
the splendour of their buildings and statuary, but for their learning
and patronage of poets and troubadours. Richard was well educated
in Latin and literature, and equally in music; it was his pleasure to
conduct the choristers in his private chapel. At the same time he was
naturally gifted as a soldier, and this was as well, for his first five
years of power were spent in reducing Aquitaine to order, and
establishing the ducal authority.

He was not born to inherit England. His elder brother Henry,
Duke of Normandy, who became heir to England after the death of
the infant Prince William in 1156, was crowned King of England in
1170 during the lifetime of his father. It was his death in 1183 which
made Richard heir. Their father, Henry II, attempted to persuade
Richard to give up Aquitaine to his younger brother, John, and
eventual successor, and this he firmly refused. Quarrelling followed,
and Richard suspected his father of trying to disinherit him. Then,

in 1189, Henry II died on 6 July: seizing the royal treasure, Richard set out at once for England, where he was crowned at Westminster on 3 September.

The news of the defeat of the Crusader army at the Horns of Hattin between Nazareth and Tiberias by Saladin on 3–4 July 1187 ended their power on all but the coast of Palestine. Richard immediately took vows to liberate the Holy Sepulchre. Henry II and Philip of France had taken similar vows in January 1188. After his coronation, Richard immediately set about organising a fleet. To raise funds he sold castles, towns, farms and manors. He dispensed William the Lion of Scotland from his oath as a vassal for 10,000 marks. To crusaders who had second thoughts he sold dispensations from their vows. To one who reproached him he retorted: 'I would sell London itself could I find a purchaser rich enough.' Here the seasoned soldier was speaking, for he well understood that he could only fight with success if he had overwhelming force.

This is not the place to detail the course of his voyage to Acre. He gathered further funds in Sicily and then in Cyprus. There he married Berengaria, daughter of the King of Navarre, at the same time putting Isaac Comnenus, pseudo-emperor of the island, in silver chains, and seizing his treasury. Then he sold Cyprus to Guy de Lusignan, ex-king of Jerusalem. He reached Acre on 8 June 1191. With his formidable wealth he afforded Saladin a formidable foe.

Acre surrendered on 12 July, for Saladin was already at war with the Atabeg of Mosul. He promised to restore the Holy Cross and to ransom the captives taken in Acre for 200,000 bezants. Here Philip of France deserted Henry, allegedly on health grounds. By 16 or 20 August the ransom money had not been paid, and Richard executed 2700 prisoners in full sight of the Saracen army. Then he advanced, defeating Saladin at Arsuf on 7 September. He took Jaffa, and opened negotiations with al-Adil, Saladin's brother. By November he was only twelve miles from Jerusalem, but heavy rain, and then snow, compelled withdrawal to the coast. The French contingent then quarrelled, and shortly Richard had to fall back to Jaffa. He was forced to accept a three-year truce.

His misfortunes were not ended. He set out for England with his Queen. Shipwreck forced him to reach England through Germany, with adventures which read more like romance than history. He was taken prisoner by the Holy Roman Emperor, Henry VI, but was released on payment of 100,000 marks, and acknowledging himself the emperor's vassal.

In England his Justiciar, William Longchamp, Bishop of Ely, had made himself unpopular by extortion and extravagance. His successor, Walter of Coutances, Archbishop of Rouen, had to hold Richard's brother John in check; he was plotting to seize the throne. By 1194 Richard had retaken the castles seized by John, and reaffirmed his own dignity by having himself crowned a second time at Winchester, 17 April 1194.

The treacheries of Philip of France and of John prevented him from what was certainly his honest intention to return to the Holy Land. In May 1194 he left England for the last time; the remaining five years of his reign were spent in his French dominions. They were infinitely more troublesome, but also more productive economically than England. His standing in Europe was evidenced when the Emperor Henry VI died, when he was summoned to take part in the election of a successor. Richard was able to secure the election of his own nephew, Otto. In 1199 he defeated his old enemy, Philip of France, in battle; when the French king fell into a river, Richard unhorsed three French knights personally.

In England government was in the hands of Hubert Walter, Archbishop of Canterbury. He not only kept the church in peace, but was able to introduce certain constitutional innovations of importance. The office of 'coroner', albeit under a different name, was established. A scutage tax was raised, requiring an oath by all persons above the age of fifteen to 'keep the peace'. Knights were entrusted with the enforcement of the oath, origin of the Justices of the Peace of Tudor times. In May 1198 a new Great Seal was made, and all grants previously made under the Great Seal were cancelled, thus reasserting the royal authority. It was probably at Richard's express instructions. Other measures were taken in the sphere of accounting for public expenditure, when the Bishop of Durham and the Abbot of Caen were ordered to make an investigation. The bishop died, while the Archbishop of Canterbury and Justiciar tendered their resignation, which Richard refused.

The term of the truce with Saladin had now elapsed, and Pope Innocent III was pressing for a renewed crusade. In April 1199 Richard went to the castle of Chalus to take possession of a newly discovered treasure that he claimed to be his. At the siege he was struck by an arrow, dying of the wound. He gave orders to spare the life of the archer who had shot him, but after Richard's death the man was flayed alive. Richard had displayed a characteristic generosity.

One historian speaks of Richard as 'a bad son, a bad brother, a bad husband, and a bad king'. From one who displayed so generous a spirit even when dying, and who had secured the admiration of a man no less noble, Saladin, this seems a distortion of historical perspective. True, in the present age the execution of 2,700 prisoners of war is shocking, but far more Jews and Armenians, not to mention others, have been wantonly put to death in the present century. Some vague charges have been made against him as a husband, but there is no hard evidence. It is true that he took less interest in England than in his French possessions. His origins and upbringing were Aquitanian, not English; he was a Frenchman by culture. His devotion to the Holy Sepulchre was wholly intelligible in the ethos of the age. It is not possible easily to convict him as a bad son. He had resisted his father only when he judged, not unreasonably, that his father's acts were unacceptable. His courage in battle could not be doubted, and was of a kind to attract legends. The attribution of his sobriquet *Coeur-de-Lion* to the tale that he thrust his arm into a lion's mouth and dragged out its heart is beyond credibility. The lion has been regarded as a symbol of courage since before the invention of sculpture, and the name is altogether reasonable. He was stern as a ruler and as a general. His men contrasted his firmness with the easy-going Philip. Soldiers admire a firm disciplinarian. Even if he did not visit England in the latter years of his reign, he had acted responsibly in his choice of ministers. He was the *preux chevalier* that his statue depicts.

JOHN

1199–1216

The long period that stretches from the accession of John in 1199 to the death of Henry III in 1272 is marked by consistently bad government. John was unpredictable, oppressive and violent, Henry feeble. It is a paradox of English history that weak kingship has been productive in constitutional advance. It enabled the leaders of the nation to develop the essential features of the English constitution, the right – eventually of the whole adult nation – to manage its own affairs by means of a representative assembly, and the duty of the ministers of the crown to be answerable, not to the king, but to that assembly. It is in these three-quarters of a century that Parliament emerges, not fully developed like Venus arising from the waves, but by slow steps taken in the face of incompetent monarchs. It is the great merit of Edward I, strong and determined, that he fostered Parliament. He could easily have destroyed it.

John was thirty-two years old when Richard I died. His whole life had been as a participant in family intrigues, quarrels and wars. His father had used him as a pawn against his brothers. He was idle and frivolous, greedy and extravagant, cruel, false, vindictive and mean. On his accession he took possession of the royal treasury at Chinon, and then, with Bishop Hugh of Lincoln, went to Fontevrault to visit the tombs of his father and brother. At Mass on Easter Day he behaved with his usual levity. The bishop refused his offering. John three times interrupted the bishop's sermon, saying he wanted his breakfast. Then he left the church without receiving communion. Next Sunday he received the insignia of the duchy of Normandy at Rouen.

John succeeded to all the possessions that Richard I had inherited from their father, from Scotland to the Pyrenees and the Mediterranean. The rich Duchy of Aquitaine that Richard had been so careful to foster was lost by a supreme act of folly. It was natural that his nephew Arthur, Duke of Brittany, son of John's elder brother Geoffrey, should have expected to succeed to the throne. Arthur was a weakling, and the barons had preferred John, as indeed Richard had done, for all his known faults. It was wholly predictable that Philip of France, with the interests of his own kingdom paramount, should back the weakling. The acme of folly was when John determined to divorce his wife, albeit retaining her property, on the flimsy ground of consanguinity, in order to marry Isabella of Angoulême, John's greatest vassal in Aquitaine. At one blow John had alienated Philip and Aquitaine. Philip and Arthur joined to invade Normandy, whereon John took Arthur prisoner.

John was not content with that. Arthur was a valuable hostage. He could have been used to cause delay until an army was brought from England. John could not resist murdering him. Then in 1204 he let the siege of Château Gaillard fall by default; and with it all Normandy, Maine, Anjou and Touraine, and the northern part of Aquitaine. Bordeaux and southern Guyenne and the Channel Islands alone remained of what had been Henry II's continental empire.

John's enterprises were now confined to England. He was now to quarrel again, first with the Church, and then with his own subjects. In 1205 Hubert Walter, Archbishop of Canterbury, died. The monks of Canterbury had by tradition the right to elect a successor. They chose their sub-prior, and sent him off secretly to Rome. This Reginald was indiscreet, and the secret reached the king. John compelled the monks to a second election, of John de Grey, more of a soldier than a prelate, and a friend of the king. He was sent to Rome.

John had not reckoned with the character of the redoubtable Innocent III. He disallowed both elections, and persuaded the monks, who had accompanied John de Grey to elect his own candidate, Stephen Langton. The king refused to allow him to set foot in England, and a struggle began. The pope replied with an interdict on the whole country. All churches were closed. Neither could Mass be said nor marriages celebrated. Even the dead could not receive Christian burial.

The bishops and the clergy could have ignored the interdict. They stood by the Pope. The king retaliated on the clergy by confiscating their lands. Innocent III replied by excommunicating John, not that it mattered to him much, for he was growing rich on the Church lands. Innocent threatened to depose John, and even invited Philip of France to expel him from the throne.

There is a saying: *Qui mange du Pape en meurt*: Whoever eats the Pope dies of it. John had challenged the clergy and the Pope, and was forced by his unpopularity to give way to them. He had to swear fealty to the Pope as a vassal and to pay a yearly tribute of 10,000 marks, some £7,500 sterling, a vast sum in those days.

John then determined to revenge himself on Philip. He formed an alliance with the Emperor and the Count of Flanders, and sent an English army to stir up trouble in Poitou. In 1214 at Bouvines, in a hard-fought action, Philip's levies and cavalry ended in the complete defeat of John's allies. John himself escaped to England.

It was only to encounter new troubles. An opposition gathered round Archbishop Stephen Langton, with a policy and a leader. It was to require the king to acknowledge the rights of his subjects and to redress their grievances. In 1213, at St Albans, an assembly met, not only of barons but of reeves and four villeins from each of the royal manors. The assembly was simply deliberative, but the lowest class of free men took part, no insignificant step. Shortly, at St Paul's Archbishop Langton read a Charter of Liberties granted by Henry I and those which Henry II had likewise promised to obey; these now John was required to accept. After Bouvines John returned, and attempted to confront the barons, importing mercenaries, imploring the help of the Pope, and even taking a vow to go on crusade so that anyone attacking him would come under the ban of the Church.

The culmination of the struggle was reached on 15 June 1215 at Runnymede, an island in the Thames. *Magna Carta*, the Great Charter, which John was now compelled to sign, contained sixty-three clauses. Only four of these had a lasting effect. The twelfth clause provided that scutage or aid – save for the three feudal aids, for knighting the king's son, the marriage of his daughter, or to ransom the king himself – should be imposed other than by the 'common council of the realm'. The fourteenth laid down that this 'council' shall consist of the archbishops, bishops, earls and greater barons. Each was to be summoned by a separate writ, and other tenants-in-chief directed to the sheriff of the county. While these clauses applied strictly only to tenants-in-chief, in practice they have been held to extend to the principle that the king may not levy any tax without the consent of Parliament.

The thirty-ninth clause stipulated:

> No free man shall be taken, or imprisoned, or dispossessed, or outlawed, or exiled, or in any way destroyed; nor will we go

upon him, nor will we send upon him, unless by the lawful judgment of his peers, or by the law of the land.

The fortieth clause read:

To none will we sell, to none will we deny, right or justice.

These clauses have been interpreted to provide for the liberty of the subjects, the right of trial by jury, the equality of all before the law, and the supremacy of the law over kings, lords and commons alike. For centuries, and still, not only in England and throughout the British Isles, throughout the British Commonwealth and beyond in the United States of America, these clauses, which were designed to limit the royal power, have provided for the liberty of the subject.

The remaining clauses have passed into desuetude because they dealt, not with fundamental principles, but with the transitory matters of daily life. They provide also for the liberty of the Church, a liberty later greatly eroded, and for the rights of cities. They were designed with a broad brush; they were not class measures intended to protect the baronage, for they were held to protect the rights of all tenants.

It was one thing for John to agree and sign. It was another for him to hold to his promises. When he learnt that twenty-five barons were to enforce the charter, he complained in fury: 'They have given me twenty-five kings.'

He gathered a party among the barons, hired mercenaries, and prepared for war. The barons of England turned for help to France. The crown was offered to Louis VIII of France, already co-ruler with Philip II. In May 1216 the French army reached London, and for the rest of the year there was civil war. By the end of August Louis was master of the greatest part of the country. In eastern England John ravaged mercilessly, even destroying churches. In October at Crowland he pillaged the church, and burnt the crops of the monastery. Then near King's Lynn, he crossed the Wash, losing all his baggage, including the crown jewels. On 14 October he reached Sleaford, having already had an attack of dysentery, brought on by a surfeit of peaches and a new kind of beer. On 16 October he reached Newark, where he died after making his confession and receiving communion. On 19 October, he was buried, as he had directed, before the High Altar in Worcester Cathedral.

HENRY III

1216–1272

Henry III was ten years old when he succeeded his father in October 1216. John had declared him his heir. There was no dispute, for there were no other close kin. The country was torn between two factions, barons who had summoned Louis of France to oppose King John, and those who now rallied round the boy king. The papal legate urged an early coronation. It took place at Gloucester on 28 November. In the absence of Stephen Langton, Archbishop of Canterbury, it was Peter des Roches, Bishop of Winchester, who placed the crown on Henry's head. The king did homage to the papal legate, since John had recognised the Pope, now Honorius III, as his suzerain. The king was given a tutor, Philip d'Aubigny, who later was buried by the door of the Church of the Holy Sepulchre in Jerusalem. William Marshall, Earl of Pembroke, was chosen by the other lords as regent, with the title *rector regis et regni*, governor of the king and of the kingdom. In 1217 Louis' army was decisively defeated at Lincoln: the justiciar, Hubert de Burgh, had destroyed a French fleet sent to relieve him, and in any case he had been losing the support of the barons who had called him in.

In 1219 Pembroke died. No new regent was appointed, but the effective power was in the hands of Peter des Roches with Hubert de Burgh as justiciar. At the Pope's direction Henry was crowned a second time in Westminster on 17 May 1220, this time by Stephen Langton, and with a far larger number of barons present than there had been at Gloucester.

The whole reign, until in 1265 when Henry ceded power partly to his heir Edward I, is taken up by intrigue and factions among the barons, dissidents who sought to enrich themselves in a state of chaos, and a constitutional party that was attempting to bring about a stable regime in terms of Magna Carta. Pembroke had reaffirmed

Magna Carta at the very beginning of the reign, significantly omitting article twelve, which referred to the need for consent to taxation. It was as inconvenient, no doubt, to regents as well as to kings. In 1223, at a council in London, Langton required Henry to confirm all Magna Carta. Henry wrote to all the sheriffs commanding them to make an inquest into all liberties men had enjoyed in the reign of his grandfather. In April 1223 the Pope declared the king of full age to rule, and ordered all castles to be surrendered to him. It was only then that the new reign truly began.

At first the king was guided by his ministers. War in France, to recover lands lost by John, proved futile, as also in Wales, where Henry was out-generalled. He now turned out Peter des Roches, and brought in a crowd of courtiers and advisers from Poitou, who were much resented by the great lords. Only with great difficulty was a great council held at Westminster in 1233, and again in 1234. By now the king was wholly isolated from the barons. At this juncture Henry married Eleanor, daughter of Raymond Bérenger, Count of Provence. She was brought to England by William, bishop-elect of Valence, who immediately established great influence over the king. Nothing would stop the king lavishing gifts on William and other Provençals, to the anger of the great magnates.

On 7 January 1238 the king's sister, another Eleanor, the widowed Countess of Pembroke, married Simon de Montfort, Earl of Leicester. The marriage was kept secret but it gave de Montfort not only great wealth but also power. It was a further insult to the magnates, as was Henry's attempt to have William of Valence elected to the bishopric of Winchester. Then Henry quarrelled with Simon de Montfort. In 1240 and 1241 there were further occasions of grievance. Heavy taxation was imposed to carry on the Emperor's war in Italy; he not only alienated the Pope, but all the minor clergy. A council of magnates was summoned in January 1242, at which many complaints were raised. Henry was enabled to make war in France, but on 20 July near Saintes he and his army fled. A great council was held in Westminster; a new Charter was to be drawn up, since the old one had so frequently been ignored, with a special office of 'guardians of liberties'; the justiciar and the chancellor were to be chosen by the common council, and certain judges elected. Wars on Wales continued. By 1249 the charter agreed in 1242 had been wholly circumvented. It is surprising that there was no general rebellion, but since the bishops and nobles fell out among themselves, there was no one to lead it. On 3 May 1253

Magna Carta was again renewed in Westminster Hall, the king swearing to keep to it 'as a man, as a Christian, a knight, a king crowned and anointed'. Then once again he set out for France, where he mismanaged the expedition in his usual fashion. There was a further futile project, to gain the crown of Sicily for his son Edmund.

In 1258 at Westminster the barons appeared before him in armour, but leaving their swords outside. The king was required to swear that he would be guided henceforth by a council of twenty-four elected magnates, who would ensure reforms. On 11 June what is known as the Mad Parliament met in Oxford. Half the council was appointed from the King's party and half elected by the barons. Parliaments were to meet three times a year. A justiciar, treasurer and chancellor were chosen, and also the sheriffs, all to hold office for one year only. Peace was now made with France, and the Sicilian episode fizzled out.

It was now rumoured that Henry's son Edward was plotting to overthrow him, in company with Simon de Montfort. Shortly they were reconciled, and in 1261 bulls promulgated by the dying Pope Alexander IV were produced, absolving Henry and everyone else from the oaths taken at Oxford. These bulls were confirmed by Urban IV in the following year. The king fell ill in France in 1262, and did not return to England until Christmas. He was again forced to agree to the *Mise*, or provisions, of Oxford. In March 1263 Henry required a general oath of allegiance to Edward as his successor, and this provoked a crisis. The barons demanded that Henry should again swear to stand by the provisions of the *Mise*. He refused, shutting himself in the Tower of London. Simon de Montfort now openly revolted, supported by numerous barons.

An arbitration by Louis of France predictably found in favour of Henry, which the barons at once refused. Finally it came to civil war, and on 14 May 1264, although he had the larger army, Henry was defeated. He took sanctuary in Lewes Priory. Commissioners were now appointed to direct the king, and Edward held as hostage. Henry was in fact the captive of Simon de Montfort: he was treated with personal respect, but was bent to do Montfort's will. On 4 June a Parliament was summoned, with four knights to be sent from each shire. The king was to act in accordance with the advice of nine counsellors. A further Parliament was held at Westminster on 20 January 1265, and to this representatives were summoned from the shires, the cities and boroughs: by now the principle of representation was firmly establishing itself. Prince Edward escaped from Montfort's custody, and set himself to overthrow him. Montfort's son, who had raised an army, was defeated at Kenilworth; and then at Evesham, on 4 August, Edward defeated the elder de Montfort. His mutilated remains were interred with his son Henry in the abbey church at Evesham.

Henry was thus restored by his son, and continued to reign. How far he ruled, and not Edward, is another question. The country had now been restored to order, and a Parliament was held at Marlborough, at which almost all the provisions of Oxford were agreed. In 1269 a great assembly took place at Westminster, when the abbey church, which the king had rebuilt at his own expense, was consecrated. With great ceremony the body of Edward the Confessor was translated to a new shrine behind the High Altar, before which all subsequent Kings and Queens – save Edward VIII – have been crowned. Here, when Henry died in 1272, his body was brought to be buried, save his heart, which was buried in the abbey church at Fontevrault.

It is always difficult for a man to perceive the spirit of the age, still less to come to terms with it. The stiff tradition that Henry, aged nine, was to receive from his mentors belonged to the Norman age where all final decisions rested with the king. Weak as he was, spendthrift, lavish, Henry had none of the tact of his grandfather, nor did he perceive the underlying currents of thought in society. It was now the age of Saint Francis and Saint Dominic, and their orders of friars who went out to preach to the masses. Unlike the great abbeys, the constitutions of their orders were essentially democratic: priors were elected for short, fixed terms of office, and then returned to the ranks. The new age was penetrated by the new philosophy of St Thomas Aquinas, born c. 1227, and dying two years after Henry. His *Summa* covered the whole realm of philosophy and theology, and was penetrated even by the mystical thought of the Muslim Sufi fraternities.

Henry was a great builder. This was the age of the cathedral and the abbey church, of which his own, at Westminster, was among the most notable. It was a new springtime, of which the elegance of Salisbury is so striking an example. It was also one of smaller, more delicate art: a satirist said of Henry that he so wanted to take away the Sainte Chapelle in Paris that if he could have put it in a cart and carried it away, he would have done so. Bishop Stubbs was surely wrong to accuse him of tyranny when he said that if Londoners were rich enough to buy the crown jewels from him, they were well off enough to give aid freely. Like many of his family he was deeply religious: he commonly attended three Masses each day. His brother-in-law, de Montfort, although a rebel, was a deeply serious man. If Henry could have come to terms with him and his reforming intentions, much bloodshed would have been saved. Henry's marriage to Eleanor, from Provence, brought a rich court culture to his palaces, which would reach its apogee under Richard II. The *Liberate* ('Deliver ye . . . ') Rolls record his personal orders to sheriffs, bailiffs, exchequer officials and others, for commodities furnished to the country: they show that he paid extraordinary attention to meticulous detail. His eye extended from clerks of the chapel to the cookhouse, the cellar and the tailors' shop, and the providers of fish and meat. There was an immense number of benefactions, and masons and craftsmen were not forgotten. It was not easy for him to reconcile himself to a new age in which men desired to reach conclusions by discussion rather than by the seemingly arbitrary decisions of the few. If he was extravagant, he was never mean as his father had been.

EDWARD I

1272–1307

Edward I's tomb in Westminster bears a simple inscription: *Edwardus primus Scottorum malleus hic est. Pactum serva*. Edward I, Hammer of the Scots, lies here. Keep troth.

The motto sums up the character of the reign: firm administration, progressive legislation, reduction of the power of the barons, bringing knights and burgesses into councils of state, settlement of Wales, diplomacy and then war with Scotland and France, and compromise with the Church. Far from resisting the current of change that was apparent in the reign of his grandfather, his Model Parliament of 1295 gave shape to a constitution that, with variations, has existed ever since. When he summoned the Model Parliament he wrote: 'what touches all should be approved of all, and it is also clear that common dangers should be met by measures agreed in common'. It was this *pactum*, this compact, that forged the parliamentary constitution of England in a form that has now developed throughout the British Commonwealth and in the United States. Only with Scotland and France could his policies be said to fail.

At thirteen he was sent to Gascony, but without a free hand in its administration. At fourteen he was sent to Wales, but the attempt to introduce English laws had little result. In Henry III's quarrels with de Montfort and the barons it looked as if he might join their cause. Then he became the prime mover in a reconstituted royalist party. Bold, athletic, with all the dash of a cavalry officer and a passion for hunting, it was his rashness at the battle of Lewes that lost the day. He and his father were taken prisoner, but in 1265 he managed to escape. With an army from the Welsh borders he defeated and killed de Montfort at Evesham on 4 August. Although Henry continued to reign, for the next five years the administration was in his hands. These were five years of peace and steady reconstruction.

In 1268 he supported St Louis' call for a crusade. By the time

Edward had found money, ships and men St Louis was dead, and a truce had been concluded with Sultan Baybars of Egypt. Edward regarded the truce as treason to Christendom, and proceeded to Acre, where he was from May 1271 until August 1272. Baybars was one of the greatest military commanders of the age, and Edward saw that any attempt at serious hostilities was futile.

He had reached Sicily on his way home when Henry died in 1272, but did not hurry. First he went to settle Gascony, reaching England only in August 1274. On 18 August he was crowned at Westminster.

Edward was thirty-five, a mature man. Almost at once he adopted de Montfort's policy. In 1275 he summoned to Parliament burgesses and citizens from the towns as well as knights of the shire. The practice did not become conventionalised at once: later knights were summoned alone, later merchants, without summoning what came to be called the Commons. The Magnum Concilium of magnates could still be summoned alone. The principle that assent of all both to statutes and grants of money was becoming accepted. In 1295 Edward was faced by enemies on three sides. In France a dispute led to fighting between fishermen, and then to Norman attacks on Gascony. The Scots joined in, and then there were three separate revolts in Wales. The Model Parliament of 1295 had summoned to it the orders of friars, two knights from each shire, cathedral priors, archdeacons, representatives of cathedral clergy and each diocese, with two citizens and burgesses from each city and borough. The clergy preferred to sit apart, and the nobility and commons sat together. Parliament was no longer an assembly of the baronial class and higher clergy; it now represented all three estates of the realm. Edward got the grants he needed, but it was the establishment of the precedent which was of greater importance. The Confirmation of the Charters of 1297 completed the work, enlarging clause twelve of Magna Carta to include all taxation, which had only forbidden the raising of scutage without consent. Parliament still depended upon summons from the king, and the responsibilities of ministers to Parliament had yet to be defined.

Further reforms were made in the administration of justice, in the institutions of lay magistrates and of juries, and in relation to land, moving towards the demolition of the feudal system. Legislation also was directed to the encouragement of commerce, breaking down the restrictions of town and city guilds. In these ways to a national Parliament was added national administration of justice and national commercial policy. It would have been strange if Edward had not looked beyond England to Wales, Scotland and finally to France.

Under William II Wales had been contained by 'lords marcher', barons who became entitled to all the land they might conquer. Thus the Welsh were slowly driven back, and pinned down by castles, from the Dee to the Conway. Edward was sent to Wales initially because of a resurgence of Welsh nationalism, led by Llewelyn ap Gruffydd, a north Welsh prince, who reconquered much of the land that had been taken. In 1269 Edward had been bought off by allowing him to surrender much of it. In 1277 Llewelyn moved to marry Eleanor, de Montfort's daughter, as a prelude to rebellion. Edward marched an army into Wales, while Llewelyn retreated into the Snowdon range. It would have been foolish to follow, and Edward therefore blocked all the passes, and assembled a fleet to blockade the coast. Llewelyn was now starved out, and surrendered. Edward treated him gently, allowing him to pay homage, but leaving him with some of his power as a vassal, and permitting him to marry Eleanor. Edward's attempt to settle Wales, and to organise it into shires and to bring English laws only provoked further rebellions in 1282, 1294 and 1295. Great castles were built at Caernarvon, Conway and Harlech. In 1294–95 Edward marched through all Wales, repairing and building castles, ringing the whole country. In February 1301 his son Edward, then aged sixteen (and not an infant as is popularly imagined), was created the first Prince of Wales. The principality had been crushed, and nationalism on any recognisable scale was not to emerge again until the twentieth century.

The earlier history of Scotland, from the ninth century until the death of Margaret, 'The Maid of Norway', in 1290, is traced in a separate chapter. Here we are concerned only with Edward's dealings with Scotland.

From the reign of William I on Kings of Scotland had from time to time done homage to the King of England. This had been done, however in respect of earldoms and land held by the King of Scotland in England, and not, at any rate, from the Scottish point of view, an acknowledgement of suzerainty over Scotland. From an English point of view the opposite was the case. The boundary between the two kingdoms was not wholly defined as it is today; at times parts or all of Northumbria, and of Cumberland and Westmoreland were under Scottish rule. In 1091, following an invasion, Malcolm III of Scots acknowledged William II. It was in order to end hostility between Scotland and England that Henry I had married Matilda, Malcolm III's daughter by Saint Margaret, granddaughter of Edward the Exile. David of Scotland was thus Henry's brother-in-law. He persuaded Stephen to cede to him Northumberland, Durham, Cumbria and Westmoreland. Henry II refused to be bound by this, and compelled David's grandson, William the Lion, to return them. He then, by the treaty of Falaise, 1174, made William do homage to him for the whole of his kingdom.

When the Maid of Norway, Margaret, died on Orkney there was no obvious heir to Scotland. Twelve competitors disputed the succession, some of then illegitimate, but with rights in accordance with Scottish law. The Scots needed a referee, and Edward was the obvious choice. He looked on the question as a lawyer, without paying too much attention to the political consequences. He tried the case in a court of eighty Scots and twenty-four Englishmen. The best claimants were John Balliol, Robert Bruce and John, Lord Hastings. Edward first refused to adjudicate the claim until the claimants had recognised him as Lord Paramount of Scotland.

Balliol, who was chosen, proved a disaster. The Scots now made up their own minds. Balliol havered, and then made an alliance with France, with which Edward was at war. Edward marched into Scotland, stormed Berwick, brutally massacring the townsfolk, and then defeated the Scottish army at Dunbar. Balliol was deposed, and Edward took Scotland for himself.

The Scots now rallied round William Wallace. At Stirling Bridge in 1297 he defeated the English, and carried war into the northern counties. By now Wallace had been named Protector of the Kingdom. Edward returned with an army, defeating Wallace at Falkirk, in 1298, where 15,000 Scots are said to have been killed. He burnt Perth and St Andrews. The war dragged on, until in 1305 Wallace was captured and hanged, drawn and quartered. It was a grave political mistake, for it united Scotland.

The next nearest competitor now seized his opportunity. Robert Bruce now hurried to Scone and had himself crowned. He fled and hid in the Highlands, where Edward could not reach him. His success belongs to the next reign, for Edward died in 1307 crossing with an army at Burgh-on-Sands. The Hammer of the Scots was no longer, but England had lost a king to whom she owed an immeasurable debt.

EDWARD II

1307–1327

Edward II was no worthy successor to his father. Edward I had done his best to train him in war and in statecraft, but his habits of extravagance and frivolity were incurable. Bishop Stubbs remarked that he 'was the first king after the conquest who was not a man of business'. Edward's chief delight was in amusements and athletics; he was lacking any serious interests. He was always in the hands of some favourite. In his early years this was a Gascon noble, Piers Gaveston, who was regent for him when he went to France in 1308 to marry Isabella, daughter of Philip the Fair. The barons were disgusted by his 'brother Piers', and in 1312 quietly murdered him. In 1311 they had forced him to accept that the kingdom should be governed by a committee of twenty-one Lords Ordainers. It was an act that reversed the constitutional progress of Edward I, for it left power solely in the hands of the barons.

Robert Bruce was now steadily conquering Scotland. In 1314 Edward and the barons were shamed into leading an army in to Scotland. On 24 June they were utterly defeated at Bannockburn. Bruce now devastated northern England, and drove Edward even more into the hands of the barons. At first the king's kinsman, Thomas of Lancaster, was his adviser, but he was soon replaced by the Earl of Pembroke. The king soon hated him, and after 1318 he depended on Hugh Despenser, a baron in no way related to the later Spencer family. The king's favourite friend was Despenser's son. In 1321 the barons met in Parliament and banished both father and son, but Edward recalled them in 1322. Civil war broke out when he made war on the barons. For the next five years the Despensers ruled England, but in 1322 a Parliament held in York revoked their ordinances, making the consent of the Commons necessary both for taxation and other statutes. It was a step forward, and the only constitutional advance in the reign.

The Despensers had unwisely angered the queen. In 1325 Isabella crossed to France, with her eldest son Edward, now heir to the throne, for him to do homage for Aquitaine to her brother, the French king. She then declined to return to England so long as the Despensers reigned as Edward's favourites.

Isabella then formed a connection with Roger Mortimer, and in 1326 landed in Essex with him. She had come, she said, to avenge the murder of Thomas of Lancaster and to rid the country of the Despensers. Edward fled to Glamorgan. She had the Despensers put to death. On 16 November Edward, deserted by his followers, was captured and imprisoned at Kenilworth.

Parliament met in January in Westminster, and chose Edward III to be king. On 20 January Edward II was force to renounce the throne. The government of Isabella and Mortimer was, however, so weak that they dared not let him live. On 3 April he was secretly removed from Kenilworth to Berkeley Castle in Gloucestershire. He was systematically ill-treated and starved in the hope that he would die of disease. His physique was so strong that he could withstand the ill-treatment. He was cruelly put to death on 21 September. It was announced that he had died a natural death; he was buried in the abbey church at Gloucester.

To judge by his effigy in Gloucester Edward II was a gentle country squire whose character in no way fitted him for kingship. He was kindly, fond of his family, suited to a routine life of reading, and a collector of rare books, legends and romances. The famous poem on his imprisonment was almost certainly from his own pen. He lacked both the political sense and determination necessary in a monarch. It would have been better for him and for England if he had never succeeded.

EDWARD III

1327–1377

Edward III had refused the throne unless his father abdicated. He was fourteen years old, and deeply attached to his father. At first he was a puppet in the hands of his mother and her paramour Mortimer. In his first year, however, he made a most fortunate marriage. Philippa of Hainault had been chosen for him for political reasons. It turned out to be a love match, which for forty years restrained his harsher character, and the violent passions which he had inherited from his mother. Philippa was crowned Queen in March 1330, and her son, the Black Prince (so called later from the colour of his armour), was born on 15 June. Then in October the Queen Mother and Mortimer were overthrown. Mortimer was executed on 29 November. Isabella was treated with every respect, and given honourable retirement. Her political life was at an end, and the reign had begun.

Isabella and Mortimer had conceded independence to Scotland by the treaty of Northampton in 1328. In 1332 Edward invaded Scotland to restore English overlordship, and won the Battle of Halidon Hill in person. The French had supported Scottish independence, and this was the beginning of the deterioration of Edward's relations with France, which led to war in 1337. In 1338 Edward made an alliance with the Emperor, Louis the Bavarian, and, with the help of German and Fleming allies, attempted to invade France in 1339 and 1340. The land campaigns resulted in his bankruptcy, but in 1340 he took part in the great naval battle off Sluys, which wholly destroyed the French navy. He then declared himself King of France in the right of his mother, the sister of the last three French kings and daughter of Philip the Fair. It was a weak claim, because France observed Salic Law, the Law of the Salian Franks, by which no woman, nor her heirs, might succeed to the French throne. This was the beginning of what came to be known as the Hundred Years War, which lasted 115 years, and which left both England and France exhausted. It began in an atmosphere of romantic chivalry. Edward wrote to Philip of Valois:

> we purpose to recover the right we have to that [our] inheritance, which you so violently hold from us . . . since the quarrel is between you and us only, . . . the discussion of our challenge should be decided by our persons, to which arrangement we offer ourselves . . . or by a battle of one hundred of the most efficient persons on your part, and as many on ours.

Some indecisive campaigning followed, but in 1343 Edward returned to England. Much time and money was now spent on rebuilding Windsor Castle, and in instituting the Order of the Garter.

War was renewed in earnest in 1346; Edward, accompanied by his son, the Black Prince, marched from La Hogue to Caen, and almost to the gates of Paris. His campaign then seemed to lose direction, and he turned again towards Flanders. The French caught up with him with a larger army at Crécy, but the decisive factor was the longbow of the Welsh archers, against whom the clumsy French cavalry were helpless. It is reckoned one of the decisive battles of history. The French lost 1,500 knights, and some 15,000 men. Edward's casualties were little over a hundred. Edward seems to have been lacking in strategical sense, and the result was no more than the capture of Calais. It was to remain English for another 200 years.

Edward was now short of money. In 1348 he had to reject the offer of the imperial throne. In that year and in 1349 the Black Death, the rat-borne plague which had come all the way to Europe from Mongolia, swept England. One-third of the English population perished. In some parts the living could scarcely bury the dead. Two-thirds of the clergy died in the Diocese of Norwich. The prior and the canons of Heveringland all died. Of the sixty monks at St Albans only thirteen survived. Whole families perished, with no one to inherit from them. Nevertheless, at Windsor magnificent revels continued, and the war with France too, with only small engagements. In 1359 Edward's army almost reached Reims, where all the French kings had been crowned. The citizens frustrated him, and in 1360 he was forced to agree to the treaty of Brétigny, and then the treaty of Calais, by which Edward renounced his claim to France, in return for the recognition of his rights to Aquitaine.

War had brought no prosperity to England. An attempt to curb the inflation brought about by the Black Death, the Statute of Labourers, ordained that payments of wages should not exceed those paid before the war. Inflation more than doubled, and many landowners were tempted to ignore the law which was intended to protect them. The economic laws of supply and demand overrode the laws of Parliament, and led only to bitterness.

Charles V of France repudiated the treaty of Calais in 1369. War was renewed, and Edward renewed his claim to France. Aquitaine was gradually lost, with all its wealth. Bayonne, Bordeaux, Brest and Calais were the only towns left to Edward. In 1375 he was glad to make a truce. He was now sinking into his dotage. The queen had died in 1369. His council was now divided between the followers of his two sons, Edward the Black Prince and John of Gaunt. The king himself was in the hands of a greedy and ambitious mistress, Alice Ferrers, who helped John to become paramount over his father. The chief opposition came from William of Wykeham, Bishop of Winchester. They were irritated by John's friendship with the reformer, John Wycliffe. Opposition to John was led by the Black Prince and Edmund Mortimer, Earl of March, husband of Edward's granddaughter, Philippa of Clarence. Indignation against the court reached its climax in the Good Parliament of 1376. Alice Ferrers was removed; John's supporters impeached. While it was still sitting the Black Prince died, and John of Gaunt regained power, reversing the acts of the Good Parliament. Then the king himself died, on 13 June 1377.

Edward III was not a great king like Edward I. He was a good knight; upright, honest, and brave, he was a tactician rather than a strategist. Froissart describes his court as the most brilliant in Europe, and he as good-tempered, liberal and kindly and easy of access. Like his father, he was self-indulgent, but until the queen died, a faithful husband.

RICHARD II

1377–1399

Richard II, Richard of Bordeaux from the place of his birth, has a paradoxical place in English history. He was ten years old when his father died, and the appointment by Parliament of a council to rule during his minority has been held to mark a new stage in Parliamentary democracy. On the other hand, no medieval English monarch had a higher concept of Divine Kingship than he. This, he believed, was conferred on him by religious coronation, as it had been conferred on David and Solomon.

Initially Richard was in the hands of a tutor, Sir Simon Burley, a man of wide culture. We have no details of the course of instruction, but for sure it included French as well as English. He was steeped in the history of regality, in theology and the canon law, and himself prepared a document requesting the Pope to canonise Edward II. His collection of books included French romances and poetry; he was a patron of Gower and Chaucer, and gave encouragement to the chronicler Froissart. He himself composed ballads, lays, roundels and songs. To him we owe Westminster Hall, the largest of its kind ever built, 240 feet long and 70 feet broad, with its innovation of hammer beams and arch ribs, together with the nave of the abbey church at Westminster and the great nave of Canterbury Cathedral. Delighting in sumptuous dress and jewellery, he was a patron of artists. The Wilton Diptych shows him at prayer in the court of heaven. He was the only king to be king of England by undisputed right for more than one hundred years to come, and the second to be compelled to abdicate.

Edward III's French wars, the Black Death and the consequent inflation caused by them both, the class struggle between land-owners and villeins – technically the landowner's property – and other related factors had brought about national insolvency. In religion Wycliffe and the Lollards had begun the quarrel which was to emerge as the Protestant Reformation, hating both papacy and higher clergy, and not least the religious orders, whether monks or friars, rich men by comparison with the parish priests.

In 1381 risings began in East Anglia, and from Kent travelled into London what is known as the Peasants' Revolt. Wat Tyler, Jack Straw and John Ball were the leaders. John of Gaunt's palace of the Savoy was burnt and gutted, and in the Tower the Treasurer and the Archbishop of Canterbury were murdered. The Court panicked.

Richard, a youth of sixteen, alone remained cool, and went out to meet the mob at Smithfield. Tyler came so close that 'his horse's head touched the croup of the king's saddle', and he began to argue with the royal attendants. The mob advanced, preparing to shoot the royal party down with arrows, when Richard rode forward and shouted, 'I will be your leader.' It was an act of great bravery, and calmed the mob. Richard promised them redress of grievances, more than he could in fact perform. It was this characteristic, repeated on many occasions during his reign, which was the real cause of his downfall. Arson, murder, brutalities continued, but slowly Richard was able to put down the rising, and with great severity.

From this time on Richard more and more asserted himself, and encouraged John of Gaunt to take up his kingdom of Castile. Shortly he was able to overcome the Lords Appellant, and by 1383 Richard had married Anne of Bohemia, daughter of the Emperor Charles IV. Although they were childless, the marriage was a happy one, and she acted as a restraining influence on his rashness. He suffered great sadness when she died suddenly in 1394.

Richard had been organising an expedition to Ireland, which no English sovereign had visited for two hundred years. The last had been King John. He planned to re-people the English 'Pale', overawing the Gaelic chiefs with magnificence and presents. He knighted all the four kings of Ireland at a banquet in Dublin. After Christmas he returned hastily to deal with a crisis caused by Lollard demonstrations in London.

It is difficult to define what Lollardy meant; it was a slang phrase which covered much, from pietism to anti-clericalism and opposition to the Church. There was emphasis on hearing and preaching the Word of God, no ill thing in itself except when it led to anti-sacramentalism and hatred of images. Its most distinguished leader was John Wycliffe, an Oxford don and Master of Balliol. Richard prudently did not make a martyr of him; he was allowed to retire quietly to his living of Lutterworth. In 1395 the Lollards nailed 'clauses' to the doors of Westminster Abbey and St Paul's. Richard firmly defended the bishops. The Lollards were said to have drawn back into their shells at his coming like tortoises.

In July 1395 Richard began negotiating for the hand of Isabelle of France, daughter of Charles VI, aged six only. She brought a dowry of £50,000, but, because of her age, the marriage was never consummated. More important, the truce with France was prolonged for twenty-eight years. France could now be relied upon to support Richard against any trouble from his subjects.

In 1397 Thomas Haxey, a clerk, introduced a bill into Parliament demanding the annual appointment of sheriffs; he criticised the defence of the Scottish borders and the expenses of the luxurious Court. Haxey was condemned to death, but later reprieved, and given appointments. It was perhaps that he had been set up by the king. On 5 February the Lords declared that it was treason for any man to excite the Commons to reform anything that affected the person, government or regality of the king. No more extreme statements of Divine Right could have been made. Said Richard: 'The laws of England proceed out of my mouth.'

Three policies are said to be the mark of his reign, although it is legitimate to doubt whether he originated them or his able group of clerks and secretaries. Three of the principal advisers were Stafford, a great magnate, Clifford, a baron, and Walden, the son of a butcher from Saffron Walden. Their relationship with the king is not certain, but they all continued to serve in the next reign. Their fault politically was they did not fully understand economics, and imposed too great a strain on the royal finances.

The first was to provide the king with a strong striking force, more than a simple bodyguard. By 1396 seventy-three cannon had been cast, and 4,000 lbs of gunpowder accumulated. The largest cannon had seven barrels and could fire ten lead bullets at once as well as a stone ball. They could be used both in battle and for sieges. In 1399 there were 1,353 bows in the Tower with arrows, and thirty-nine brass and iron cannon. There were paid reservists all over England.

The second policy was to form a group of magnates on whose loyalty the king could rely absolutely. In 1397–99 there were nine such magnates. All were of ancient family. Nine owed their titles and six most of their wealth to the king. Land was distributed too as well as money, and this all diminished the royal purse.

The third policy was to increase royal authority in local

government. By 1399 eleven shires were ruled by sheriffs who were members of the royal household. Other minor royal officials served as Justices of the Peace. The offices of the Privy Council, the Privy Seal, the Signet, and the Great and Privy Wardrobes grew as a central bureaucracy, casting further burdens on the royal finances. Forced loans and fines of 'La Plesaunce' were necessitated, but the kingdom was fundamentally insolvent, and kept going only by financial ingenuity. The twenty-first article of Richard's deposition was to state that he had forced the people of seventeen shires to submit to him as traitors in order that he might recover fines from them. These and other practices were political mistakes even when regarded as necessities.

Richard's scheme to absorb the possessions of John of Gaunt was political as well as financial. John had first married his cousin Blanche of Lancaster, the greatest heiress of her time. At twenty-two he was created Duke of Lancaster. His income, over £12,000 a year in England, made him the richest man in England. By his second marriage he had become King of Castile in right of his wife. John of Gaunt died on 3 February 1399: on 18 March Richard took possession of all his estates. It was an act of supreme folly.

John of Gaunt's only son by his first marriage was the future Henry IV. He is frequently known as Henry of Bolingbroke, not a title but the name of the castle where he was born. Initially he was known as Earl of Derby. At the age of thirteen he married his sister-in-law, one of the co-heiresses of the earldom of Hereford, a name he assumed as a ducal title. On his father's death he became Duke of Lancaster, where he had officiated as Warden for his father. Henry now contested Richard's throne.

Early in July Henry landed from France, with a small force. He quickly acquired a following, and by a brilliant forced march seized Chester on 9 August. About 13 August the Earl of Northumberland went to him from Richard, offering terms: Richard would restore John of Gaunt's estates to Henry, but himself remain king.

What followed is very obscure. Richard and Henry travelled to London together, Richard being lodged in the Tower. Government was carried on in his name throughout September. Then, on 30 September, it was announced that Richard had abdicated. The document stated that Henry should succeed him. Richard was first imprisoned at Leeds Castle, in Kent, than at Pickering, then at Knaresborough, and finally at Pontefract. There he was either strangled or suffocated.

5   *House of Lancaster*

John of Gaunt, Duke of Lancaster, King of Castile
and León, b. 24 June 1340, d. 3 Feb. 1399,
m.1, 19 May 1359 Blanche (d. 31 Sept. 1369), d.
and heir of Henry, 1st Duke of Lancaster, great-
grand-daughter of King Henry III

35. Henry IV, b. 30 May 1366, usurped the
throne from Richard II 30 Sept. 1399,
d. 21 March 1413, m.l, 1380, Lady Mary de
Bohun (b. 1370, d. 4 July 1394), d. of
Humphrey, Earl of Hereford; he m. 2, 7 Feb. 1403,
Joanne (d. 10 June 1437),
widow of John V de
Montfort, Duke of
Brittany,
d. of Charles, King of
France, without issue

Philippa, b. 31 March
1360, d. 9 June 1415,
m. 11 Feb. 1386 John I,
King of Portugal

issue—Kings of
Portugal

Elizabeth, b. 1362,
d. 24 Nov. 1425, m.l,
24 June 1380
(annulled), John
Hastings, Earl of
Pembroke; m. 2, 1384
John Holand, Duke of
Exeter (beheaded
9 Jan. 1399-1400)

issue

Isabel
d. you

36. Henry V, b. 9 Aug.
1387, s. 21 March 1413, d.
31 Aug. 1422, m. 3 Jan.
1420 Catherine (b. 1401,
d. 3 Jan. 1437), d. of
Charles VI, King of France;
she m. 1428 Owen ap
Meredith Tudor and was
grandmother of King
Henry VII

Thomas, Duke of
Clarence, b.c.
May 1388, k.
at battle of
Baugé 22 March
1421, m. 1411
Margaret (d.
c. Dec. 1439),
widow of John
Beaufort, 1st
Earl of Somer-
set, d. of
Thomas Holand,
2nd Earl of
Kent

John, Duke of
Bedford,
Regent of
France during
Henry VI's
minority, b.
20 June 1389,
d.s.p. 15 Sept.
1435, m.l, 17
Apr. 1423,
Anne (d. 14
Nov. 1432), d.
of John, Duke
of Burgundy;
m. 2, 20 Apr. 1433,
Jaquetta (d. 30 May
1472), d. of Peter
of Luxembourg

Humphrey, Duke of
Gloucester, b. 3
Oct. 1390, d.s.p.
23 Feb. 1447, m.l,
Jacqueline,
Countess of Holland
and Hainault
(annulled c. 1430);
m. 2, c. 1430,
Eleanor (d. 1454),
d. of Richard, 2nd
Lord Cobham

Blanche,
b. 1392, d.
21 May 1409,
m. 1402 Louis
III, Elector
Palatine

issue

Philipp
b. 1393,
5 Jan. 1
m. 26 O
1406 Er
King of
Denma
(d. 1455
s.p.

37, 39. Henry VI, b.
6 Dec. 1421, s. 31 Aug.
1422, dep. by Edward IV
4 May 1461 (see Table 6,
38, 40); restored 9 Oct.
1470, again dep. Apr.
1471, d.c. 21 May
1471, m. 22 Apr. 1445
Margaret (d. 25 Aug.
1482), d. of René, Duke
of Anjou

Edward, Prince of Wales, b. 13 Oct. 1453,
k. at battle of Tewkesbury 4 May 1471,
m. Aug. 1470 Lady Anne Nevill (b.c. 1454,
d. 16 March 1485), d. and co-heir of
Richard, Earl of Warwick; she m. 2,
King Richard III

John of Gaunt m. 2, June 1371, Constance, (d. June 1394), d. of Peter I, King of Castile and León

Katherine, d. 2 Jan. 1418, m. 1393 Henry III, King of Castile and León

issue

John of Gaunt m. 3, 1396-7, his former mistress Katherine (d. 10 May 1403), widow of Sir Hugh Swynford, and d. of Sir Payn Roët. Their children were born in adultery, and surnamed Beaufort, and although legitimatized by Statute 20 Richard III (1397) were allegedly debarred from the throne. The eldest son

John, Earl of Somerset, Marquess of Dorset, b. c. 1372, d. 16 March 1410, m.c. 1399 Margaret, d. of Thomas Holand, 2nd Earl of Kent, s. of Joan, 'The Fair Maid of Kent', d. of Edmund of Woodstock, Earl of Kent·

Henry, 2nd Earl of Somerset, b. 25 Nov. 1400, d. unm. 25 Nov. 1418

John, 3rd Earl and Duke of Somerset, b. 25 March 1404, d. 27 May 1444, m. Margaret (d. 8 Aug. 1482), d. of John Beauchamp, Lord Beauchamp of Bletso

Margaret ('The Lady Margaret'), b. Apr. 1441, d. 5 July 1509, m.l, 1455, Edmund Tudor (d. 1 Nov. 1456), 1st Earl of Richmond, s. of Owen ap Meredith Tudor and Catherine, widow of King Henry V

43. Henry VII

See the House of Tudor on page 108

Thomas, Earl of Perche, b. 1405, d. unm. 1432

Edmund, Marquess of   2d. Dorset, Duke of Somerset, b. 1406, k. 22 May 1455 at battle of St Alban's, m. Eleanor (d. 12 March 1467), widow of Thomas, 9th Baron de Ros, d. of Richard Beauchamp, 2nd Earl of Warwick and Albemarle

issue

HENRY IV

1399-1413

When the Parliament summoned by Richard met at Westminster on 1 October it followed no normal Parliamentary procedure. No speaker was elected; no petitions were heard; and a London mob mingled with the members. Thirty-three articles were read to show that Richard deserved deposition, with emphasis on his having perjured himself. Henry then claimed the vacant throne 'by right of descent vindicated by conquest'.

Henry issued new writs and Parliament met again on 6 October. On 13 October Henry was crowned with great splendour, and anointed with the sacred oil, which, it was claimed, the Virgin Mary had given to St Thomas of Canterbury.

Henry then set about arresting Richard's supporters. He could not feel any certainty. Politically he did not accept, any more than Richard had done, that the king ruled by the authority of Parliament. He was king, he asserted, by the will of the *communitas regni*, the common will of the people of the kingdom. Such a view was certain to be disputed. Richard II had succeeded as the only surviving son of the Black Prince, Edward Prince of Wales, son of Edward III. Edward's next surviving brother had been Lionel of Antwerp, whose daughter Philippa had married Edmund Mortimer, third Earl of March. His son Roger, the fourth earl, had been killed in battle in 1398, leaving a child, another Edmund, fifth Earl of March, then eight years old. Henry's throne was never safe until 1406.

First Richard's half-brothers, the Earls of Kent and Huntingdon, rebelled, and then, inevitably, the Mortimers. They were backed by a rising in Wales, led by Owen Glendower, a descendant of the princes of the ancient house of Powys. Henry campaigned in Wales, but was frustrated by the Welsh withdrawal into the mountains. In the meantime the Percies in Northumberland had won a brilliant victory against the Scots at Homildon Hill in 1402. They had hoped to make an enormous profit by the ransom of prisoners, when Henry forbade it. The northern families made an alliance to restore Richard if he were alive, and if not, to enthrone the child Edmund Mortimer. This alliance was defeated in 1403 at the battle of Shrewsbury, with victory to the king.

The Percies now combined with Mowbray, Earl of Nottingham, and Archbishop Scrope of York. Scrope charged Henry with winning the crown by treachery, with conniving at Richard's murder, with putting men to death without trial and by ruining his subjects by illegal taxation. Scrope and Nottingham were seized and beheaded. It was rumoured that Henry's subsequent ill-health was God's judgment on him for his sacrilege.

Mattathias Percy, Earl of Northumberland, had been too prudent to have been present at Shrewsbury, or to have been caught like Scrope and Nottingham. He travelled into Scotland, Wales, Flanders and France to gain support against Henry. Then he risked his fortune by attacking the local levies at Bramham Moor in 1408, half way between York and Leeds across the road to Scotland. He was routed, and killed in battle. Thus ended the first round in what later became known as the War of the Roses, and the establishment of the House of Lancaster on the throne for the next six decades. There was no outbreak of civil war until 1455, but conspiracies rumbled on beneath the surface.

Henry's funeral effigy at Canterbury shows him as a stout, burly man of undoubted determination. He was able and not unintelligent, but, unlike his predecessor, unhampered by shortage of funds. He now had all the Crown possessions, all the greater possessions of the House of Lancaster, and half of the inheritance of the de Bohuns. Unlike Richard, he had a wide knowledge of other courts, Paris, Bohemia, Venice, and had even travelled as a pilgrim to Jerusalem. Paradoxically his mistakes arose from foreign policy.

He first asked for a French princess for his eldest son. He had only been on the throne for three months, and the French court regarded him as a usurper. Knowing Paris intimately he now fell into the trap of playing with French politics, which led to war in 1401. In 1402 he intrigued in Brittany, and married the widow of the Duke of Brittany, Joanne of Navarre. There was sporadic fighting. He joined in other feuds, first allying with the Duke of Burgundy, and then allying with the Armagnacs against him. At the end of his reign he was planning to invade Aquitaine.

All these adventures and a splendid court cost money, and by

1406 he was insolvent. Already in 1402 he was raising money from Florentine and Genoese bankers, and from the German Hanse merchants. Thus in 1406 he was forced by Parliament to submit to the audit of his accounts and a reform of his household. It was the longest Parliament that had ever sat. On 22 May he was forced to nominate a council which supervised the reforms. He was now altogether a constitutional king. In 1407, in return for a liberal grant, he had to concede the right of the Commons to originate all money grants.

He was forty-one, and had apparently developed sciatica. His health was declining. He seems to have taken little part in the struggles that went on in the Council. More and more the business of state was falling into the hands of his son. In 1408 he was seized with a fit, and for a time was thought to be dead. There were rumours that he had leprosy, but this has never been confirmed. Now he was no longer allowed to nominate his counsellors, and Parliament refused him a revenue for life. In 1411 an attempt was made to make him abdicate in favour of his son, which he indignantly refused. Prince Henry declined to come into open conflict with his father, and retired for a time from public life. In 1411, when the king proposed to lead troops into Aquitaine he was unable to walk, and could scarcely ride. Then he toyed with the idea of a crusade. In 1413 he had a fit while praying in front of King Edward the Confessor's shrine, and lay in a trance in the abbot's house. He had wished to die in Jerusalem, and this was granted to him in a strange way, for he died in the Jerusalem Chamber of Westminster Abbey on 21 March 1413.

HENRY V

1413–1422

Henry V has a reputation unsurpassed by any other English king, and is equalled, in popular imagination, only by Alfred, William the Conqueror and Richard I. Like Richard he is seen as the very embodiment of chivalry. Shakespeare, to whom much is owed in perpetuating his fame, was in truth only reflecting the opinions of his contemporaries. Even in the Second World War a version of Shakespeare's play was produced to raise public morale when spirits were low. Yet there was a darker side of his character, and his policies led only to disaster in his son's reign. His great misfortune was his early death at thirty-five – when he was within two months only of being crowned King of France.

Shakespeare paints 'Harry of Monmouth' as a wild and irresponsible youth. This can hardly have been so. Richard II had already taken him to Ireland in 1399. He was only eleven. At Henry IV's coronation he carried the heavy sword Curtana, and then was heaped with honours: Knight of the Bath, Earl of Chester, Duke of Cornwall, Prince of Wales. These were not empty honours. In 1400 he accompanied his father into Wales, and in October was left in authority at Chester. There can hardly have been time for frivolity. 'Hotspur', the famous Henry Percy, was for a time chief of his council. Thereafter he was almost continuously at war, in Wales, in 1402, against the conspiracy of the Percies in 1403, again in Wales, and in 1405 against Scotland. In 1410 the Commons prayed the king to thank the prince for his services. By 1410 the king was almost entirely disabled by illness, and he now sat in his father's place at the council.

On 21 March 1413 Henry IV died, and Henry V succeeded as king. He was still unmarried, although several brides had been suggested for him. Some chroniclers recount that he was a wild and reckless youth; Bishop Stubbs, never slow to condemn when he found evidence, speaks only of 'the frolics of a high-spirited young man, indulged in the open air of the town and the camp; not in the deliberate pursuit of vicious excitement in the fetid atmosphere of a court'. Shakespeare's tradition is not supported by any contemporary authority, but, like his many other fancies, it made good theatre. One of the earliest acts of the new reign was his removal of the body of Richard II, which had been buried unceremoniously at King's Langley, to an honourable place in the abbey church at Westminster. Almost at once Henry was faced with a Lollard rebellion, which was put down with firmness.

Henry now took the first step to asserting his right to the French throne. Already proposals had been made for his marriage with Catherine of France, daughter of Charles VI. Henry waived his right to the French throne, but claimed the former English possessions of Normandy, Touraine, Anjou, Maine and Poitou, and all the other lands that had been ceded by the treaty of Brétigny. Even in a country in chaos, and distracted by a mad king, this was unacceptable. Henry prepared for war, and the story that the Dauphin sent him a box of tennis balls in reply appears in contemporary writers.

As he prepared to embark a conspiracy was uncovered to proclaim the Earl of March king. The principal leaders were executed. Henry set sail in about 1,500 ships, with 2,500 men-at-arms and 800 archers, disembarking on 13 August 1415. After some skirmishing Henry marched on Calais, and came up with the French at Agincourt. The French spent the night dicing for the prisoners they hoped to take; the English spent the night in preparing for battle and in prayer. The French force far exceeded theirs, some fifty thousand. Henry commanded in person, the flanks of his army protected by woods which prevented the whole French force being committed at the same time.

The French relied on their cavalry, and at first had some advantage. Soon they were in confusion, for the English longbowmen had wounded the horses, and there was no room to rotate their charges. The result was a massacre, and by evening some ten thousand French were dead, and numerous others taken prisoner. The English were too exhausted to pursue them, but next day continued to Calais, which they took. Henry then returned briefly to London, where he remained until 1417. Peace was made with the Welsh and Scots, and a representative sent to the Council of Constance to end the schism in the Church. Aided by the Roman emperor and envoys from Holland and Burgundy, attempts were

THE 'HUNDRED YEARS' WAR, Third Phase 1415-20

ENGLAND

London

Southampton

Calais

Agincourt
25 Oct.

PONTHIEU

Second campaign in
Normandy 1417

Harfleur
11 Aug.

Seine R.

NORMANDY

Paris

HOLY ROMAN EMPIRE

BRITTANY

Treaty of Troyes
Troyes 1420.
3 June 1420. Henry V of
England m. Catherine,
Princess of France (and
later grandmother of
Henry VII)

Loire R.

F R A N C E

POITOU

Henry V's brief
campaign 1415

English possessions
under the Treaty
of Troyes

Battle

AQUITAINE

0   50 miles

0   50 km

Bordeaux

QUERCY

ROUERGUE

GASCONY

NAVARRE

ARAGON   CATALONIA

made to make a permanent settlement with France. Henry visited France briefly, but without a successful settlement.

Henry now prepared for war in ways that seemed almost modern. Arrangements were made not only to victual the army but to provide a regular medical service. Great ships were built, and others provided from the ports: it has been suggested that we should date a permanent royal navy from this time. Then on 23 July 1417 Henry set sail again, but this time with an army of 50,000 and some 1,600 ships.

Henry at once showed his ability as a general. Instead of marching on Rouen, the capital of northern France, he set about securing Norman castles, severing the communication of Rouen with central France. Shortly he had Normandy in his hands, and had neutralised Brittany. Then, in 1418, he cut off Rouen altogether, by land and sea, demanding unconditional surrender. In the middle of winter Rouen was reduced to famine, and drove out from the city 12,000 *bouches inutiles*, who ate up rations, but could not fight, old men, women, children. They were left to perish between the Norman and English lines. Henry has been criticised for what superficially was an act of monumental cruelty. He had not, however, made provision for such a callous use of helpless civilians, which could have destroyed his own army, and the crime should rest as much, if not more, on those who had expelled them. Henry entered Rouen on 19 January 1419, and at once provided food for the starving inhabitants.

Normandy was once again organised, and money struck with the legend *Henricus, Rex Francie*, Henry, King of France. He made peace with Burgundy and Brittany, and at Mantes at the end of the month met the Queen of France and the Princess Catherine, whose hand he immediately demanded in marriage. By May a treaty had been concluded. Henry accepted only to become heir to France, for he held it unbecoming to take the throne so long as Charles VI lived. He was recognised as *Henricus, rex Angliae et haeres Francie*, King of England and heir of France. Henry and Catherine married at Troyes on Trinity Sunday, 2 June 1420. There was still work to be done in making a general peace, and they only entered Paris, together with Charles VI and the Duke of Burgundy, on 1 December. She was crowned at Westminster on 24 February.

England had been quiet during Henry's long absence. The court now made a progress through the Midlands, keeping Easter at Leicester. They then went north to York, and as far as Beverley and

Bridlington. The peace with France did not hold, and in early May Henry was preparing yet another expedition to France.

It was not to be thought that the French would accept English domination willingly, and now the reign of Charles VI was drawing towards its close. The Dauphin had rebelled against the treaty in Chartres, and other cities and towns had followed suit. Henry held Paris after news that there was a move to surrender it to the Dauphin. He was beginning to be short of men, and he had applied to his allies in Germany and Portugal for men-at-arms.

Henry's health was visibly failing; it seemed that he had some form of chronic dysentery. His chamberlain, however, described it as pleurisy. It became clear that he had not long to live, and his last days were spent in arranging for the education of his son and for the government after his own death. When he was told that the end was near, he made his confession, and received the last sacraments, and then ordered that the penitential psalms be read. When they reached the words 'Build thou the walls of Jerusalem' he interrupted them, saying: 'Good Lord, thou knowest that mine intent hath been, and yet is, if I might live, to rebuild the walls of Jerusalem.' As the clergy continued, he breathed his last on 31 August 1422. His body was embalmed, and carried in state to Westminster.

No medieval king has been loved more by his subjects. His private life was temperate, chaste and frugal; he spoke little, answering with a straight yes or no. He was stern, but inflexibly just. If at times he would seemed harsh, as at the siege of Rouen, it was from a serious regard for the best interests of his country and his army. He treated his soldiers with consideration, the first king to provide them with medical services. He was more than a soldier; he was a diplomat of the first order. His system of alliances was arranged quietly, and without fuss. He knew how to depute power to others; in the field this is particularly noticeable in his second and third expeditions to France, when he took no personal part in the warfare. After the initial troubles with Wales and Scotland had been ended, he was able to confide the administration of England to others. Unlike his predecessors, he never had any confrontation from Parliament.

We cannot predict what his future policies would have been. Like his father, his last words were of Jerusalem, and of the crusade. On this he would have seemed fixed.

HENRY VI

1422–1471

Henry VI succeeded when he was only nine months old. The Council appointed the Duke of Bedford his protector, and Bedford's younger brother, the Duke of Gloucester, as protector in his absence in France. His grandfather, Charles VI of France, died on 21 October, and he was at once proclaimed King of France. At first in his mother's care, at three years old he was taken to open Parliament, and 'shrieked and cried' as he was carried in. In 1428, Richard Beauchamp, Earl of Warwick, was appointed his tutor, a devout and cultivated man whom the Emperor Sigismond hailed as the 'Father of Courtesy'. His instructions were,

> to be about the king's person . . . to teach him to love, worship and dread God, draw him to virtue by ways and means convenable, lying before him examples of God's grace to virtuous kings and the contrary fortune of kings of contrary disposition, teach him virtue, literature, language, and other manner of cunning, to chastise him when he doth amiss, and to remove persons not behovefull nor expedient from his presence.

In France the campaigns of Joan of Arc were meeting with success, and Charles VII was crowned at Reims on 17 July 1429. Henry was crowned King of England at Westminster on 6 November 1429; Joan of Arc was shortly captured in France. He was in Rouen during her trial, and probably attended some of the sittings. On 2 December he entered Paris and was given a triumphant welcome. He was crowned in Nôtre Dame on 16 December, but the Parisians were disappointed by the absence of the usual largesse. Shortly he returned to England, where he seems to have behaved tactlessly, for he was reproved by the Council. He was further warned in 1434.

The story that he grew up an idiot, scarcely able to distinguish right from wrong, is baseless. Rather he would seem to have been precocious. In 1437 he was admitted to preside at the Council; and exercised his powers with such recklessness that he was again warned. Proposals were then made for his marriage. Candidates were suggested from Scotland, France, the Empire and Armagnac; he was to be sent portraits of their daughters. France could only accept on condition that he renounce his claim to the French throne, and this was once again stated in 1443. On 22 May England concluded a treaty with René of Anjou, brother-in-law of Charles VII of France, Duke of Lorraine and Count of Provence. Henry was finally married to his daughter Margaret on 22 April 1445, and settled to a happy domestic life. He began his great educational foundations of King's College, Cambridge, and Eton College. Progresses, tours, became frequent, staying at numerous monasteries in 1446, as far as Durham in 1448, and others. The accounts of these journeys concentrate rather upon their religious aspects, and say little or nothing of their political effect. It was at this time that he was rebuked by the Pope for interference in an episcopal appointment.

At Whitsun 1450 Jack Cade's rebellion broke out, and Henry showed the extent of his weakness. At first his appearance at the head of an armed force caused the rebels to retire. They returned again, and he fled with his panicked troops. The mayor and council in London begged him to stand fast, but he fled to Kenilworth, while his troops dispersed. Cardinal Kemp and Bishop Wayneflete managed to contain the rebellion, and Henry made a progress through Kent and Sussex, giving sentences of great severity. There was a 'great harvest of heads'; he would have done better to be conciliatory.

In the prevailing anarchy Richard, third Duke of York, and father of the future Edward IV, returned from Ireland and took a hand in the matter. In November Parliament agreed that York should be declared heir to the throne; in February 1452 he marched on London with a Welsh army, and reached Blackheath. Once again, Bishop Waynflete negotiated a compromise.

Henry travelled the country seeking support, in Norfolk, then in the West Country, then on the Welsh borders, then in the Midlands and East Anglia. On 6 July 1453 he fell ill with what seems to have been a stroke. He lost his reason and memory, and could neither stand nor move. On 13 July the Queen gave birth to their only child, Edward. Margaret and York were now rivals, she for her son, he for himself. York became regent, and she was quietly put aside. Living at Windsor, Henry was incapable, not even knowing he had a son. In 1454 he showed some improvement, and by 30 December he was able to recognise both his wife and the Prince of Wales. York was now excluded from the Council. Margaret and the Duke of Somerset ruled; the king simply obeyed their will.

In May 1455 York assembled another army. At St Albans he took the town easily, capturing the king, who was wounded by an arrow. He had not been wounded seriously, but had a relapse of his illness. He opened Parliament on 9 July, and allegiance to him was renewed. He had a further relapse, and resigned affairs to his council, with York as chief counsellor. The queen, however, managed to remove York from office in 1456. Henry continued to travel the country, but power was wholly in the hands of the great lords. Civil war seemed inevitable, even though in the council the queen was supreme.

War finally broke out in 1459. For a time Henry regained power, and in November the Yorkist leaders were attainted. 'The king, it was said, was simple and led by covetous counsel and owed more than what he was worth. The hearts of the people were turned away . . . '

In July 1460 the Yorkists again had a victory at Northampton, and took the king prisoner in his tent. He was taken to London. On 16 October York claimed the throne, but, after discussion, it was agreed that Henry should keep the throne for life, and that York should then succeed, disregarding the young prince Edward.

On 29 December Queen Margaret, who had raised an army in the north to maintain her son's right, met York at Wakefield, defeating his army and killing him on 29 December. The new Duke of York, Edward, then took up arms, winning a victory at Mortimer's Cross. Then, at the second battle of St Albans on 17 February 1461, York utterly defeated Margaret's northerners, leaving the king to his fate. The king met Margaret and his son, whom he blessed and dubbed a knight. On 4 March 1461 Edward was solemnly proclaimed in London, without waiting for Parliament. He at once set out to attack the northerners, and won a decisive battle at Towton. The king had remained in York, for it was Palm Sunday, and he preferred to spend it in prayer.

Henry fled northwards, and subsequent movements are unclear. By 1462 he was in Edinburgh, and in 1464 gave the citizens a charter to trade in England. More realistically, the Lord of the Isles

THE WARS OF THE ROSES, 1455–71, 1485

North Sea

Irish Sea

■ Lancastrian castle
■ Yorkist castle
✕ Lancastrian victory
✕ Yorkist victory

Northam
Wark
Bamburgh
25 Apr 1464
Hedgeley Moor
Dunstanburgh
Alnwick
Warkworth

Hexham
8 May 1468
Newcastle
Carlisle
Lumley
Brancepeth
Raby
Appleby
Barnard
Castle
Richmond
Skelton
Bolton
Middleham
Masham
Sheriff Hutton
Lancaster
Knaresborough
York
Spofforth
Cawood
Ravenspur
29 March 1461
Towton Moor
Wressell
1471
10 Oct 1460
Wakefield
Pontefract
Sandal
Tickhill
Conisborough
Bolingbroke
Rhuddlan
Liverpool
Henry VII defeats
Lambert Simnel's rebellion
Tattershall
Beaumaris
Conway
Chester
Stokefield
16 June 1487
Newark
Denbigh
Ruthin
Newcastle-
under-Lyme
Belvoir
Castle Rising
Harlech
23 Sept 1459
Blore Heath
Tutbury
Bosworth Field
22 Aug. 1485
Caister
Stokesay
Ludlow
Kenilworth
Fotheringhay
Wingfield
Ludford Bridge
Warwick
Northampton
10 July 1460
Framlingham
2 Feb. 1461
Mortimer's Cross
Tewkesbury
4 May 1471
1468
Edward IV restored 1471–83
St. Davids
Grosmont
Skenfrith
Edgcott
1469
Pleshey
Haverfordwest
White Castle
Gloucester
St. Albans
22 May 1455
Milford Haven
Kidwelly
Abergavenny
Pinlan
17 Feb. 1461
Barnet
London
Pembroke
Swansea
Usk
Berkeley
Wallingford
14 Apr. 1471
Manorbier
Caerphilly
Windsor
Leeds
Ogmore
Cardiff
Farnham
Reigate
Dover
Tiverton
Arundel
Steyning
Herstmonceux
Okehampton
Portchester
Bramber
Pevensey
Corfe
Carisbrooke
Compton

English Channel

0   25   50 miles
0   25   50 km

and Douglas signed a treaty with Edward IV. Nevertheless Margaret continued the struggle, and in the spring of 1464 the north again rose for Henry. The Yorkists crushed the rising, and Henry went into hiding in the wild borders between Lancashire and Yorkshire. Eventually he was captured and taken to London. Various accounts have been given of his treatment, the Lancastrians maintaining that he was treated with cruelty, the Yorkists that he was treated with 'humanity and due reverence'. For himself Henry professed that he was indifferent to the loss of his earthly kingdom, provided that he was allowed to receive the sacraments of the Church. So long as Prince Edward lived, it was obviously in Edward IV's interest to keep Henry alive.

After five years imprisonment the wheel of fortune turned for a brief spell. Margaret, with Warwick and Clarence, formed a league against Edward IV, and restored Henry VI. Edward fled to Flanders. Officially his restoration took place on 9 October 1470. In March 1471 Edward IV returned with an army, and so little support was found for Henry that Archbishop Neville thought it best to treat with Edward. On Easter Day at the battle of Barnet, Edward was victorious, and on 4 May 1471 Margaret was defeated at Tewkesbury, and her son killed. There was no longer a motive for keeping Henry alive, and on 21 May he was murdered. It is not clear who the murderer was, or who gave the order.

In Yorkshire Henry was venerated as a saint and as a martyr. Later Henry VII sought Henry's canonisation from Pope Julius II, and evidence was collected by Henry's former chaplan, Blakman; he claimed that many miracles attested Henry's holiness. Nothing came of it. According to one source Henry VII found the fees demanded by Rome too heavy, and dropped the case. It has never been pursued.

Henry had been weakly in body, and had inherited from his grandfather, Charles VI, a feeble and irresolute mind. He was never more than a puppet in the hands of factions, and not least of the queen. He was not stupid nor unintelligent. His heart was not in kingship. Early in life he had been made a *confrater* in the Abbey of St Edmund at Bury St Edmund's, a lay associate of the order. His preferred life was that of a pious recluse, learned and occasionally enjoying hawking and hunting. He wore his hair shirt whenever he assumed his robes of state.

6 House of York

Edmund of Langley, Duke of York (see Table 4 above),
b. 5 June 1341, d. 1 Aug. 1402, m.l, March 1371-2, Isabel (d. 23 Nov. 1392), d.
of Peter, King of Castile and León; he m. 2, 4 Nov. 1393 Joan, d. of Thomas
Holand, Earl of Kent, without further issue

Edward, 2nd Duke of York and Duke of Albemarle,
b.c. 1373, k. at the battle of Agincourt 25 Oct.
1415, m. Philippa (d.s.p. 17 July 1431), d. of
John, 2nd Lord Mohun of Dunster

Richard, Earl of Cambridge, b.
1375, beheaded 5 Aug. 1415, m.l,
Anne Mortimer (d. Sept. 1411), d.
of Roger, 4th Earl of March; m 2, c. 1411 15, Maud, d.
of Thomas, Lord de
Clifford (d. 26 Aug.
1446), without further
issue

Richard, 3rd Duke of York,
heir to the throne on the
death of his uncle Edmund
Mortimer, 5th Earl of
March (see Table 4) and
Earl of Ulster, b. 21 Sept.
1411, m. *ante* 18 Oct. 1424 Cecily
(d. a nun 31 May 1495), d. of Ralph
Nevill, 1st Earl of Westmoreland, k.
at the battle of Wakefield 31 Dec. 1460

Constance, d. 28
Nov. 1416, m. 1386,
Thomas le Despencer,
1st Earl of Gloucester

Henry of
Hatfield,
b. 10 Feb,
1440-1, d.
young

38, 40. Edward IV, b. 28 Apr.
1442, seized the throne
4 March 1461; dep. 9 Oct.
1470; restored 4 May 1471, d.
9 Apr. 1483, m. 1 May 1464
Elizabeth (b.c. 1437, d.
7 June 1492), d. of Sir
Richard Widville (or
Woodville), Earl of Rivers,
and widow of John Grey,
Lord Ferrers

Edmund, Duke of
Rutland, b. 17
May 1443, k. at
battle of Wake-
field 31 Dec.
1460 unm.

George, Duke of Clarence,
b. 21 Oct. 1449, murdered
18 Feb. 1477, m. 11 July
1469 Isabel (d. 12 Dec.
1476), d. of Richard
Nevill, Earl of Warwick

Edward, Earl of Warwick,
b. 21 Feb. 1475,
beheaded 24 Nov. 1499,
the last male to be
born a Plantagenet

Margaret, Countess
of Salisbury, b. 14
Aug. 1473, beheaded
27 May 1541, m. 22
Sept. 1494 Sir
Richard Pole (d. Nov.
1504). She was the
last surviving
Plantagenet

41. Edward V, b. 4 Nov.
1470, s. 9 Apr. 1483,
dep. 23 June 1483,
and murdered in
the Tower of London
with his brother,
Richard, Duke of
York

Richard, Duke of
York, b. 17 Aug.
1473, d.c. 23 June
1483, when he
was murdered
with his brother,
Edward V: m.
1477-8 Anne
(d.s.p. 16 Jan.
1480-1) d. of John
Mowbray, Duke of
Norfolk

George, Duke of
Bedford, b. March
1476-7, d.c. 1481

Elizabeth ('Elizabeth
of York'), b. 11 Feb.
1465, d. 11 Feb. 1502-3,
m. **43. Henry VII**—
see Table 7; she was
heir presumptive to the
throne, but not so
recognised, on the death
of her brothers, Edward
V and Richard, Duke of
York

42. Richard III, b. 2 Oct. 1452, seized the throne 23 June 1483, k. at battle of Bosworth Field 22 Aug. 1485, m. 12 July 1472 Lady Anne Nevill, widow of Edward, Prince of Wales (see Table 5) (b.c. 1454, d. 16 March 1485), d. of Richard Nevill, Earl of Warwick

Edward, Prince of Wales, b. 1473, d. 31 March 1484, buried at Sheriff Hutton, York

Anne, b. 10 Aug. 1439, d. 14 Jan. 1475-6, m.l, (annulled 1472) 30 July 1447, Henry Holand, Duke of Exeter (d. 1473), having 1d.; she m. 2, 1472, Sir Thomas Leger, and had 1d.

Elizabeth, b. 22 Apr. 1444, d.c. 1503, m. Oct. 1460 John de la Pole, 2nd Duke of Suffolk

issue

Margaret, b. 3 May 1446, d.s.p. 16 Apr. 1503, m. 9 July 1468, as 3rd wife, Charles the Bold, Duke of Burgundy

Ursula, d. young

Mary, b. Aug. 1466, d. 23 May 1482

Cecily, b. 1469, d.s.p. 24 Aug. 1507, m.l, c. Dec. 1487, John, 1st and last Viscount Welles, (d.s.p. 9 Feb. 1498-9); m. 2, 1503, Thomas Kyme

Margaret, b. 19 Apr. 1472, d. Dec. 1472

Anne, b. 2 Nov. 1475, d.s.p. 23 Nov. 1511, m. 4 Feb. 1494-5 Thomas Howard, 3rd Duke of Norfolk, as his 1st wife

Katherine, b. 1479, d. 15 Nov. 1527, m. Sir William Courtenay, later Earl of Devon (d. 9 June 1511)

issue

Bridget, b. 10 Nov. 1480, d. a nun 1517

EDWARD IV

1471–1483

When Edward IV's skeleton was exhumed at Windsor in 1789 it was found to measure six feet three inches. His portraits show him to have been strikingly handsome, and his familiarity with the wives of London citizens was a by-word. He was affable and ingratiating in manner, but firm and decisive when action was needed.

The backcloth to his reign, and to that of Richard III who followed him, is what is known as the Wars of the Roses, although in fact the White Rose was not used as a badge until the very end. In essence it was a dynastic quarrel between the descendants of Edward III, muddied by murder and rebellion, treachery and treasons, beheading even without trial, and squalid family intrigue. In all this the ambitions of married women may be discerned, and not least the hand of Margaret of Anjou, the 'she-wolf' of France, the strong-minded wife of the meek and pious Henry VI. It was complicated above all by the ambitions of the family of Neville, of which the head, the Earl of Warwick, had, both by inheritance from his father and from other relatives, acquired lands and fortune far outweighing those of the Crown. Inevitably he was cast as King-maker – and paid with his life for it.

It is convenient to divide this war into four phases. In the first it was a struggle for the regency, beginning in 1455, between the Dukes of York and Somerset, in which York triumphed at the battle of St Albans in 1455. Then, in a second phase, from 1459, Queen Margaret sought to overthrow him, but was defeated by the Yorkists at the second battle of St Albans on 17 February 1461; Edward IV succeeded his father when he was killed at the battle of Wakefield on the last day of 1460, and seized the throne. He declared himself king in Westminster Hall on 4 March, but once again had to hasten north to attack Queen Margaret, who had regrouped Henry VI's supporters. On Palm Sunday, 29 March, the

Lancastrians were utterly defeated at Towton, and Henry and Margaret fled to Scotland. It is claimed that 28,000 dead were counted on the field by the heralds, but the figure seems exaggerated. Edward was crowned on 28 June 1462, and seemingly felt secure on the throne by January 1463, when Alnwick Castle capitulated. Nevertheless a new, young, Duke of Somerset, and other northern barons, intrigued against him, and raised an army, which was defeated at Hedgley Moor on 25 April 1463.

Edward now turned his thoughts to marriage. Various ladies had been proposed to him, among them a princess of Castile, Isabella, later joint ruler with Ferdinand of Aragon; and Bona of Savoy, sister-in-law of Louis XI of France. Edward was already enchanted with Elizabeth, widow of Sir John Grey of Groby, a daughter of Sir Richard Woodville, who himself had married *en secondes noces* the Duchess of Bedford, the widow of the Duke of Bedford who had governed France in the youth of Henry VI. Edward's marriage was kept secret, and the truth emerged only towards Michaelmas when Warwick was about to go to France to negotiate the marriage with Bona of Savoy. Warwick was offended, and so were many of the peers. Unperturbed, Edward raised his father-in-law to be Earl Rivers, and honoured his relations with leading offices of state. It caused further offence.

In May 1468 Edward declared his intention of invading France, where the king was known to be intriguing with Margaret of Anjou, as also was Warwick and other nobles, among whom was Edward's brother, the Duke of Clarence, and the Earl of Pembroke. There were insurrections in 1469 in Yorkshire and in the Midlands, and Edward himself was taken by the Archbishop of York near Coventry. He was later released by Warwick, for London was still loyal to him. A new rebellion broke out in Lincolnshire in March 1470, but shortly the rebels were defeated at Stamford. The King of France took a hand, backing Warwick, who invaded before Michaelmas. Warwick's brother, the Earl of Northumberland, raised an army as if for the king, and then, having drawn near him, changed sides to support Henry VI. Edward escaped to Holland with about 800 men, while his wife and children sought sanctuary in Westminster. Henry was released from prison, and proclaimed king once more.

Edward now obtained 50,000 florins from the Duke of Burgundy, and landed again in Cromer on 12 March 1471. Finding the area hostile, he sailed further north to the Humber. He travelled in Yorkshire, raising support, and then moved south to near Banbury, where he met an army raised by his brother Clarence. Battle was not joined, and Edward was able to proceed to London, where he was received with warmth. Some thought that they might recover debts Edward had left behind; others that the citizens were encouraged by the attentions Edward had paid to their wives. Edward now had possession of the person of Henry. Marching out of London, he met Warwick's army at Barnet on 14 April, and then that of Queen Margaret on 4 May. Margaret was taken prisoner, and her son, Edward Prince of Wales, was either slain in battle or murdered after it. Two days later the Duke of Somerset and fourteen others, who had sought sanctuary in the abbey at Tewkesbury, and delivered after a promise that their lives would be spared, were beheaded. A further insurrection took place in Kent. Edward retired on London, arriving on 21 May. On the same night Henry VI died. It was pretended that he died of a broken heart.

Edward could now reign tranquilly. The direct line of Lancaster was extinct. So too was the line of John of Gaunt: his only surviving descendant was the son of Edmund Tudor, Earl of Richmond, whose father had married Catherine of France, the widow of Henry V. This son, in the near future, would be Henry VII. His uncle, the Earl of Pembroke, prudently took him to Brittany.

In 1472 Edward proposed to invade France, and received funds from Parliament. Finding these insufficient he invented a new kind of tax, that any might give what he pleased 'by way of benevolence'. A chronicler records that a rich widow gave him £20, no unhandsome sum, and was rewarded with a kiss – whereon she doubled the sum. In 1474 Edward landed in France, but, after some bargaining, agreed to be bought off, 75,000 crowns were to be paid to Edward during the life of both monarchs, and the hand of Elizabeth, Edward's eldest daughter, given to the Dauphin. Aged nine, she was to await marriage until she reached a more suitable age. Her destiny, rather, was to be the bride of Henry VII.

Of the king's opponents there now remained one, the Duke of Clarence. He angered Edward by aspiring to the hand of the only daughter of the Duke of Burgundy, Mary, heiress to the duchy. Edward had him sent to the Tower, and in 1478 accused him before Parliament. Those present sat in silent horror, and he was condemned to be executed. This was delayed, until the Speaker requested on behalf of the Commons that the sentence should take effect. It was ordered to be done in the Tower, secretly. No one could now oppose Edward's will.

Edward next began using the law officers of the crown to search out nobles and gentlemen of means for penal offences. Fines became a convenient source of income. It must be remembered that at this time the monarch had to bear all the expenses of government apart from war and defence. As Edward I had done, Edward IV maintained profitable relations with the City of London, engaging in the wool trade, the principal export of the time, but more regularly than his forebears had done. It was a rich and extravagant court, and the pension from the King of France inclined him to a French alliance. This was imprudent, for the principal trade in wool was with Burgundy and the Low Countries, and less with France. When Louis XI invaded Burgundy and Picardy, Duchess Mary appealed to Edward for help. He ignored it, preferring the pension and the prospect of the marriage of his daughter to the Dauphin.

Relations with Scotland now deteriorated, and an army was sent in 1482 under Richard, Duke of Gloucester, later Richard III. His campaign was made easier by the rebellion of some Scottish nobles, which enabled the invading force to retire in August. Duchess Mary of Burgundy was then killed by a fall from a horse. By way of making peace with France and facilitating trade, the merchants of Flanders contrived the treaty of Arras, by which her daughter Margaret was to marry the Dauphin, and receive as dowry Artois and lands in Burgundy taken from her brother Philip. This violated Edward's treaty with France, and in January he summoned Parliament to raise supplies for war. The clergy likewise were required to make a contribution. Quite suddenly, he was taken ill, dying on 9 April 1483. French writers believe he died of mortification as a result of the treaty of Arras.

All in all, it had been a chaotic reign until the last years. If the king became absolute, it was only at the cost of war. These wars had been fought largely by retainers, men paid in the service of great lords. It does not seem that the country had been devastated or that the commonalty had much suffered. It is perhaps because of this that the Commons voted supplies willingly enough. Now Edward's heir succeeded, aged only twelve, with the threat of another minority, and more quarrelling and even war between such lords as had survived.

EDWARD V

1483

Edward V was the eldest son of Edward IV by his Queen, Elizabeth Woodville, born during the time that his father was in exile. His father recovered the throne on 26 June 1471, and created him Prince of Wales while still an infant. Grants were made for his maintenance, including the Duchy of Cornwall, and ordinances drawn up for the 'virtuous guiding' and education of the child. Various honours were bestowed on him. He was in his thirteenth year when his father died on 9 April 1483, and his short reign, until he was deposed on 23 June 1483, is entirely a history of the struggle between the Woodvilles, his maternal relations, and his uncle Richard, Duke of Gloucester, from which, backed by the all-powerful family of the Neville, he later emerged as King Richard III. Edward's coronation was appointed for 4 May, and then deferred until 22 June, and then until 12 November.

On Sunday 22 June, at St Paul's, a sermon was preached by a Dr Shaw, the Lord Mayor's brother, on Wisdom 4.3: 'Bastard slips shall not take deep root.' It impugned the validity of Edward IV's marriage, and claimed that his children were bastards. A Parliament, whose validity has been questioned, met on 25 June, and argued in a similar vein, declaring Richard king. The Lords, Commons and the Lord Mayor and citizens of London sent a deputation to that effect to Edward V. His brief reign was over.

The precise time and date of his murder, with his brother, Richard, Duke of York, is not known, but it is clear that it took place in the Tower of London. The matter was later investigated by Sir Thomas More, the Chancellor, who found that it had been carried out at the behest of Richard III. The evidence has been much questioned, and perhaps certainty will never emerge. At least Sir Thomas More's information where the bodies were to be found, at the foot of the White Tower staircase, is certain, even if it can be questioned whether these were indeed their bodies.

Sadly, no account survives of the character of this pathetic child-king.

RICHARD III

1483–1485

An old lady, Katherine, Countess of Richmond, whom Sir Walter Raleigh knew, and who died early in James I's reign, having lived to the astounding age of 140, said that as a girl she had danced with Richard at court: 'He was the handsomest man in the room except his brother Edward, and he was very well made.' We may perhaps prefer her reminiscence to that of Archbishop Moreton, that Richard was a hunchback with a deformed hand and a monster of abominable cruelty. The tale was relayed to Sir Thomas More and others, and eventually, via Holinshed, reached Shakespeare. His play builds up a fine drama of plots and suspicion, but assuredly of the greatest number of murders of which Richard has been accused he can be acquitted for the lack of sufficient evidence. For the past two centuries Richard's enigmatic character has been the subject of speculation and controversy, whether or no he murdered his nephew Edward V and his brother, the princes in the Tower.

It is of course true that the Plantagenets were men of violence. Judicial murder is commonplace, save for Henry VI, who himself was murdered. Murders run like a scarlet thread through to Henry VIII's reign, and beyond to his daughters. When Edward IV died, Edward V was in the hands of his grandfather Lord Rivers and Sir Richard Grey: Richard had them imprisoned at Middleham. Lord Hastings, following a quarrel provoked by Richard at the Council, was summarily beheaded over a log; Rivers and Grey were executed later.

The court chaplain, in a public sermon, had cast doubt on the validity of Edward IV's marriage. It was curious that the question had not been raised long before. Edward V first, for his protection, and then his brother, for companionship, were inveigled by Richard into the Tower. They never left. Murdered, Richard never made any demur. It is hard to condemn on negative evidence, but harder still to acquit.

Richard was the reputed murderer of Prince Edward, Henry VI's son. Anne Neville had been betrothed to the prince, and her death, in March 1485, by then Richard's wife, has also been laid at his door. It is claimed that he wished to marry the Princess Elizabeth of York, Edward's eldest daughter. She is reported to have said that she would sooner be buried. Nevertheless, Richard is believed to have been deeply attached to Anne Neville. It may well be another court canard. He would hardly have wished to marry his own niece, against all the laws of the church.

Richard's first appointment was as Admiral of the Sea, at the age of only nine. He received a number of other appointments, largely sinecures to provide him with an income; the first serious appointment was when he was made Constable of England for life and Chief Justiciar of South Wales. He shared Edward's exile in Holland. On their return in 1471 he commanded the vanguard at Barnet and at Tewkesbury, and showed himself a skilful and brave commander. On 14 July he was given the castles of Middleham and Sheriff Hutton in Yorkshire, and Penrith in Cumberland. These had belonged to Warwick the Kingmaker, and Richard now was to marry his daughter, Anne. His brother, Clarence, already married to her sister, attempted to frustrate the marriage, but unsuccessfully; it led to ill-will between the brothers for many years. It is unlikely that he had any responsibility for the death of his brother in 1478, whether or no he was drowned in a butt of malmsey. On 12 May 1480 he was made the king's lieutenant-general in the north. He punished a Scottish raid, returning to Sheriff Hutton. In 1482 he campaigned against Scotland, for which he had the thanks of Parliament in 1483. Then Edward IV died on 9 April.

Edward V, whose fate has already been related, was to have been crowned on 22 June; it was postponed until 2 November. On 24 June the Duke of Buckingham spoke to some citizens at the Guildhall, urging Richard's claims. They stood silent, until the recorder asked whether they would have Richard for their king. A few at the back called: 'King Richard!' Parliament met the following day, or what seemed to be one, at which Richard was acclaimed. A deputation was sent to him at Baynard's Castle, asking him to take the throne. He did this on 26 June, the following day. A splendid coronation took place on 6 July.

Buckingham now turned on Richard, crossing to Brittany, where Henry of Richmond had prudently kept himself secluded. A general rebellion was about to break out all over the country, which, it was rumoured, Buckingham would lead. He was prevented by unseasonable floods which kept him in Wales. He was caught in Shropshire, brought before Richard, and executed on 2 November.

Parliament met on 23 January 1484, confirming the king's title, and attainting a hundred persons who had been implicated in the rebellion. Some laws were enacted, including one against 'benevolences'. Richard sent a curious letter to the bishops, ordering them to repress and punish immorality. At the end of the year there was a proclamation punishing lying rumours and seditious writing. Offensive to Richard was the rhyme which coupled him with his chief counsellors:

> The catte, the rat and Lovell the dogge
> All ruled England under the hogge –

an allusion to Lord Chancellor Catesby and the badges of the others, including Richard's own badge of the Boar's Head.

A general rebellion was now expected. The Princess Elizabeth was sent, a virtual prisoner to Sheriff Hutton castle, where Richard already kept his brother Clarence's son Edward, Earl of Warwick.

Commissions of array were sent to every county ordering troops to be ready at an hour's warning. Having hesitated in March, and having denied that he had ever entertained it, Henry of Richmond landed at Milford Haven on 7 or 8 August. Richard had some difficulty in assembling troops, and excuses were made. Henry wasted no time, and shortly reached Lichfield. By 20 August Richard had reached Leicester, with what was reputed as the largest army ever seen in England. On 22 August the armies met near Market Bosworth, but Lord Stanley and his brother joined Henry openly. A contingent dispatched from York, with Yorkshire prudence, arrived too late for the battle. The battle lasted some two hours only, and in a last desperate attempt the king himself charged into the mêlée. It was a suicidal act, for he was surrounded and killed. His golden coronet fell from his helmet, and was later picked up and placed on Henry's head by Lord Stanley. Scarcely a hundred men had perished on either side. Richard's body was unceremoniously trussed on a horse's back and carried to the Grey Friars in Leicester. After two days exposure to the public gaze it was quietly buried. Later the remains were exhumed and thrown into the River Soar from Bow bridge. An inscription was placed on a nearby building: *Near this spot lie the remains of Richard III, the last of the Plantagenets, 1485.*

Richard is said to have been an able administrator, but his principal ministers, Lovell and Catesby, made him unpopular. The death of his only legitimate son left the succession with his sister, Elizabeth. His proposal, after the death of his wife, to marry Elizabeth of York, his niece, was regarded as scandalous. Yet he was not the monster of Shakespeare's play. Several portraits of him survive. He had a thin, intellectual face with a somewhat blank expression. Controversy is still kept alive by the Richard III Society, with the object of exculpating him from the murder of his two nephews in the Tower.

7   *The House of Tudor*

43. Henry VII, b. 28 July 1457 (see Table 5), proclaimed King of England by right of conquest 22 Aug 1485, d. 22 Apr. 1509, m. 18 Jan. 1486 Elizabeth (b. 11 Feb. 1465, d. 11 Feb. 1502-3), eldest d. of Edward IV (see Table 6)

Arthur, Prince of Wales, b. 20 Sept. 1486, d.s.p. 2 Apr. 1502, m. Catherine, Princess of Aragon, (b. 16 Dec. 1485, d. 6 Jan., 1536), d. of Ferdinand V, King of Castile and Aragon; she m. 2 his brother, Henry VIII

44. Henry VIII, b. 28 June 1491, s. 22 Apr. 1509, King of Ireland from 1540-1, d. 28 Jan. 1547, m.1, 11 June 1509, his brother's widow Catherine (marriage diss. 23 May 1533)

Edmund, Duke of Somerset, b. 20 Feb. 1498, d. Jan. 1499

Henry, Duke of Cornwall, b. 1 Jan., d. 22 Feb. 1510-11

Duke of Cornwall, b. and d. Nov. 1513

a prince, b. and d. Dec. 1514

47. Mary I, b. 18 Feb. 1515-16, s. 19 July 1553, d.s.p. 17 Nov. 1558, m. 25 July 1554 Philip II, King of Spain, etc., (d. 13 Sept. 1598)

Henry VIII m. 2, 25 Jan. 1532-3, Anne (b. 1501, marriage diss. 17 May 1536, beheaded 19 May 1536), d. of Sir Thomas Boleyn

a son, b. and d. 29 Jan. 1535-6

48. Elizabeth I, b. 7 Sept. 1533, s. 17 Nov. 1558, d. unm. 24 March 1603

Henry VIII m. 3, 20 May 1536, Jane (b.c. 1500, d. 14 Oct. 1537), d. of Sir John Seymour

45. Edward VI, b. 12 Oct. 1537, s. 28 Jan. 1547, d. 6 July 1553

Henry VIII m. 4, 6 Jan. 1539, Anne (b. 22 Sept. 1516, d. 17 July 1557) (marriage annulled 13 July 1540) d. of John, Duke of Cleves; m. 5, 8 Aug. 1540, Catharine (b.c. 1521, beheaded 13 Feb. 1542), d. of Lord Edmund Howard; m. 6, 12 July 1543 Katharine, (b. 1513. d.s.p. 5 Sept. 1548), d. of Sir Thomas Parr

Margaret, b. 29 Nov. 1489, d. 18 Oct. 1541, m. 8 Aug. 1503 James IV, King of Scotland (k. at the battle of Flodden Field 9 Sept. 1513)

See Table 11 for the Kings of Scotland on page 226

Elizabeth, b. 2 July 1492, d. 14 Sept. 1495

Mary, b. 1498, d. 26 June 1533, m.1, 9 Oct. 1514, Louis XII, King of France (d.s.p. 1 Jan. 1515); she m. 2 as his 3rd wife, 13 May 1515, Charles Brandon, Duke of Suffolk (d. 14 Aug. 1545)

Henry, Earl of Lincoln, b. 11 March 1516, d. unm. 8 March 1534

Frances, b. 16 July 1517, d. 21 Nov. 1559, m.1, 1535, Henry Grey, 3rd Marquess of Dorset, later Duke of Suffolk (beheaded 23 Feb. 1554); she m. 2 Adrian Stokes (d.s.p.c. 1581)

Eleanor, b.c. 1520, d. Nov. 1547, m. 1537 Henry Clifford, 2nd Earl of Cumberland (d. 8 Jan. 1569)

issue, from whom descend the Earls of Derby

46. Jane (commonly known as Lady Jane Grey), b. Oct. 1537, s. 6 July 1553 in accordance with the Wills of Henry VIII and Edward VI, dep. 19 July 1553, beheaded 12 Feb. 1553-4

Katherine, heiress presumptive to her sister, m.l., 21 May 1553 Henry Lord Herbert, later 2nd Earl of Pembroke; m. 2., Dec. 1560, Edward Seymour, 1st Earl of Hertford (d. 6 Apr. 1621) and d. a prisoner in the Tower of London 26 Jan. 1567

issue—heir-general Lady Kinloss

Mary, m. Aug. 1565 Thomas Keyes, from whom descend the Lords Keyes

HENRY VII

1485–1509

If not the cleverest, certainly the shrewdest King of England, Henry VII had a somewhat tenuous claim to the throne. Descended from John of Gaunt by his third wife, their Beaufort descendants were born in adultery; although legitimated by Statute (20 Richard II, 1397), they were allegedly barred from the throne. By his mother, he was the sole surviving descendant of John of Gaunt. The son of Edmund Tudor, Earl of Richmond, his grandfather, Sir Owen Tudor, was a descendant of Welsh princes, who had married Catherine of France, widow of Henry V. Conscious, perhaps, of his Welsh descent, he bore the Dragon of Wales as his personal standard at the battle of Bosworth, and this, carved in stone and endlessly repeated, is portrayed in King's College Chapel, Cambridge, where he completed the work of Henry VI. Born posthumously, he was Earl of Richmond from birth. He was brought up under the care of his uncle, Jasper Tudor, Earl of Pembroke. His tutor, Andreas Scotus, reported that he had never seen a boy so quick in learning. After Edward IV had regained the throne in 1471, it was no longer safe for him to remain in England, and Pembroke took him to Brittany. Edward tried to persuade the Duke of Brittany to give him up, but the order, first given, was then revoked. With the death of the princes in the Tower there was none left nearer to claim the throne.

Henry was in Brittany from 1471 until 1485. An only child, he was reserved and inward-looking; he formed no intimate friendships, except perhaps with the future Cardinal Morton. He, while still Bishop of Ely, with the Duke of Buckingham, agreed to promote Henry's claim to the throne against Richard's usurpation of his nephews and tyranny. A rising was planned for 1483, but was foiled by foul weather.

At Christmas 1483, in the cathedral at Rennes, friends who had escaped from Richard bound themselves to Henry, who in turn took a solemn oath to marry Elizabeth of York, the heir of her line. Finally, after careful preparation, Henry embarked at Harfleur on 1 August 1485, reaching Milford Haven within a week. He was accompanied by English refugees and troops provided by Charles VIII of France. Welshmen and English gathered around him, and by 22 August he had about 5,000 men, half the number of Richard's opposing army. Henry had no battle experience, but a rivulet on his left and a morass on his right protected his flanks. After some two hours of fighting, Sir William Stanley, who had hung back, changed sides to support Henry, while Richard plunged into the mêlée in a reckless action that cost him his life. Henry's success was established.

Disorder did not die with Richard. In 1487 Lovell set up Lambert Simnel to personate an heir to George Duke of Clarence, and provided an army of Yorkists, Irish levies and German mercenaries. Simnel was crowned in Dublin on 24 May; he crossed to England, and was defeated and taken prisoner at Stoke-on-Trent on 16 June. It was the last battle of the Wars of the Roses. Then, from 1492 to 1499, Henry was pestered by Perkin Warbeck, who intrigued against him in Burgundy, Kent, Ireland and Scotland. When he landed in Devonshire, he was taken prisoner. In the Tower he intrigued with Edward, Earl of Warwick, Clarence's son: Henry had them both executed.

A portrait in the House of Lords painted from Henry's death mask shows him about this time. His face is calm, scholarly and calculating, without malice, with the sword Curtana, the unpointed sword of mercy, in his hand. Rather he was slow to punish, and preferred pressure and diplomacy. It is a mistake to think that it was a time of growth of Parliament. Henry used Parliament to raise taxes; it did not control him. He manipulated it. Only twenty-three peers were summoned to his first Parliament; their numbers had been reduced by the wars. He was in no haste to increase them. In November 1487, immediately after his coronation, Henry revived the Court of Star Chamber, so called from the decoration of the walls. It was a prerogative court which had existed at least from the reign of Edward III. In it the king had sat with the Chancellor and principal officers of state to try 'over-mighty' subjects, who could not easily be made amenable to the ordinary courts. It was in no way an instrument of injustice. Parallel to this revival were two new statutes. The Statute of Livery denied private armies of retainers, forbidding the wearing of liveries, the badge of their leaders. This was fortified by the Statute of Maintenance. It forbade all, and so the great lords whose practice it had been, from overawing juries by crowding the courts with their own supporters and men-at-arms. Where the local courts could not deal with a case, the Star Chamber was available. The king no longer sat. His prerogative was administered by the Lord Chancellor, the Treasurer and the Privy Seal, with a bishop and two chief justices. They could impose fines and imprisonment and deal with juries which gave perverse or unsatisfactory verdicts. In these ways Henry reformed justice and suppressed the barons who had subverted it.

Edward III had created a new rank in the peerage, that of duke. Primarily the honour was given to his sons; slowly it was given to others, so creating, together with the marriage of princesses, para-royal families. These even provided queens to England. With Henry VII this policy ended: his son was to marry a princess of Spain, his daughters to the Kings of Scotland and France. Thus began a new policy in which the monarchy was enhanced by its royal connections, and the nobility further weakened. It was a policy which Henry VIII partly deserted, but to which Mary I adhered, and to which Elizabeth I partially adhered in her dalliances that led to nothing. There was nothing new in this; it was the practice of all Europe. For England it spelt the emergence of what was to become a world power.

Henry is an enigmatic character, to a great extent because he left no papers, no diary, no letters. There is something secret, and secretive about him. He loved pomp and splendour, but much, like the dragons in King's College chapel, is allusive. So is the great rose window in the south transept of York Minster, with its patterned red and white roses, which commemorates his marriage to Elizabeth of York. Although the marriage was for dynastic reasons, it seems there was a genuine love between them. Henry could be avaricious in building up taxation, in increasing, often by the devious means of benevolences, the wealth of the crown. Yet he could show great generosity. Richard III's body was brought from Greyfriars in Leicester to lie with his queen in Westminster Abbey. He gave his enemy, Richard III, a splendid marble tomb, with an effigy in alabaster. It was destroyed at the Reformation. He was orthodox in religion: there is an account of £4,000 given 'for the Pope's use'. There is a touching account of how, when their eldest son, Prince Arthur, died, he went to comfort the queen. God, she told him, had left him yet 'a fair Prince and two fair Princesses';

and, 'God is where He was, and we are both young enough.' Sadly, she died in childbirth the following year.

When Arthur died, Henry hastened to have his widow, Catherine of Aragon, marry his son Henry. The negotiations for obtaining a dispensation were protracted, even though a church law (as distinct from a law of God) can always be dispensed by authority. Henry's motive, however, was impure. It was that he wished to retain the dowry she had brought. Then he bullied her, making her write to her father, Ferdinand of Aragon, after the death of Queen Elizabeth, asking for Henry the hand of Catherine's sister Juana, the widow of Philip of Burgundy. The squalid affair ended only when Henry discovered that she was in the habit of carrying about the embalmed body of her deceased husband. Henry now directed his attentions towards the widowed Queen of Naples. An account of his detailed enquiries about her is meticulous in examining and questioning the most intimate of her features. It's true that long distance courting has its disadvantages, in that too little inquiry can lead to more than disappointment. To mention only one instance, one may consider George IV and the repellent Caroline of Brunswick.

Henry VII's reign coincided with the discovery of the New World and of the Indies, with the consequence of a complete revolution of the directions of world trade. In the same year that Vasco da Gama set out for the Indies, John and Sebastian Cabot became the first Europeans to land on the American mainland. It was the seed of what was to follow. Where da Gama had led, England was later to follow, to her greater profit. How much the king knew we cannot tell, but it is hard to credit that he was not aware of what was taking place. His reign coincided with great building activity, in the universities, in the enhancement of cathedrals, and above all in his most elegant chapel that he added to Westminster Abbey. In its harmonious proportions one can perceive most cultivated taste.

Henry was above all a good manager. By 1492 the royal accounts show a surplus, and that he had repaid all he had borrowed. When he came to the throne the Crown was heavily in debt; now the income from the Crown lands had risen from some £13,000 to over £32,000. Trade, which he had been at pains to foster with Flanders, had increased the customs revenue from £20,000 to over £40,000. In the first five years of his reign his income averaged £52,000; the last five years it averaged £142,000. After 1497 he was able to save large sums annually, and at his demise to leave some one and a half million pounds. Moreover, save for the brushes with the pretenders, there had been no civil war. Except for a pointless expedition to France, there had been no external war either. Justice had been restored for all men, high and low. There was peace with all his neighbours, and peace with the Church.

HENRY VIII

1509–1547

If Henry VII had succeeded, by hard work and rigorous financial policies, in placing the finances of the Crown on a firm footing, Henry VIII surpassed his father beyond all possible expectation. An inventory, in the hands of the Society of Antiquaries, shows that at the end of his reign his income had reached £250,000 a year; and that his accumulated fortune, taking into account 90,000 listed items, was no less than £10 billion, that is to say, in English (not American) usage, ten million times one million. By comparison the present Queen is a pauper, with an estimated fortune of only £450 million.

Henry VIII is celebrated in all sorts of ways. As a romantic figure, with his six serial marriages – of which one or two only were possibly romantic; as founder of the Protestant Reformation – although, apart from his schism from the Papacy, he was a strictly traditionalist Catholic; as the founder of the Royal Navy, although he was no seaman; as a respecter of the rights of Parliament, whereas in truth he used it masterfully.

Erasmus, the most distinguished scholar of the Renaissance, was struck by Henry's intellectual precocity as a child and his polished manner. As a youth he excelled at tilting and tennis, while at twenty-nine at hunting he could exhaust eight or ten horses in a single day. He took great delight in music, and was devoted to religious observances.

In 1509, after his father's death, he married his brother Arthur's widow Catherine of Aragon, following a papal dispensation. They were crowned together on 24 June; a general pardon for prisoners and debtors of the Crown was proclaimed; Empson and Dudley, his father's financial ministers, were sent to the Tower amid popular acclaim. Next year they were beheaded. His reign falls into two fairly distinct halves; the first, in which he established himself in the devious web of European politics; the second, in which his main preoccupations centred round relations with the Church, the dissolution of the monasteries, and his attempt to arrange for the succession to the throne.

In foreign politics he wavered between the Empire and France. In this the Pope was a factor, not so much because he was a spiritual figure but rather as the ruler of a number of Italian states, which it was needful to keep on good terms with the Empire. It was by the papal consecration that the Emperor received his title, but the actuality of power derived from his election by European sovereigns. Among these was Venice, which still retained much of its commercial importance, until its wane during the eighteenth century. So, in 1511 Henry entered the Holy League, of Aragon, and Venice with Papacy, to expel the French from Italy. In the following year Aragon united with Castile by the marriage of Isabella with Ferdinand, who now took the title of King of Spain. Henry, having gone to war in their support, was deflected by an invasion from Scotland as French allies; James IV of Scotland was defeated at Flodden Field on 9 September 1513. Henry's French war pursued a futile course, and, when both the Emperor Maximilian and Ferdinand deserted, made peace with France. Henry's sister Mary was married to the aged Louis XII at Abbeville on 9 October. He died on the following 1 January. Henry then allowed his sister to marry Charles Brandon, later Duke of Suffolk. In Parliament, when it met in November, the Cardinal's hat was received by Wolsey, who now became Henry's closest friend and adviser. He was as shrewd as Henry, and clever in amassing money. It was he who guided Henry through a veritable thicket of foreign relations, with the Swiss, with the Duchy of Milan, with Germany and the Empire, with Spain, with the Low Countries, and with the Pope.

In May 1520 Henry received the Emperor at Canterbury; they crossed to meet Francis I of France at 'the Field of the Cloth of Gold' at Guines, a diplomatic meeting of unparalleled splendour. Henry had a further meeting with Charles V in July. During 1521 Francis and Charles were at open war, in which Henry joined in 1522. Little came of it, save demands on Parliament for money, grudgingly given. Riots followed in southern England and London. By 1525 Henry was able to make peace, because Charles V was unable to continue the war, and Henry himself unable to continue without him. Thus Henry made peace with France which, by Wolsey's diplomacy, was made to pay a high price in the form of tribute and pensions. Charles V's sack of Rome in May 1527 further strenghtened the Anglo-French alliance, and greatly weakened what was a greatly secularised papacy.

This set the background for the royal divorce. Henry had already had a by-blow by Elizabeth Blount, Henry Fitzroy, created Duke of Richmond. His fancy was now caught by Anne Boleyn; if he could have illegitimate progeny, he could have legitimate heirs. So in May 1527 the question was raised, whether the Pope had been right in giving him a dispensation to marry Catherine of Aragon. Wolsey, with Cardinal Campeggio, were ordered to hear the case.

In January 1528 England declared war on Spain and the Empire. It was an act that could only be unpopular, for it spelt the end of trade with the Netherlands as well as with Spain, the staple of English commerce. Campeggio let the case drag on, and Henry referred his case to the universities. Oxford and Cambridge were subjected to not a little cajolery and intimidation; opinions favourable to the king were obtained from universities and corporations in France and Italy. Wolsey, Archbishop Warham with four bishops and twenty-two abbots memorialised the Pope, asking him to dissolve the marriage without further delay. The attorney-general took action against the bishops as a body, on the grounds that all the clergy had incurred the penalties of *praemunire* by acknowledging Wolsey's authority as legate of a foreign power. It was a crude way of obtaining both money as a fine, and the admission that they had no right to appeal to a foreign power: they were required to acknowledge Henry as supreme head of the Church in England. The clergy concurred, adding the words 'in so far as the law of Christ allows'. Parliament and the Speaker remonstrated, but gave in; except for Bishop Tunstall of Durham, so did the Convocation of York.

By May Henry moved further. Spiritual men, he told the Speaker and twelve of the Commons, were only half his subjects. They had an obedience to the Pope as well as himself. Thus on 15 May the Commons made a full submission. Sir Thomas More, the Chancellor, immediately resigned his seal of office. Two friars also protested, and were arrested. On 15 November the Pope himself sent a further brief of disapproval. He had already sent two.

When Archbishop Warham died in August 1532 the King was able to nominate a compliant successor, Thomas Cranmer. Parliament had already decreed that the payment of the first fruits of dioceses to Rome should cease. The peers had agreed, but it had a stormy passage in the Commons.

On 25 January 1533 Henry went through a ceremony of marriage with Anne Boleyn. This was not made known until Easter, by when she was known to be pregnant. In spite of opposition, Parliament now passed an act forbidding appeals to Rome. Cranmer declared the king's marriage to Catherine of Aragon as invalid on his own authority. In Rome, on 11 July, Henry was excommunicated personally. In September Anne gave birth to a daughter, later Elizabeth I; Henry's daughter Mary was deprived of her title of princess, and treated as a bastard.

In 1534 the Council decreed that henceforth the Pope should be called only 'the bishop of Rome'; bishops would for the future be appointed by royal authority, and without recourse to the Holy See. Further statutes dealt with appeals and the succession, by which all the king's subjects were required to swear to the entailment of the crown on Henry's children by Anne Boleyn. This oath Sir Thomas More and Bishop Fisher of Rochester refused, and were committed to the Tower at once. By now the Pope had declared Cranmer's actions invalid, but there was no longer room for argument.

A reign of terror had now begun, and even some bishops expected to be sent to the Tower. Preachers were appointed to execrate the Pope; every cleric and every monk was required to sign a declaration that the 'bishop of Rome' had no more authority in England than any other bishop. In June two cart loads of friars were sent to the Tower; the Observant Franciscans were suppressed entirely. Other recusants were imprisoned or chained. On 15 January 1534 Henry's title as head of the church was added to the royal titles; paradoxically the title conferred on him by the Pope, Defender of the Faith, was allowed to remain. Other acts were passed, giving the king the first fruits of benefices and ordering a valuation of all ecclesiastical property. It was treasonable to call the king a heretic.

In 1535 the weight of persecution and tyranny was increased. In the middle of the year Carthusian monks were martyred, a strange choice, for they lived in a vow of silence. Cardinal Fisher, as he now had become, was beheaded on 22 June, Sir Thomas More on 6 July. For reasons of their own, no other monarchs found themselves able to support Henry; and his papal deposition was everywhere ignored. From 1529 until 1535 it had been tyranny by manipulation of Parliament. It was now directed at the monasteries.

A mass of misinformation was spread abroad, calling attention to their abominable and filthy lives. It has been shown to be without justification. Thomas Cromwell was appointed Lord Privy Seal, with the express object of dealing with the monasteries. In its final session the king was given possession of every monastery which had a revenue of less than £200 a year. It was the beginning of Henry's immense accretion of wealth.

Catherine of Aragon died of natural causes on 8 January 1536. The king had now sickened of Anne Boleyn; on 2 May she was convicted of incest with her own brother and intercourse with other members of the court. She and her alleged accomplices were beheaded forthwith. The king's formal betrothal to Jane Seymour was announced the day after Anne's execution, and their marriage two days later, 22 May. A new Parliament met on 8 June, and passed a new act of succession. It declared the marriages of both Catherine and Anne invalid, and their children bastards. The king himself, in default of issue to Jane, was entitled to dispose of the Crown by Will; it was said that the king's intention was to appoint his bastard son, Duke of Richmond. He died, however, on 23 July 1536, five days after the dissolution of Parliament.

Local rebellions now broke out, in Lincolnshire, in Nottingham and in Yorkshire, where it was known as the 'Pilgrimage of Grace', and then in Westmoreland. Members of the nobility of Ireland were hanged, while others fled abroad. Queen Jane gave birth to a child on 12 October, the future Edward VI; then she died on 24 October at Hampton Court.

Henry remained a widower for two years, although the names of various ladies were mentioned. From 1538 his health was giving anxiety. He had a fistula in one leg; at times his face grew black, and was speechless from pain. His later portraits show him as extremely gross. He now continued his work of spoliation. Images and shrines everywhere were demolished; pilgrimages were forbidden. Monasteries were suppressed beyond the financial limits set by Parliament; he was said to have shown some inclination towards the Lutherans. In November 1537 he issued a proclamation against the Anabaptists, and asserted his power as head of the Church by hearing an appeal from the court of the Archbishop of Canterbury. Thomas Cromwell, as his vicegerent, was ordered to have the man burned. The rich shrine of St Thomas of Canterbury now caught his attention, and Rome this time had the support of Charles V and Francis I in condemning him. In 1539, seemingly to reassure the people that the old religion still remained intact, Parliament passed the Statute of the Six Articles. Entirely orthodox, it enjoined the doctrines of transubstantiation, the reception of the sacrament in one kind, enforced the celibacy of the clergy, upheld monastic vows, defended private Masses and auricular confession. Yet during 1538 and 1539 almost all the great abbeys were suppressed; by early 1540 not a single monastery remained in England. Protestant doctrines had already penetrated deeply, and Bishops Latimer and Shaxton resigned, while a Catholic reaction was growing.

In 1539 a marriage was arranged with Anne, daughter of the Duke of Cleves. Its purpose was to make an alliance with German Protestants, and wholly political. It came to nothing, and shortly in 1540 Thomas Cromwell was executed, and Anne of Cleves divorced. On August 8 Henry married his fifth wife, Catherine Howard. His health was now improved, and he could rise, hear Mass at seven, and ride until ten. A series of executions took place. The French ambassador reported that at this time men did not know of what they had been accused. Henry went on progress as far as York. On his return he learnt that the new queen had been unchaste before their marriage, and even during the progress. Her accomplices were executed in her presence in December; she was beheaded on 13 February 1542.

Henry now had himself proclaimed King of Ireland by Act of Parliament. There had been trouble on the Scottish border, and the Duke of Norfolk was sent northward. He was forced to retreat for want of provisions, but in November routed the Scots at Solway Moss. James V's infant daughter Mary was now heir to the Scottish kingdom. Henry thought to marry her to his son Edward, but the Scottish Parliament did not concur.

Henry's reign, which had at first looked so promising, was approaching a miserable end. He was now immensely gross and suffering from his fistula. Still, on 12 July 1543, he married his sixth wife, Catherine Parr. In 1544 he made her regent, while he went on a brief and fruitless campaign to France. He tried to raise funds, but the people were unwilling. He then debased the currency, coined his own plate, and mortgaged his estates. By 1546 he had made peace with France for the last time.

The Parliament of 1545 gave him the endowments of numerous chantries, schools and colleges, for which he thanked them with great satisfaction. He now could do little but die. He was an extraordinary sovereign. He had acted throughout with all the clothing of legality. He had never been unconstitutional. Legal means had always been found for persecution and spoliation. He had cut off England from the Roman obedience and destroyed monasteries. At Oxford he had become the second founder of Wolsey's Cardinal College, now Christ Church. He had reorganised the episcopate, making six new dioceses, Bristol, Chester, Gloucester, Oxford, Peterborough and Westminster. Of these Westminster did not survive. The distribution of the former monastic lands, although he could neither have intended nor foreseen it, was to have lasting social consequences. Many hostages had been given to the future.

EDWARD VI

1547–1553

Unique among English rulers, the personal diary of the child-monarch Edward VI details his life from his accession until the Christmas before his death in 1553. The only parallels as diarists are King Alfred and Queen Victoria. He was Henry VIII's third child by his third marriage, to Jane Seymour. To make way for a male heir Henry VIII had divorced Katherine of Aragon, mother of Mary I, and executed Anne Boleyn, mother of Elizabeth I, whose crime was to have provided him only with daughters.

Historians have represented Edward as a sickly child, yet there is no hint of illness in his *Chronicle*, as he called it, until 2 April 1552. It records the public and private events of his reign, and would appear to have been kept at the behest of his tutors. On that day he 'fell sick of the measles and the smallpox', but was sufficiently well as to be able to attend the Garter celebrations on 23 April, a swift recovery indeed if the diagnoses were correct.

What is clear is that he enjoyed active sports, tilting, hunting, hawking, 'running at base', shooting at random as well as fixed targets, and archery, by then beginning to be archaic, with no less than one hundred of his guards. His descriptions do not suggest those of a sickly child.

Until he was six Edward was brought up 'among the women', but then had a series of tutors, some men of real distinction. By the age of eight he could correspond with his godfather, Archbishop Cranmer, in Latin. Three of his exercise books survive, with extracts from Cicero and Aristotle. He was conversant with most of the Church Fathers. He knew French, but his knowledge of German and Italian is dubious. He could play the flute, and took an interest in astronomy, on which he wrote a paper which has survived. Unlike other heirs to the throne, he did not lead a sequestered life, but was brought up with other youths, the sons and often heirs of peers.

He was never Prince of Wales, although this had been intended. He was scarcely nine when Henry VIII died, and was designated successor by his Will. This, dated 30 December 1546, named eighteen executors as a council of regency, and twelve assistant executors who could be summoned at pleasure. Because many of these were raised to the peerage with additional titles, his uncle, the Earl of Hertford, became Duke of Somerset, and Viscount Lisle, Duke of Northumberland. The contest between these two, the families of Seymour and of Neville, underlie the chief political movements of the reign.

Henry VIII had died an orthodox, if schismatical, Catholic. The new reign implied a major religious shift. It was marked by Cranmer's coronation sermon, which Edward's *Chronicle* does not mention. Cranmer told the king that his coronation was not strictly necessary, and that his coronation oath was 'without earthly sanction'. 'Your Majesty,' Cranmer told him, 'Your Majesty is God's vicegerent and Christ's Vicar within your own dominions.' No king of England has ever been assured of such absolute power or so unconditionally as this nine-year-old boy.

For the first two years of the reign Somerset ruled as vicegerent alone from his palace at Somerset House, treating his nephew with the same disdain that he accorded to his fellow-councillors. As Lord Protector it was naked dictatorship. In 1549 his fellow-councillors arose against him. By then an Act of Uniformity had been published together with a *Book of Common Prayer* to supersede the Mass and the Breviary Office. The parishioners of Sampford Courtenay scoffed at it as 'a child's Christmas play'. There was war with France, and on 13 October 1549 Somerset was dismissed. He was beheaded in 1552 and succeeded by Northumberland.

Edward's *Chronicle* scarcely mentions religion. Nevertheless, he showed enthusiasm for sermons. Latimer, Hooper and even John Knox occupied the pulpit. One reported: 'A more holy disposition has nowhere existed in our time.' Bucer reported that daily the king read ten chapters of the scripture, and told Calvin that 'the king is exerting all his power for the restoration of God's kingdom'. Later, Knox wrote of his experience at court as 'unsurpassable'.

At first Catholic opinion welcomed the change of vicegerent. They soon learnt that Northumberland intended no change of policy. Permission for Princess Mary to have Mass celebrated was refused by the council. She categorically refused the new prayer-book. The king noted the execution of Somerset with great complacence: he was wholly subject to Northumberland's influence.

By January 1553 it was clear that Edward was suffering from a fatal illness, and rapid consumption was soon diagnosed. A new Parliament sat from 1 until 31 March. The king had been much touched by the sufferings of the poor, and the royal palace of Bridewell was handed over to the corporation of London as a 'workhouse for the poor and idle people'. Christ's Hospital was given to poor scholars, and St Thomas's Hospital put in funds for the reception and treatment of the sick.

By May it was evident that the king was very weak. On 21 May Lady Jane Grey, great-niece of Henry VII, married Lord Guilford Dudley. In June Northumberland had Edward draw up a 'devise of the succession' to her, excluding his natural sisters and the Scottish descendants of his aunt Margaret, Queen of Scotland, who had died in 1541. The 'devise' was witnessed by the Lord Chief Justice and many others the following day. Edward died peacefully on 6 July.

JANE

1553

Lady Jane Grey was the eldest surviving of the three daughters of Henry Grey, Marquis of Dorset, later Duke of Suffolk; his mother had been Frances, daughter of Henry VIII's favourite Charles Brandon, Duke of Suffolk, and his wife Mary, Queen of France and Duchess of Suffolk, the younger daughter of King Henry VII. She was born in 1537, about the same time as her cousin Edward VI. She had two younger sisters, Catherine and Mary.

She was remarkable for her beauty and sweetness of character, equalled only by the distinction of her mind. She was a pupil of John Aylmer, Bishop of London. In 1550 Roger Ascham found her reading Plato while her family were out hunting. He reported on her almost unbelievable skill in writing and speaking Greek. At fifteen she started to add Hebrew to French, Greek, Italian and Latin. At the age of nine she became a member of the household of Queen Catherine Parr, Henry VIII's widow, and was chief mourner at her funeral. She then became a ward of Queen Catherine's second husband, Lord Seymour of Sudely, brother of the unfortunate Duke of Somerset. Some thought of her as a bride for Edward VI, but Somerset wished him to marry his own daughter, also Jane; and destined her for his son, the Earl of Hertford. The schemes of dynastic marriage account in great measure partly for Somerset's fate, and partly for her own. Her father became Duke of Suffolk in 1551, and she was frequently at court and in the company of Princess Mary. It was against her will that her father forced her marriage to Lord Guilford Dudley, procuring it only by violence.

Edward had died on 6 July: on 8 July Northumberland brought her before the council. She fainted when she was told that she was Edward's successor. On 10 July she was brought in an elaborate procession to the Tower of London, where later in the day she signed a proclamation announcing her accession. On the previous day Princess Mary, Edward's half-sister by blood, had written to the council claiming the throne. On 11 July Northumberland, with twenty other councillors, replied that Queen Jane was already Queen of England. Next day the crown jewels were surrendered to her. Her husband then claimed the title of king, which she refused, leaving the question to Parliament.

By 19 July, Mary's supporters had proclaimed her throughout the country, and Northumberland himself deserted Jane, proclaiming Mary at the gates of the Tower of London. There she was kept in virtual imprisonment. On 14 November she was arraigned for high treason, to which she pleaded guilty. She could do little else. She and her husband were both sentenced to death. The sentences, however, were held in suspense, until, in the winter of 1533–34, her father, the Duke of Suffolk, was imprudent enough to participate in Wyatt's rebellion. She and her husband were both beheaded on Tower Hill on 12 February 1554, he first, and she having to witness the still bleeding body of her husband. On the scaffold she spoke, saying that she had never desired the crown, and that she died a truly Christian woman.

She held strongly Calvinist opinions, and strongly defended her views against those bishops who visited her in prison and wished to return to unity with Rome.

MARY I

1553–1558

When Mary, daughter of Catherine of Aragon, ascended the throne in 1553, there had never been a Queen Regnant of England; nearly 900 years before Queen Seaxburgh had ruled Wessex, but briefly. There had been little serious support for Queen Jane and an anti-Protestant tide had set in. Mary had popular support as the daughter of her father, 'the good old days of King Harry'. She could scarcely have had a more unfortunate upbringing. As a little child, the lords of the council had thought her of great precocity. At the age of two she was betrothed to the Dauphin; Wolsey changed his mind, and at five she was betrothed to Charles V, already twenty-three. Then even James IV of Scotland was suggested. Charles changed his mind, since no dowry had been paid; and James IV was no longer considered. She was having a rigidly classical education, Greek as well as Latin, with French and Spanish, as well as astronomy, geography, mathematics and natural science. Aged ten, Wolsey attempted to marry her to Francis I of France, by now a roué of thirty-two. Next his son, Henri of Orléans, was proposed, and then rejected because of consanguinity.

Henry VIII's divorce from Catherine of Aragon was now brought forward. To divert public attention, it was proposed that she should marry the Duke of Richmond, Henry VIII's natural son. Application for a dispensation from the Pope for so unnatural a union received the reply that it could only be considered if the divorce were dropped. Anne Boleyn then suggested a marriage with the Duke of Norfolk's heir, which gained Clement VII's full approval. This was dropped, and she went to live with her mother. In 1531 they were parted; Anne Boleyn, now Mary's greatest enemy, after the birth to her of a daughter, Elizabeth, 1533, exerted every influence to humiliate Mary. Parliament now reordered the succession. Mary was pronounced illegitimate because her mother's marriage had been declared null and void. Anne's children alone were to inherit the throne, and Mary was ordered to cease to use the title of princess. Her household was broken up, and she was treated as little better than a servant. She fell seriously ill. At the beginning of 1535 Queen Catherine died, and Mary's grief was made more intense by the refusal to let her visit her dying mother. Then in 1536 Anne Boleyn was executed, and Jane Seymour took her place. Mary wrote to her father but was told that she must acknowledge her mother's marriage as unlawful, and herself as a bastard. She was to acknowledge the king's supremacy over the church. This she refused to do, as against the laws of God. Eventually such pressure was put upon her that she consented and was reconciled with him.

In October 1537 the future Edward VI was born, and Jane Seymour died twelve days after. Mary now displeased her father and Thomas Cromwell by entertaining some dispossessed nuns, and was kept in Hertford Castle. It was at this time many of her friends were executed for not recognising the royal supremacy over the Church. Next further dynastic marriages were suggested, but nothing came of them in spite of some reconciliation brought about by Catherine Parr. In 1544 a statute entailed the crown on her in default of Edward and his heirs, but without any mention of her legitimacy.

When Henry lay dying in 1547, he bade Mary to be a mother to her brother. Shortly she criticised Edward's religious policy. In 1549 the Act of Uniformity was passed, and then the Mass outlawed. This she resolutely refused. She was intermittently ill: she told her brother that 'her soul was God's, and her faith she would not change'. She had the support of the Imperial Ambassador, and again in 1551 the council pressed her to submit. Bishop Ridley visited her. She entertained him to dinner, but declined to let him preach before her. Amidst all the intrigue and turmoil Edward VI died. Northumberland, now in power, supported Lady Jane Grey in the Protestant interest, but the tide of support for Catholic Mary was too strong.

She was still unmarried. She dismissed all her brother's previous councillors, and worked incessantly. Bishop Gardiner urged restraint in matters of religious policy. The 'old religion' was restored, but there was to be no restitution of former church property, save some plate. Pope Julius III was told of her intention to restore the papal supremacy in matters of religion.

Her council now urged her to marry. Some six persons were named, from England, Denmark, Portugal and Spain. Charles V, ever her supporter, recommended his son, Philip II of Spain, who had been widowed in 1546. It was said he wished for a youthful bride. He had a reputation of being a fanatical Catholic, and Mary appreciated that a strong hand would be needed to re-establish Catholicism. All laws concerning religion of Edward VI's reign were rescinded. Parliament petitioned her to choose an English nobleman, but she persisted in negotiating a marriage with Philip. It was agreed that Philip might assist Mary in the government of the kingdom, but that no Spaniard should be employed in government. If Mary had a child, it should succeed to her throne, and also to all Philip's inheritance in Burgundy, that is, the rich provinces of Holland and Flanders. Philip would not engage England in his father's wars in France; peace between England and France would remain. If she died without heirs, neither he nor his heirs would have any claim.

Agitation began to restore Lady Jane Grey, and risings took place in Cornwall and Kent. The latter, led by Sir Thomas Wyatt, reached London. Sixty persons were hanged in London, and Lady Jane Grey and her husband executed. Mary now increased pressure on the Protestants. Married clergy were ordered to leave their parishes or be separated from their wives. Altars were to be restored in village churches. Philip landed in England on 20 July 1554, and the couple were married in Winchester Cathedral on 25 July. Their titles were proclaimed at the close of the Mass:

> Philip and Mary, by the Grace of God King and Queen of England, France, Naples, Jerusalem, and Ireland, defenders of the faith, Princes of Spain and Sicily, Archdukes of Austria, Dukes of Milan, Burgundy, and Brabant, Counts of Hapsburg, Flanders and Tyrol.

For all this, Philip exercised no apparent influence on English public life. In November, after twenty-three years exile, Cardinal Pole returned to England as Papal Legate; he gave England formal absolution on the Pope's part and freedom from all censures. Amid much rejoicing public pleasure was increased by the announcement that Mary was with child. The Dean of Westminster composed a prayer for her safe delivery; another prayer was for a male child 'well favoured and witty'. In January Parliament passed acts repealing all those affecting religion since 1529, and recognising the papal supremacy over the Church. Penal laws against heresy were restored, but there was no question of the restoration of confiscated church property. Westminster Abbey, and three other abbeys, however, were revived. Mary herself disliked the idea of persecution, but she was persuaded to the re-enactment of the laws against Lollardy, punishable by burning at the stake. The term Lollardy has never been clearly defined, but 275 persons were executed during the following three years. Taken in isolation it is this that has given her the name 'Bloody Mary'. Set in the historical context Henry VIII's acts of tyranny and persecution must be taken into account, and not less the penal laws persecuting Catholics enacted under Elizabeth I, and in other following reigns until the Roman Catholic Relief Act of 1829.

In May 1554 Mary's confinement was expected immediately. All was ready and letters to announce the birth prepared to send to foreign courts. It proved to be a false pregnancy, which had deluded both her and others. Relations between Mary and Philip had for some time been strained, and his behaviour had not been beyond reproach. On 29 May he departed to Spain, leaving her disconsolate.

Mary now increased pressure upon the Protestants. She and Philip quarrelled over his proposal that Elizabeth should marry the Prince of Savoy. Elizabeth was averse to the proposal, and Mary would not press her. It was clear that the heir to the throne could not marry outside the country. She and Philip quarrelled further over episcopal appointments. In 1557 Philip returned, but not out of affection. Charles V had now resigned to Philip the Netherlands as well as Spain, and he wished to draw England into a renewal of his quarrel with France. 8,000 men were dispatched under the Earl of Pembroke to the Netherlands, and Philip followed. Mary never saw him again.

Paul IV, now Pope, recalled Pole to Rome. He was unsatisfied that all had been done that could be done to re-establish Catholicism in England. William Peto, an Observant Friar, was made Cardinal and Papal Legate. Mary refused him entry, nor let Pole depart. She was now at war with France, and in late 1557 the Scots too declared war against her in support of France. On 5 January the Duc de Guise took Calais, the last English possession on French soil. It was a national humiliation.

Mary now believed herself to be pregnant once again. In August 1558 she was suffering from fever and dropsy, believing pregnancy the cause of the swelling. By November it was clear that she was dying. At Lambeth Pole too lay on his deathbed, and messages passed between them. Early on 7 November she asked for unction, and that Mass might be celebrated in her room. She died as the blessing was given. She had suffered endless humiliations, as a child, as a young princess, as a wife, in the expectation of motherhood, and finally as a queen. A lady-in-waiting suggested that Philip's absence contributed. 'Not only that,' she said, 'but when I am dead and opened you shall find Calais lying upon my heart.'

It was James I who ordered the inscription above the tomb which she shares with her sister: *Regno consortes et urna hic obdormimus Elizabetha et Maria sorores in spe resurrectionis*: Here lie the sisters Elizabeth and Mary, sharers in the kingdom and in the grave in the hope of the resurrection.

ELIZABETH I

1558–1603

All the portraits of Elizabeth I are idealised. They show, even in a young woman, a suave and dignified beauty. Her auburn hair rather suggests a fiery temper, her dignity an air of imperturbable command. She is a creature of contrasts, a woman with a masculine temperament, at the same time intensely feminine. Anne Boleyn's daughter was bereft of her mother when she was less than three years old. On 7 January 1536 Queen Catherine died; Anne Boleyn was executed on 19 May; Henry VIII married Jane Seymour the following day; and on 1 July Parliament compliantly declared both princesses, Mary and Elizabeth, illegitimate, and that the succession to the throne would be from the descendants of Queen Jane Seymour.

Like her sister Elizabeth was carefully educated. Cicero and Livy, and for Greek, Isocrates and Sophocles' tragedies; and for religion St Cyprian, *De disciplina virginum*. When Edward VI died, she entered London on horseback beside her sister; she did nothing, said nothing, wrote nothing. For all that she was sent to the Tower following Wyatt's rebellion. After six months detention she was again received at court; she was cheered by the people as she went to Hatfield, but prudently made no response. Then Mary died, and so too had many men of eminence during her reign. Elizabeth's heir presumptive was now Mary Stuart, the sixteen year-old Queen of Scotland. Elizabeth was twenty-five.

Elizabeth now had to be crowned. The archbishopric of Canterbury was vacant. The Archbishop of York refused to administer the oath, for it spoke of the ruler as supreme head of the Church. It was repugnant to him as a Catholic, and to the other bishops Mary had appointed. Eventually the Bishop of Carlisle officiated. It was the old Mass of the *Liber Regalis*, the Royal Book, but significantly of compromise the Gospel was sung in Latin and said in English. Parliament met, and petitioned her to marry; she had already refused Philip II, and now she declared once again that she would remain a virgin.

About mid-March Mary of Scotland assumed the royal arms of England, and had her husband assume the titles of King of France, Scotland, England and Ireland. The eighteen-year contest with Mary, Queen of Scots, had begun. Elizabeth's position now began to be made clear. On 15 May the bishops were required to take the oath of Supremacy. All but one refused. She sent them back to the Tower to consider their position. For herself, she showed herself to her subjects in magnificent costumes and jewellery, with banquets, masques, jousting, pageants and plays. Meanwhile new bishops were consecrated, and the Act of 1554, which had restored the Roman allegiance, repealed. A new Act of Supremacy proclaimed the Queen 'supreme of all persons and causes ecclesiastical as well as civil'. An Act of Uniformity accepted Edward VI's Second *Book of Common Prayer* with some revisions; the vestments of the clergy and church ornaments were to be the same as those established by Parliament in 1549. Edward VI's Articles of Religion were reduced from forty-two to thirty-nine, and re-enacted. It was a conspicuously tactful settlement. It uttered no threats; Rome was not attacked or vilified, merely denied in the Articles; to these only the clergy were required to subscribe. The wording of the Holy Communion was amended, so that those who accepted the Real Presence and those who did not could both accept it. On the other hand things were made difficult for Catholics. All the bishops had refused the oath, and some two hundred clergy; they were retired. The new appointments were all in sympathy with Elizabeth. A shilling fine was imposed on those who declined to attend the Anglican rite; a man could compound for himself and his family at £1 a month. The 'recusants' had to pay their own clergy; slowly the country gentry succumbed, so that Catholics dwindled.

Two great powers now dominated Europe, France and Spain, for with Spain one has to count the might of the Empire. In the past, whenever England had been at war with France, Scotland had intervened to attack the English in the rear. Elizabeth had also to reckon that whereas Spain was warm in the support of the Papacy and the Counter-Reformation, France, with Gallican sympathies, inclined the other way. The Reformation was now gathering ground in Scotland, and not less because Mary, who was half French, and surrounded by French courtiers, lacked popularity.

(The history of the Scottish ruling house is dealt with separately, below, p. 230.) Nevertheless, until Mary sought shelter in England from her enemies, and so put herself in Elizabeth's hands, she was a perpetual danger to her. By playing the card of possible marriage, but always withdrawing before committing herself, Elizabeth played an elaborate diplomatic game, while at the same time toying with members of her own court. In 1566 Mary gave birth to a son, the future James VI and I of England; by 1567 he was King of Scotland and aged only thirteen months.

It was a casual remark of the Duke of Norfolk in 1569 that now set off a new series of troubles. It was that he might be considered a suitor for the hand of Mary, Queen of Scots. It provoked a rebellion known as the Northern Rising, where Catholics were still numerous. Pope Pius V did not react until 1570. On 25 February he issued the Bull *Regnans in excelsis*, excommunicating Elizabeth by name, and absolving from their oaths any of her subjects who had taken oaths of allegiance to her. How successful her policy of moderation had been is shown by the fact that, when the Bull was published in London on 15 May, it was received with indifference. The Parliament which assembled in the following year was more Protestant than ever. In the north, however, the rising had been put down with vigour. Eight hundred persons were hanged, three times the Protestant martyrs of 'bloody' Mary's reign. Over the next seventeen years a series of plots threatened Elizabeth's life, gathering momentum after 1580, Throckmorton in 1583, and Babington in 1586. In 1587 it made the execution of Mary, Queen of Scots, an inevitability.

Already in 1497 John Cabot, a Bristol merchant, had sailed as far as Newfoundland, and possibly Nova Scotia and New Brunswick. In 1509 his son Sebastian penetrated the Hudson Strait. In mid-century Sir Hugh Willoughby explored Nova Zembla and Lapland, and perished with his crew, in 1553-4. At the same time Richard Chancellor reached Russia via Archangel. A period of great voyages had begun, with attention now on the Americas. It was the interest of Cornwall and Devon, and the Bristol merchants. Sir John Hawkins visited the West Indies in 1562 and again in 1564. He was there again in 1567, when he was accompanied by Sir Francis Drake. In 1570 the latter sailed alone, on what was openly a privateering voyage; so too in 1572 and 1574. The object of these voyages, in which the Queen had a commercial interest, turning a blind eye to their conduct, was to seize Spanish bullion; it was a covert war against Catholic Spain. In 1577–80 Drake accomplished his greatest exploit, circumnavigating the entire world, sailing for the first time into the Pacific. He returned with much gold. Fur was of no less importance, and it was this that took Frobisher to Baffin Island and the Hudson Strait in 1576–7, and Sir Humphrey Gilbert to make a colony, or trading settlement in Newfoundland in 1583. He was lost at sea on the return voyage. Similar intentions inspired Sir Walter Raleigh, who sent Sir Richard Grenville to Roanoke in 1585. The colony, the first in what was named Virginia in compliment to the Queen, disappeared without trace. A further attempt in 1587 was also a failure. Drake was in the West Indies again in 1586, as a privateer, and successful in plundering.

War with Spain was now inevitable. In the late 1570's there was a distinct revival of Catholicism, engendered by priests trained in Douai and Reims, in Lisbon and Valladolid. Their activities, the plots against the Queen's life, set off an uprush of national feeling. Drake's voyage of 1586, with its heavy losses to Spain, was followed by a daring raid into Cadiz harbour, on 19 April 1587. He burnt and sank thirty-three ships, and captured four more which were already laden with provisions for the conquest of England. Philip could have had no idea what he was encountering.

England had never had a standing army, and no more than a nucleus of a navy. A militia was ready to muster in every county in England to resist invasion; on the coast there was a similar liability to provide ships for defence. Of the vessels which encountered the Armada probably not one third were victualled nor their crews paid at royal expense. 120 vessels were fitted out and manned by the London merchants, and better supplied than those of the Queen.

On 20 May 1588, blessed by the Pope and clergy, the great Armada sailed from Lisbon. There were 130 ships, 8,000 seamen and 19,000 men-at-arms. The intention was that they should join 30,000 Spanish troops assembled in the Netherlands. Meeting shocking weather, it did not arrive off the Lizard until 19 July. For long Elizabeth refused to believe that the invasion would ever take place. She was proved right, but not in the way expected.

Lord Howard of Effingham had only some seventy ships, but most of them small and of little fighting value. They were wholly different in type from the Spanish vessels. Huge and unwieldy, they were constructed like castles, whereas the English ships were small and could move like terriers. At this time ship's guns could not be raised or lowered. The Spaniards therefore were at a disadvantage, firing over the small vessels. These could heave close, and fire into the castles. These had been successful for the Spaniards against the Turks at Lepanto in 1570; the English were a wholly different enemy.

Howard and Drake let the Spaniards sail up the Channel. The Armada could not turn round, and those ships that were not sunk or set on fire, were at the mercy of storms. Of 130 vessels only fifty-three returned to Spain. Only two Englishmen were killed in the first day's fighting, and only sixty during the whole running battle.

With the departure of the relic of the Armada, the last fifteen years of Elizabeth's reign were ones of fading glory. Pageants and masques continued. In the last thirteen years Parliament assembled only three times, in 1592, 1597 and 1601. It met only to grant supplies. The persecution of Catholics continued: between 24 July and 25 November 1588 twenty-two priests and eleven of the laity, including a woman, were executed. One priest, William Richardson, was hanged, disembowelled and quartered at Tyburn merely for being in England. Yet freedom of religion was granted to resident foreigners, and the chapels of ambassadors continued to be thronged. After 1567 Puritans, as they came to be called, suffered also, by imprisonment. There was some difference: Catholics were guilty of a political offence, the Puritans only of offences against the established religion, as troublemakers, and handed over to ecclesiastical courts.

Elizabeth was now seventy. In January 1603 she caught a bad cold. She recovered, but fell ill again on 28 February. She grew steadily worse, refusing all medicine, and declining to go to bed. She ate little. She had always refused to name a successor. On 24 March she became speechless. Her council stood around her. A sign was interpreted that she accepted that James VI of Scotland should succeed her.

8 *The House of Stewart*

49. James I of England, VI of Scotland, great-grandson of James IV of Scotland and his Queen Margaret, d. of King **Henry VII** (see Table 11—Kings of Scotland), b. 19 June 1566, King of Scotland from 24 June 1567, s. to throne of England 24 March 1603, d. 27 March 1625 m., 21 Nov. 1589, Anne (b. 14 Oct. 1574, d. 2 March 1618-19), d. of Frederick II, King of Denmark and Norway

| Henry Frederick, Prince of Wales, b. 19 Feb. 1593-4, d. unm. 6 Nov. 1612 | **50. Charles I**, b. 19 Nov. 1600, s. 27 March 1625, beheaded in Whitehall 30 Jan. 1649, m. 11 May 1625 Henrietta Maria (b. 25 Nov. 1609, d. 10 Sept. 1669), d. of Henry IV, King of France† | Robert, Duke of Kintyre, b. 18 Feb. 1601-2, d. unm. 27 May 1602 |

| Charles James, Duke of Cornwall, b. and d. 13 May 1629 | **51. Charles II**, b. 29 May 1630, s. 30 Jan. 1649, restored to the throne 29 May 1660, d. 6 Feb. 1685, m. 21 May 1662 Catherine of Braganza, Princess of Portugal (b. 25 Nov. 1638, d. 30 Nov. 1705), d. of John IV, King of Portugal | **52. James II**, b. 14 Oct. 1633, s. 6 Feb. 1685, deemed to have abdication on 11 Dec. 1688, d. 16 Sept. 1701, m.1, 24 Feb. 1659, Anne (b. 12 March 1637, d. 31 March 1671), d. of Earl of Clarendon; he m. 2, 21 Nov. 1673, Mary (b. 25 Sept. 1658, d. 8 May 1718), d. of Alphonso IV, Duke of Modena | Henry, Duke of Gloucester, b. 8 July, 1640, d. unm. 13 Sept. 1660 | Mary, Princess Royal, b. 4 Nov. 1631, d. 24 Dec. 1660, m. 2 May 1648 William II, Prince of Orange (d. 6 Nov. 1650) | 3ds d. young |

| 4s., 2d. died young | **54. Mary II**, b. 30 Apr. 1662, s. with her husband **53. William III**, 13 Feb. 1689, d.s.p. 28 Dec. 1694 | **55. Anne**, b. 6 Feb. 1665, s. 8 March 1702, d. 1 Aug. 1714, m. 28 July 1683 George, Prince of Denmark, s. of Frederick III, King of Denmark and Norway

issue, all of whom d. in childhood | James Francis Edward, 'The Old Pretender', b. 10 June 1688, d. 1 Jan. 1766, m. 28 May 1719 Mary Clementina (d. 30 Dec. 1735), d. of Prince James Sobieski | **53. William III**, Prince of Orange, b. posthumously 14 Nov. 1650, d.s.p. 8 March 1702, m. 4 Nov. 1677 his first cousin **54. Mary II**, with whom jointly he was summoned to the throne 13 Feb. 1689 |

| Charles Edward Louis Philip Casimir, 'The Young Pretender', 'Bonnie Prince Charlie', b. 31 Dec. 1720, d.s.p. 31 Jan. 1788, m. 1772 Louisa Maximiliana (d. 29 Jan. 1824), d. of Gustavus Adolphus, Prince of Stolberg-Gedern | Henry Benedict Mary Clement (Cardinal Stewart 1747), b. 21 March 1725, d.s.p. 13 July 1807, when the representation of the line passed to Charles Emanuel IV, King of Sardinia (d.s.p. 6 Oct. 1819) |

†**Commonwealth 1649-1660**
Oliver Cromwell, Commander-in-Chief March 1649; Protector 16 Dec. 1653; d. 3 Sept. 1658; Richard Cromwell, Protector 3 Sept. 1658-25 May 1659

Elizabeth, b. 19 Aug. 1596, d. 13 Feb. 1662, m. 14 Feb. 1613 Frederick V, Count Palatine of the Rhine, Elector, King of Bohemia (d. 29 Nov. 1632)

Margaret,	Mary,	Sophia,
b. 24 Dec. 1598, d. March 1600	b. 8 Apr. 1605, d. 16 Dec. 1607	b. 22, d. 23 June 1606

| Henrietta Anne, b. 16 June 1641, d. 30 June 1670, m. 31 March 1661 Philip Duke of Orleans (d. 9 June 1701) | Henry Frederick, King of Bohemia, b. 1 Jan. 1614, d. 7 Jan. 1628 | Charles Lewis, Count Palatine, Elector, b. 12 Dec. 1617, d. 9 June 1701, m. 12 Feb. 1650 Charlotte (d. 26 March 1686), d. of William V, Landgrave of Hesse | Rupert 1, Count Palatine, Duke of Cumberland, b. 17 Dec. 1619, d. unm. 29 Nov. 1682 | 2s. Sophia, b. 13 Oct. 1630, d. 8 June 1714, declared heir presumptive to England, Ireland and Scotland 6 March 1701-2, m. 30 Sept. 1658 Ernest Augustus, Duke of Brunswick and Lüneberg, King of Hanover, Elector (d. 23 Jan. 1698) | 3d. Louisa Hollandine, Abbess of Maubuisson, b. 18 Apr. 1622, d. 11 Feb. 1709, passed over by the Act of Settlement, 1701, as a Roman Catholic |

issue

Dukes of Bavaria, present representatives of the Stewart lineage

| 56. George I See Table 9 —House of Hanover *Continued on page 168* | Frederick Augustus, b. 3 Oct. 1661, k. in battle against the Turks, unm., 30 Dec. 1690 | Maximilian William, b. 23 Dec. 1666, d. unm. 16 July 1726 | Charles Philip, b. 13 Oct. 1669, k. in battle against the Turks 1 Jan. 1690-1, unm. | Christian, b. 19 Sept. 1671, d. by drowning 31 July 1703, unm. | Ernest Augustus, Duke of York and Albany, b. 7 Sept. 1674, d. unm. 14 Aug. 1728 | Sophia Charlotte, b. 20 Oct. 1668, d. 21 Jan. 1705, m. 6 Oct. 1684 Frederick I, King of Prussia |

issue

JAMES I

Scotland, 1567–1625; England, 1603–1625

James VI of Scotland, I of England, and later to call himself King of Great Britain, succeeded to the Scottish throne in his thirteenth month. He was crowned at Stirling on 29 July 1567. His mother having fled to England, he was put in the care of the Earl and Countess of Mar, the most ancient of Scottish titles, said to be 'lost in its antiquity'. His tutor was the Presbyterian divine George Buchanan, with four others; while he respected Buchanan's learning he later expressed detestation of his doctrines. By the age of ten he was remarkable for his learning; he was able, *extempore*, to read a chapter out of the Bible in Latin, translate it into French, and then into English. Buchanan wished to make him a constitutional king, the servant of his people. This was not in James's temperament. The Scottish Parliament was a single house in which Lords of Parliament sat with Commons. A 'constitutional king' would have been the mere servant of the nobility. It was his genius that by tact and diplomacy, and with very slender funds, he was able to master warring clan leaders and commons who were no less divided in religion. Some satisfaction was given to the Presbyterians by his marriage in 1589 to the Lutheran Anne of Denmark. It was not to last long, for she turned to Catholicism.

James was early conscious that, as the great grandson of Henry VII of England, he was heir to the English throne. In 1587, following his mother's execution, he sent Sir Robert Melville and the Master of Gray on an exploratory mission to England. In 1598 and again in 1601 further missions were sent under the Earl of Mar, son of his former protector, and Edward Bruce, Lord Kinloss, James's distant cousin. Thus his accession passed smoothly in 1603, although he had to pause at York for funds to enable him to make his way south with suitable pomp. Elizabeth I had died virtually penniless, but to James England had seemed Eldorado. His lavish generosity and extravagance always left him short of money. In Scotland he had exerted power by force of character. He was highly conscious of his intellectual attainments and superiority. He had developed a high concept of kingship, the Divine Right of Kings', which, in 1611, he explained to the English Parliament. He sowed future trouble.

He said:

> The state of monarchy is the supremest thing upon earth; for kings are not only God's lieutenants and sit upon a throne, but even by God Himself they are called gods; as to dispute what God may do is blasphemy, so it is sedition in subjects to dispute what a king may do in the height of his power.

James, indeed, was prolix and pedantic, as well as tactless in a country in which Parliament, and in particular the Commons, was beginning to be conscious of its powers.

So, in 1604, in Godwin's case, when James intervened in disallowing the election of an outlaw, and again in Bate's case, where a merchant had refused to pay excise dues, he involved himself with quarrels which would best have been left to the courts. His first Parliament sat from 1604 to 1611, managed largely by Lord Salisbury, Elizabeth's great minister. A second Parliament met for six weeks in 1614; it passed no laws, and is known to history as the Addled Parliament. Between 1612 and 1625 James ruled either alone or through his catamite favourites, Robert Carr and Lord Buckingham. A third Parliament met in 1621, called by James to support Frederick, his son-in-law, with supplies, in his war in the Palatinate. He had married James's daughter, Elizabeth, who even in old age enjoyed such popularity that she was known as the 'Queen of Hearts'. Parliament granted subsidies, but was concerned rather with other matters. It was an occasion for voicing grievances. The right of the Commons to impeach ministers or office holders before the House of Lords, not invoked since 1449, was raised, against holders of monopolies. Francis Bacon, the Lord Chancellor, was accused of receiving bribes. It is true in one case that he received a purse from a lady, containing £100, and decided her case against her.

The Commons further upheld their liberty of speech. As a body they were fanatically anti-Catholic and anti-Spaniard. James at this time had proposed that his son should marry a Spanish princess, and the Commons received this with fury. Charles and Buckingham went to Spain. They had one formal interview only. Informally, Charles jumped over a garden wall, to make his acquaintance with the lady – who fled shrieking. James's fourth Parliament, in 1624, ran smoothly, for the Commons had got the war with Spain that they wanted, although it came to nothing.

The issue of religion arose early in the reign. There were three Catholic plots. The Bye plot, in 1603 raised by a single Catholic, who was delated by another, intended to kidnap the king. More serious was the Main Plot, whose object was to put Lady Arabella Stuart, a granddaughter of Henry VII, on the throne with Spanish aid. It was alleged that Sir Walter Raleigh, who had been condemned for treason, and then reprieved in 1603, had attacked the Spaniards on the Orinoco River. James, on the insistence of the Spanish ambassador, executed Raleigh on the old charge, for which he had been forgiven. It is difficult to forgive James.

The third plot, in 1605, was the Gunpowder Plot, organised by Robert Catesby, who sent a Yorkshire soldier of fortune, Guy or Guido Fawkes, to blow up the House of Lords during the State Opening of Parliament, when the Commons would be present in the Chamber, as well as the king. One of the conspirators wrote a letter to warn a peer who was his cousin; he passed the letter to the government. None of these plots had any popular support, but laws of extreme severity were passed: Catholics were excluded from all professions; they could not appear at Court or within ten miles of London unless employed there; fines were increased. Neither James or his successor took much trouble to enforce them.

At a different level from James's relations with Parliament were his relations with the Church of England, itself of very complex character. Aside from the Catholics, the official Church, with its royally appointed archbishops and bishops, had not yet lost what had been reckoned at no less than 170 sects by 1649. It is simplest to define these divisions as Anglican, loyal to Episcopalianism, known sometimes – but inaccurately – as Arminian, and, on the other side of the divided, bodies known as Puritans, a term they did not use themselves; rather it was a term of abuse used by their opponents. Their principal divisions included Independents, Presbyterians (whom privily James hated) and Congregationalists, although these terms did not emerge in any organised manner until the next reign. On only one point could all these be said to be united, in detestation of Catholicism and of the papacy. Even so, the Anglicans themselves were not solid, but covered a spectrum, what later would emerge in terms difficult to define, High Church, Broad Church, Low Church. It was in the interest of national unity that James had to confront them all, and not less as supreme governor of the Church within the terms of the monarchy that he had, as we have seen, defined in Parliament.

His remedy was to call the Hampton Court Conference following what was known as the Millenary Petition; it was so called because it was supposed to have been signed by 1000 ministers, although in fact only 800 had signed it. James presided, with the two archbishops, and six bishops, together with four Puritans on the other side. At first the king behaved with impartiality. He thought of himself in terms of being a second Constantine, who had called the Council of Nicaea in 325. All went well until the end of the second day, when one of the Puritans mentioned the Presbyterian form of government. To James this was anathema, in the form it had taken in Scotland. 'A Scottish Presbytery agreeth as well with a monarchy as God with the devil. Then Jack and Tom and Will and Dick shall meet, and ensure me and my Council.' With the king as supreme, James saw the Anglican episcopate as part of the social order: 'No bishop, no king' was his maxim. If the episcopate were overthrown, the monarchy would be also.

The conference thus broke up, but with one most important result, the translation of the Bible known as the Authorised Version. It was the king himself who fleshed out the form of the original proposal that had been prepared by the President of Corpus Christi College, Oxford. The work was carried out by sixty scholars divided in committees of ten. Each man made his own version, and then the versions were compared and revised into a single form. It was further to be revised by the bishops, then by the Council, and finally to be presented to the king for his approval. It took until 1611 before the first edition could be published. Since 1870 many different revisions have been published, some of great merit. So greatly did the Catholic Vicar Apostolic, Bishop Challenor, admire it in the late eighteenth century, that in making his translation of the Latin Vulgate, he followed the wording of the Authorised Version, he said, whenever he could. In taking command of this great venture James not only showed a true grasp of scholarship, but made a contribution to the English language and its literature which has endured to this day. The most recent revision, with the approbation of every ecclesiastical authority in England, was issued in 1989.

For all this, James was given to hesitancy and inconsistency. This was most marked in his foreign policy, in which he veered from one line to another. In spite of his high Anglican attitude, and in the face of Parliament, he had not only cherished the hope of a Spanish marriage for his first son Charles, but eventually moved him towards a marriage with a French princess, which took place early in the latter's reign. This could not please the Anglican hierarchy, nor the people at large.

At the end of his reign James was showing signs of senility. He had always shambled, and always overindulged in drink. He was coarse in speech and obscene, and shameless in hugging and fondling his catamites. Taken together his reigns in Scotland and England amounted to some fifty-eight years out of a life of fifty-nine. He had always been isolated, first as an orphan, then by his inheritance. In any sober assessment he must be accounted a wholly remarkable man.

CHARLES I

1625–1649

When he was brought to England in 1604 many ladies refused to look after him. He was so weak, and especially in his ankles; he had a speech defect that he never wholly outgrew. He was intensely shy and introspective. He was wholly unreceptive to the opinions of others and lacked all imagination. He was untrustworthy, not out of ill will, but out of thoughtlessness. As he grew up, he learnt to ride well, to enjoy tennis and tilting. Morally he was irreproachable, and even blushed if an immodest word was uttered in his hearing. The long, sad face of his portraits displays a lack of character, albeit he was dignified.

His visit to Spain has already been described. It was in every way a fiasco. He was wholly under the thumb of Buckingham. Having failed to get a Spanish wife, he determined on a French one. The Commons had already voted, urging him to marry a Protestant. He ignored their wishes. Even the French ambassador was baffled by him. When James I died in 1625, he said that either he was an extraordinary man, 'or his talents are very mean'. He married Henrietta Maria on 1 May 1625, after his father's death. Strongly Catholic, and without any sympathy for Protestants, and wholly ignorant of England, she was less fitted to be Queen, it is said, even than Cleopatra or the Queen of Sheba would have been. She never ceased to intrigue.

Between 1625–29 Charles called three Parliaments. He quarrelled with them all. Parliament was Puritan and anti-Catholic. Charles was High Anglican, and inclined to be tolerant of his wife's co-religionists. He quarrelled likewise over money, over Buckingham and his hot-headed expedition to Cadiz. From 1629 until 1640 the 'Eleven Years' Tyranny' followed. He governed without Parliament, as indeed Elizabeth I had done. His two principal advisers were Thomas, Earl of Strafford and William Laud, Archbishop of Canterbury. Macaulay wrote of Strafford as 'The First of the Rats'; he was arbitrary and inconsistent, as self-interest might move him. Laud was devoted to the king. He had distinguished himself as President of St John's College, Oxford, where he had pioneered the study of Arabic. As archbishop he was constant in visiting all the dioceses under him. His motto 'Thorough' applied equally to his theological views, an unbending High Churchman. Remarkably, he so inclined to Rome that the Pope even offered him a Cardinal's Hat.

A regime of fines even for the smallest infringements on the part of the laity, and flogging, branding and the cutting of of ears for disobedient clergy, could only lead to trouble. For W. E. Gladstone Laud saved the Church of England from Calvinism, but undoubtedly it drove moderate Protestants into the Puritan camp.

England was now ripening for rebellion. In 1634 Charles wished to enlarge the fleet, and revived a tax called 'ship-money'; it was levied on the coastal towns in Anglo-Saxon times. It was successful, however, and Charles then enlarged its scope to inland counties. It was collected but with much grumbling. In 1637 an extraordinary scene took place in Palace Yard, Westminster, where in Richard II's Hall the Courts of Justice were then situated. A lawyer, a clergyman and a doctor had their ears removed, for scurrilous attacks on bishops. Admittedly, one had written that the bishops were the enemies of God and the king, and that the Church was as full of ceremonies as a dog is of fleas. They were further sentenced to fines of £5000 and imprisonment for life.

A little later a Buckinghamshire squire, Hampden, refused to pay ship money. Twelve judges heard his case, which he lost by seven to five. Nevertheless, his opinions were echoed all over the kingdom. In Scotland the situation was even more critical. The single-chamber 'Council of Estates' was controlled by 'Lords of Parliament', a feudal assembly in essence. Thus the only representative body was the General Assembly of the Kirk, of Presbyterian ministers and elders. In the same year as Hampden's case in England, Charles attempted to recover some of the Church lands which had been lost at the Reformation, and to impose a new Service Book and bishops. One Presbyterian called them 'bunchy knobs of papist flesh'. At St Giles's, Edinburgh, when the Service Book was introduced, one Jenny Geddes threw her stool at the Dean who was conducting the service. In 1638 an Assembly in Glasgow Cathedral ruled in a Presbyterian sense, abolishing all bishops, and sentencing some for heresy. This was the origin of the First Bishops' War, when Charles led an

English army, reaching Berwick, where he had to agree to Scottish demands. A second Assembly met at Edinburgh, confirming the first. In 1640 the Second Bishops' War began when Charles refused to acknowledge it. The Scots accordingly invaded England and occupied the northern counties.

In this way Scottish affairs gave England a Parliamentary system, for only Parliament could give the king funds to prosecute a war against Scotland. Charles called Parliament. It refused him subsidies and ship money, and demanded a peaceful settlement with Scotland. Parliament was dissolved, but, after some wrangling, Charles was compelled to give way to the Scots. Then, in November 1640, what is known as the Long Parliament was called. It was to last, although no one could foretell it, until 1660. In 1641 it tried and executed Strafford; Laud also was condemned, but not beheaded until 1645. It was in this Parliament that the arbitrary power of the Crown became abolished. It determined its own length, and that a new Parliament should meet each three years. The courts of the Star Chamber and High Commission were abolished. In October an Irish Catholic rebellion compelled Charles to seek funds, to which Pym, now the Puritan leader in the Commons, replied with the Grand Remonstrance.

It detailed all the misdeeds of which Pym and his friends held Charles and his advisers to be guilty. It required the approval of Parliament for the appointment of ministers and a Synod of Divines for the appointment of bishops. It went far beyond anything hitherto advanced, and was the watershed between Puritans and moderate Royalists in Parliament. It was carried on 23 November 1641 by eleven votes only.

Charles now attempted a coup d'état. On 4 January 1642 Parliament determined to impeach the Queen. Charles went down to the Commons in person to arrest five members for high treason, for plotting with the Scots. It was a failure: 'the birds had flown'.

Charles had made no attempt at conciliation. Both he and Parliament knew war was inevitable, and prepared to fight. On the side of Charles was the greater number of the nobility and gentry, with their tenants: the majority of yeomen and townsfolk backed Parliament. It was not a war of class. Of 130 peers, eighty fought for him, while 175 members of the Commons were royalists. The real alignment was religious, Anglican against Puritan. It was also territorial: a line drawn from the Humber to Southampton formed a rough division, Parliamentary east of the line, Royalist west of it, save for the cities of Bristol, Gloucester and Plymouth. The City of London was crucial, in possessing the bulk of the wealth of the country. Parliament had the better infantry, but the pikemen were no match for the royalist cavalry, and the dash and panache of the king's nephew, Prince Rupert. Charles's first object, to take London, was barred by 24,000 Londoners at Turnham Green in 1642; in 1643 a series of battles were lost by Parliament, as shown on the map, until the House of Lords proposed to the Commons that they should negotiate with the king. It was lost by only seven votes.

At the end of 1643 Pym had negotiated for 20,000 men with the Scots. The Solemn League and Covenant – with some equivocation – promised the reform of the Church of England 'according to the word of God' and the example of the best reformed churches. Charles countered by bringing troops from Ireland, but they were regarded with horror by the English, as Catholic and undisciplined. In July 1644 the battle of Marston Moor, near York was important, and for the first time a cavalry general who was more than equal to Rupert emerged, a squire from Huntingdon, Oliver Cromwell. It was his New Model Army and the Ironside cavalry which were to prove decisive. At Naseby in 1645 Charles lost half his cavalry, and all his artillery and infantry, with most of his best officers. In Scotland the Marquis of Montrose campaigned on Charles' behalf against the Earl of Argyll and the Presbyterians, but was defeated at Philiphaugh in September 1645. In May 1646 Charles surrendered to the Scottish army. With the fall of Oxford in June the war was over.

Yet no one knew quite what to do. No one wished to abolish the monarchy. The Scots were determined to establish Presbyterianism in England. Parliament itself would have accepted a constitutional monarchy, and feared the New Model Army. There were extremists, Levellers, Democrats who wanted annual Parliaments and universal suffrage, and Fifth Monarchy Men. In the army Independents predominated, with 'tender consciences' that would not accept either bishops or Presbyterian divines. It was out of this situation that Oliver Cromwell at length emerged.

Charles's own situation was complex. The Scots had possession of him, but he refused the Solemn League and Covenant. Finally they sold him to Parliament for £400,000, and retired across the Tweed in February 1647. Parliament then quarrelled with the Independents, and by 1648 war broke out again. There were royalist risings in Scotland, in Wales and in southwest England. The Scottish army reached near Preston, where Cromwell destroyed an English Royalist force, and then went on thirty miles to destroy the Scottish invaders, whom he pursued into Scotland. In London, on 6 December 1648, Colonel Pride 'purged' Parliament of 143 members, leaving some ninety, who now agreed to set up a court to try the king.

It was a foregone conclusion. Charles met his death outside Whitehall Palace on 30 January 1649. He behaved with great dignity. He asked, it is said, to wear two shirts lest he should shiver and seem afraid.

Andrew Marvell summed it up:

> He nothing common did or mean
> Upon that memorable scene:
> But with his keener eye
> The axe's edge did try.

The nation regarded the execution with horror. A few days later *Eikon Basilike* was published. It purported to contain the king's last thoughts and meditations. Many regarded him as a martyr.

THE CIVIL WAR, 1642-53

SCOTLAND

Area controlled by Parliament
at 1 May 1643
Area controlled by Parliament
at 1 Nov. 1644
Battle

Philiphaugh
1645

NORTHUMBERLAND

Newburn   Newcastle
1640

Durham

Marston Moor   York
1644
Preston   Adwalton Moor   Hull
1648   1643

Gainsborough

Winceby

Rowton Heath   1646 May: Charles
1645   surrenders to Scots
Nantwich   Newark
1644   Nottingham

Lichfield

Naseby
1645
Holmby House   Huntingdon   Newmarket
Edge Hill
1642   Cropredy
Worcester   1644   EASTERN ASSOCIATION
to raise Parliamentary
Oxford   Army 1643
London
Lansdown Hill   Uxbridge
1643   Windsor   Farnham   Ockham
Donnington   Hampton Court
Roundway Down   Castle   Basing House
1643   Newbury   1645
1644

Langport
Bideford   1645
Stratton   Hurst Castle   Carisbrooke Castle
                                        IS. OF WIGHT
Held for the King   Bradock Down
by John Grenville   Lostwithiel
until 1653   1644   Plymouth   Dartmouth

SCILLY ISLES

CHARLES II

1649/60–85

Charles took his seat in the House of Lords in the same year that the Royal Standard was raised at Nottingham; he was only ten years old. We know very little of his extreme youth other than the names of his tutors. After various honorary appointments while remaining in the king's train, in 1646 he was made general in the four western counties, a nominal appointment with Lord Goring and Sir Richard Grenville (grandson of the Admiral) in effective command. Shortly the king ordered him to France for his greater safety. In 1648 he was put in charge of a fleet which sailed from the Low Countries up the Thames, with very little effect. During these years, according to Bishop Burnet, the Duke of Buckingham and Lord Percy introduced him to the impieties and vices of the age. He had a son by Lucy Walter in 1649, and a daughter by Lady Shannon in 1650. Other of his mistresses were Lady Byron and the widowed Duchesse de Châtillon, a lady of 'a presence very graceful and alluring'; many others were to follow, 'la belle Stuart' and Nell Gwynn, who referred to herself as 'the Protestant whore', to mention only two.

He had exerted every effort, direct and indirect, to save his father from the block. Six days later he was proclaimed king in Edinburgh, but in England in only one or two places. The Parliamentary fleet in Portsmouth prevented him and hindered him from going further up the Channel than to the Netherlands, where he took refuge. It was not until June 1650 that he reached Scotland. He was depressed by what he met: the presbytery, he said, was 'not a religion for gentlemen'. He was forced into various concessions, and not least by his father's blood-guiltiness and his mother's idolatry, while at the same time writing to Pope Innocent X in Rome and promising concessions to Catholics in England. On 3 September 1650 Cromwell's army settled matters at Dunbar so far as Edinburgh was concerned. Nevertheless he was crowned at Scone on 1 January

1651, having sworn to the Presbyterian Covenant and to parliamentary rule equally in England as in Scotland. Then at the end of July he set off to England with an army of 10,000. It had no hope against Cromwell's force of between 30,000 and 40,000 which virtually annihilated his army at Worcester on 3 September. He lived as a penniless refugee until he reached Fécamp in February in 1651.

In battle he had shown great bravery as well as dash; even in defeat he showed equal endurance and sang-froid. His exile was spent first in France and then in Germany, and for a time with his widowed sister, the mother of the future William III. For a time he lived with the Jesuits in Cologne, moving later to Brussels. It was there that he was settled in 1658 when he learnt of Cromwell's death.

It was not long before negotiations for his restoration began in which Sir John Grenville, later Earl of Bath, negotiated successfully with his cousin George Monk, later Duke of Albemarle. His army, brought down from Scotland, had reached London unopposed. So, on 8 May Charles was proclaimed in Westminster Hall, and arrived on person on 26 May at Dover, to be acclaimed in a Convention Parliament on 29 May. A basis of agreement between the king and Parliament had been reached at Breda on 8 May.

The terms of agreement covered a wide field. It included an Act of Indemnity for wrongs done previously in the name of Parliament, save for the actual regicides; for the disbandment of the army and navy, except for the regiments of guards; of liberty of conscience, although without toleration for sectaries or papists; and an Act of Uniformity, which, in 1662, restored the *status quo* of the Anglican Church. Parliament also settled a fixed income for the king and for his brother, the Duke of York. Charles was then crowned on 23 April 1661.

Parliament met shortly, with further constitutional legislation; it vested the command of the militia in the crown, excluded heretics and papists from public office, and raised a benevolence. The king himself announced his marriage to Catherine of Braganza, daughter of the King of Portugal, bringing him a substantial dowry, and the ports of Bombay and Tangier. Later the latter was relinquished, but Bombay was the beginning of what became the Indian Empire. The marriage took place according to both the Anglican and Roman rites. Charles found her unattractive, preferring Lady Castlemaine's company. He slept with the queen from time to time, but the marriage was childless. Charles's toleration of Catholics stretched the patience of Parliament. His Declaration of Indulgence, which he had pressed on both houses in 1662, was shelved; it led to the Conventicle Act of 1664 and the Five Miles Act of 1665.

War now broke out with the Dutch, but in the winter of 1664–5 plague swept through London, and brought commerce to a standstill. The court moved to Salisbury. The only benefit was the departure of the Queen Mother, an inveterate intriguer, to her native France, from which she never returned. Then, from 2 to 6 September 1666, occurred the Great Fire, destroying the greatest part of the city of London; it coincided almost with the fall of Charles's principal minister, who had been his adviser since his restoration, the Earl of Clarendon.

The second part of Charles's reign, from 1667 to 1674, was marked by the slow formation of what came to be known as the Cabal, from the initials of the ministers who composed a committee of five from 1672. Buckingham was virtual prime minister, although the term did not come into use until the following century. It was Charles's objective to govern without calling on Parliament for supplies; to do this he could only depend on foreign subsidies, and his foreign policy became more and more devious and entangled. His motives were mixed, and once more the question of religion raised its head. Slowly France under Louis XIV gained an ascendancy, and Charles himself found a new mistress, Louise de Kérouaille, later Duchess of Portsmouth. Charles was under constant pressure to convert to Catholicism, and on 15 March 1672 he issued a further Declaration of Indulgence suspending all penal laws against Protestant nonconformists and Catholics. War continued with Holland, and it is from this time that many have dated the superiority in commerce and in the Royal Navy over the commerce of the Netherlands and France. Parliament declined to accept the Declaration of Indulgence, and only granted supplies when the king agreed to a Test Act, which excluded Catholics not only from public office but also from all the professions. The Dutch War was ended by the Peace of Westminster on 9 February 1674. Three years later Charles's niece, Princess Mary, was to marry William of Orange, thus consolidating the position.

In August 1678 a fraudulent charlatan, Titus Oates, claimed to 'discover' a popish plot. Charles went off to Newmarket to enjoy the racing, and was accused of frivolity. He had seen through Oates's mendacity, but Parliament seized the occasion to exclude all Catholics from Parliament except the Duke of York. The Bill failed. Charles sent him abroad, to avoid further trouble. Public opinion nevertheless had been inflamed, and was in no way soothed when the king suffered from a number of fits. There were rumours of attempts against the king's life. Further trouble was fomented by suggestions that the Duke of Monmouth, an illegitimate son of Charles II's, should be legitimated by Act of Parliament. The Commons then passed an Exclusion Bill, but the king dissolved Parliament. In March 1681 it met in Oxford, only again to be dissolved by the king. The tide was now turning against the Exclusion Bill, and in favour of the king. He visited Newmarket, and the queen in Cambridge; they both dined at the Guildhall on their return to London. The foundation stone of the Chelsea Hospital, for sick and elderly soldiers, was laid by the king in person. In September 1682 the so-called Rye House Plot was discovered against the lives of both the King and the Duke of York, in which a number of Whig peers were involved, together with Monmouth.

The King's health was now fading, and rumours spread of his imminent intention of joining the Church of Rome. Somewhat enigmatically, he remarked that he was too old to go on his travels again. One night, when he was at supper with the Duchess of Portsmouth, he had an apoplectic fit. Three days later he worsened. Tales that he had died of poison have no historical foundation. He died as a professed Catholic, and was given the last sacraments by Father Hudleston, who had hidden him at Boscobel after the battle of Worcester.

If the song 'The Vicar of Bray' echoes the sentiments of the period, it is to Charles's credit that he – with others – salvaged the monarchy at a moment when it seemed that the whole fabric of the constitution had perished. If his actions appear devious, they may be excused that no other policy was within the bounds of possibility. His adventures with women began during a difficult childhood and youth, in which he was in no way helped by a dominant and overbearing mother. He was perhaps in search of a mother. To the last he maintained a gift of wit and vivacity, even when he apologised that he was 'an unconscionable time a-dying'.

JAMES II

1685–1688

There is a contrariness and superficiality about the character of James II which makes him hard to depict, let alone to comprehend. As a Catholic he was a conventional bigot, yet he kept two mistresses, Arabella Churchill and Catherine Smedley, intermittently for the whole period 1665–87, both Protestants. His court was almost exclusively Anglican, and he even envisaged an English Catholic Church modelled on Rome. In the illegitimate Duke of Monmouth he was surprised that he showed none of the supposed attributes of royalty. He was given to labels: republicans, atheists, rogues, for all those who did not share his opinions. He expected to be followed blindly, and without discussion. He saw himself as a despot in the true meaning of the word, but lacked the ability to fulfil his intentions.

He was perhaps happiest when he was allowed to serve in the French army. He joined as a lieutenant-general; no doubt he was well supported by experienced officers. Later he took service in the Spanish army, but refused the office of Lord High Admiral. Shortly he had to disclose that he had fathered an illegitimate child by Anne Hyde, whom he at first married secretly, mother of the future queens, Mary II and Anne. At the same time he had other *amoureuses*, at least five, but it is not certain how far they rewarded his attentions.

At his brother's restoration he was appointed Lord High Admiral of England. Samuel Pepys records that he took a genuine and deep interest in naval matters, but his writings seem rather to belong to the hand of Pepys himself. Nevertheless he showed courage in the war against the Dutch, and some determination in reforming the navy. It is not known when his mind first turned to Rome. In 1668 or 1689 he applied for a papal dispensation to remain outwardly a Protestant while inwardly conforming to the Roman Church.

Fr Symonds, S.J., replied he could not, and this was later confirmed by Pope Clement IX. The turning point may have come when his duchess died on 31 March 1671, with full Catholic rites. At Christmas 1672 he refused to receive the sacrament with his brother according to the Anglican rite, and resigned his admiralty in accordance with the Test Act.

Then on 30 September 1673 he was married by proxy to Mary, daughter of the reigning Duke of Modena. The House of Commons passed violent addresses against the marriage, and Anglican bishops, and even Archbishop Sancroft, urged him to recant. He was not swayed, but allowed that his daughters should continue to be brought up in the Church of England. For a time he retired to Holland, but an Exclusion Bill, passed by the Commons, which would have denied him the succession, was scotched when Charles II dissolved Parliament. There was some talk that Monmouth might succeed, but the king sent him away from court, and made James High Commissioner in Scotland. Although he was well received, he shortly returned to London. The struggle went on through 1680 when James was back in Scotland, where generally he was conciliatory towards the Presbyterians. He was back in England when Charles II died, and present at his deathbed conversion.

James's succession passed off peaceably, much to his own astonishment. Monmouth's rebellion, 11 June to 15 July 1685, proved a failure. Parliament voted James a large income. The organisers of the Popish Plot were now barbarously treated, and Oates himself received 3,400 lashes in three days. Public opinion felt that his fabrications had got what they deserved. A second rebellion, on Scotland, was put down. Of Monmouth's followers the Lord Chief Justice, Jeffreys, with four other judges, hanged more than 300, and deported over 800. Never had so much cruelty been seen in England, nor since.

For the first nine months James behaved moderately. He accepted coronation, but declined the Anglican sacrament. Louis XIV of France urged on him an immediate proclamation of liberty of worship. James, however, initiated a policy of exercising what he claimed was inherent in him, the dispensing power, the power to dispense from laws in particular cases. So not only were Catholics given commissions in the army, but even permitted to become ministers of the crown; at Magdalen College, Oxford, some were appointed Fellows, and one even Dean of Christ Church. A

Declaration of Indulgence suspended all penal laws against Catholics and Protestant dissenters on 27 April 1688. Seven Anglican bishops protested, and were imprisoned in the Tower for rebellion, only to be acquitted on 30 June 1688. Significantly, already on 10 June the Queen had borne a son, James Francis Edward, to be known to history as 'The Old Pretender'.

So long as there had been no Catholic heir apparent, but only the king's two Protestant daughters, Mary and Anne, there had been no great nervousness. Relations with Holland, now ruled by William III of Orange, the husband of his eldest daughter, Mary, since 4 November 1677, had for some time deteriorated. For dissenters the prospect of a Catholic dynasty seemed disastrous, and the affair of the Seven Bishops had made clear the difficulties facing the Church of England.

In these circumstances four peers, the Earls of Danby, Devonshire and Shrewsbury, Lord Lumley, and three others closely related to the peerage, Henry Sydney and Edward Russell, together with the Bishop of London, wrote to William of Orange. They complained of James's interference with Parliamentary elections, and the rumours – which have never been substantiated – that the young prince was no son of James II, but had been introduced into the palace in a warming-pan. It offered William support if he would invade and accept the crown.

It is easy to mistake the origins of the movement. It was no national movement. The greater number stood aside, whether Anglican or Dissenter, 'Whig or Tory', Protestant or Catholic. The decision to invite William came from members of the nobility, those who had suffered most from James's policies. The nobility, that is, in its broadest sense, the peerage and the families that composed it, were emerging at this time to the dominance which became wholly apparent as the eighteenth century wore on, and which extended long after. Catholics had supplanted them as lords lieutenant; Catholics were taking their places at court; Catholics were supplanting them in commissions in the army. Others were sent to the country for the slightest reason; Lord Lovelace was actually reprimanded and threatened with prosecution when he ostentatiously used as lavatory paper a writ which had been sent against him by a papist magistrate.

Louis XIV offered James support. He refused. Louis accordingly moved his troops to attack Germany. William was thus secure by James's own act, for James had not realised his danger. He was shortly to repent. William eventually set out on 1 November, and landed at Torbay on 5 November. By 18 December he was in St James's Palace at Westminster, following events which are recounted in the next chapter.

Until 21 September James had done nothing. That day he announced that Catholics would be ineligible to sit in the approaching Parliament. Next day he told the Bishop of Winchester that he would stand by the Church of England, and issued a royal proclamation appealing for support against an imminent Dutch invasion. Many Protestants were restored to their former posts, and the former order re-established. On 22 October he made a formal declaration to an extraordinary council of peers and dignitaries of the genuineness of the birth of the Prince of Wales. A fleet was collected, and an army of 40,000, so the king said, was mustered. By 6 November James knew of William's landing at Torbay. Once again he had been outwitted; he had expected a landing in Kent. There was no enthusiasm for James, nor at first did William's army attract volunteers.

James set out to confront William near Warminster, but was seized by a violent nosebleed on 19 November. He withdrew to Andover. Here John Churchill (later Duke of Marlborough) deserted him with others, followed shortly by Prince George of Denmark, husband of Princess Anne, and other notables. Anne herself had fled, with Lady Churchill. It was now clear that there was a conspiracy in the army, and on 26 November James returned to London. Some forty or fifty peers, including nine bishops, met him next day to discuss summoning a Parliament. Negotiations took place, but it was clear that the game was up.

On 11 December, between 2 a.m. and 3 a.m. James left Whitehall Palace. A hackney coach conveyed him to Millbank, and he was ferried to Vauxhall. It was then that the Great Seal is supposed to have been thrown into the river by him. Of this, Bishop Burnet says: 'With this his reign ended.'

At Sheerness he had ordered a hoy to be ready, but he was recognised, and held by fishermen. He was rescued by Life Guards, and brought back to London on 16 December. Many messages were sent to him urging him to yield, and on 23 December he crossed to France. He landed on Christmas Day at Ambleteuse, near Boulogne.

He continued to Paris, but was received by Louis XIV at St Germains, where the Queen was awaiting him, given the palace as a residence and a pension. He had a fancy that he would receive general support from the European powers. It was a delusion. In 1689 he crossed to Ireland, where, on 1 July, he was defeated at the battle of the Boyne. He returned to France, and continued to scheme and intrigue until 1697, when, at the Congress of Ryswyck, Louis XIV made peace with William III, recognising him as King of England.

James had no longer any political significance or occupation. He now gave himself up to religious exercises and austerities, and composed religious treatises. He still went hunting with the French court. Then in March 1701 he had a stroke, and died on 6 September 'like a saint'. He had forfeited his throne for a fantasy.

WILLIAM III

1688–1702

&

MARY II

1688–1694

With James II's two flights from London the whole situation was completely altered. Those who had invited William had not seen him as more than a regent, or as a Prince Consort, or as a Protector. Now William was the only restraint against political anarchy or warring religious enthusiasm. Louis XIV had offered James support, and he had refused. Louis – for forty years, much of them occupied by war – had never lost a battle. William could no longer fear his opposition. Nevertheless, William advanced cautiously, avoiding battle, which, if he had offered it, he could quite likely have lost. He let time do its work. By degrees leading men gathered round him; not a blow was exchanged.

William now took responsibility for the administration of justice and the collection of taxes. He summoned a 'Convention' Parliament to Westminster in January 1689. Although Mary was the senior as the daughter of a king, whereas he was a grandson, he made it clear that he would accept nothing but the Throne. On 13 February they accepted it jointly. There was no doubt who would be the dominant partner.

Whatever view one may take of 'The Glorious Revolution of 1688', there can be no doubt that 1689 opened up a new era for Britain. Between 1688 and 1815 Britain was engaged in seven great wars. Of these, two began and five ended with France as Britain's chief opponent. Of these 127 years fifty-six were spent at war. It is in the beginning of this era that William's reign in England is set.

He was the posthumous son of William II, born eight days after his father's death. He was not declared stadtholder, captain– and admiral–general until 1672, although the medal struck in that year declared that it was by hereditary right. Until then forces of republicanism had been too strong in the Netherlands. There, Holland, or the United Provinces, were independent; Spain held most of modern Belgium until 1713, and then Austria. French ambition was to reach the Rhine as a frontier, and, if possible, to control Spain. For William to preserve the independence of Holland was paramount; later, he was to say: 'Without the concurrence of the realm and power of England it was impossible to put a stop to the ambitions and greatness of France.' It was within this context that his youth was spent fighting and from which he emerged a plodding, rather than a brilliant, general. In the same context, in 1677, with the encouragement of Sir Matthew Temple, the English ambassador, he sought the hand of Princess Mary, James's elder daughter, who had been brought up a Protestant.

As Queen, Mary II was cursed by her father, who wrote disowning her utterly. Already at six years old she delighted in dancing, then an elegant, polite art. Drawing she learnt from dwarfs. She was informed of her father's consent to her marriage on 21 October 1677, and married on 4 November. There was little joy in the marriage. William was engaged in peace negotiations, and took little notice of her; she refused to leave St James's Palace, where her sister Anne was ill with smallpox. William, in any case, was twelve years older, taciturn and in feeble health since his smallpox in 1672, and suffering from asthma. She was devoted to religion, and said to live the life of a nun. There was to be no heir. While acting for William and dealing with state papers during his absences in Holland, she lived a life of solitude; she nevertheless loved him devotedly, as her letters to him attest: it was 'a passion that cannot end but with my life'. William gave her the little attention he could spare from his life's work.

From 1689 until 1697 he was absorbed by the War of the League of Augsburg, or the War of the English Succession. While fighting began at sea and in Scotland on behalf of James, in Ireland William intervened in person. With James were French forces, some two-thirds, otherwise with locals. William, apart from English, had 7,000 Danish mercenaries, as well as German and Dutch troops. The decisive battle was that of the Boyne, 10–11 July 1690, after which James fled to France with his French troops on 14 July. At sea from 1691-7 England maintained supremacy; on land William in person lost battles, but Luxembourg, his principal opponent failed to exploit his victories. Thus William, by sheer tenacity, fought the French to a standstill, until peace was made at Ryswyck in 1697.

Mary died of smallpox in 1694 aged only thirty-two. She had long complained of infirmities, and described herself, in spite of her age, as an old woman. Her funeral was celebrated with great pomp in Westminster Abbey, with both houses of Parliament in attendance. There were new plots against the life of the king, who now began to show himself in different parts of the country.

In 1701, when James II finally died, Louis XIV recognised his son as James III (the Old Pretender), in defiance of the Treaty of Ryswyck. It made England enthusiastic for renewed war, what was to be known as the War of the Spanish Succession. Almost all Western Europe fought against France, Spain and Bavaria. It had hardly begun when William died, having taken no part in the fighting.

William's absorption with foreign affairs, with Holland, and with wars forms the necessary backdrop to constitutional changes of which they were partly the cause during his reign. Parliament made the king annual grants of taxation only, necessitating the assembly of Parliament annually. Thus the power of the Commons was increased as the result of William's military needs. A second major shift arose from the Declaration or Bill of Rights, made in 1689, which defined the limits of the power of the Crown. It was the first enactment to define the succession, declaring William and Mary King and Queen, and then the succession to their expected off-spring, failing whom, to Mary's sister Anne. It provided that no person who was a Catholic, or who married one, could succeed to the throne. It declared illegal the 'pretended' power of the Crown to suspend or dispense from laws, the Court of High Commission and other similar courts, and forbade a standing army. A Mutiny Bill, however, enabled the existence of the nucleus of an army, but had to be renewed annually. Parliament itself was to be freely elected, to enjoy freedom of speech, and to meet frequently; there was to be no taxation without its consent. In this the foundation of a new constitution was laid, which was to develop in the following century. As yet the doctrine of ministerial responsibility had not evolved. William thus could, and did, select his ministers and dismiss them as he pleased.

Almost the last act of William's reign was the Act of Settlement,

1701. William and Mary had been childless, and all the eleven children of Princess Anne by Prince George of Denmark had died. The Act therefore settled the Protestant succession on the Electress Sophia, the granddaughter of James I, who was married to the King of Hanover, and to her descendants. Other limitations were placed upon the sovereign. The monarch was not to leave England without the consent of Parliament, England was not to be obliged to engage in any wars for the foreign possessions of the monarch. Judges were no longer to hold office during the royal pleasure; but only *quamdiu se bene gesserint* – so long as they behaved themselves. The Crown could no longer influence the Judiciary.

In the sphere of religion a Toleration Act allowed liberty of worship to all who could subscribe to thirty-six of the thirty-nine Articles in the *Book of Common Prayer*, thus excluding all Nonconformists, Catholics and Jews. Later some toleration was allowed to Protestant Nonconformists. In spite of this Act some Anglican consciences were not at ease. One archbishop, four bishops and 400 other clergy, refused to take an oath of allegiance to William and Mary on the grounds that they were already under oath to James II. They were known as Non-Jurors. England had tired of religious squabbles, and the laws against Catholics were less stringent and lightly applied. For all this, William, a strict Calvinist, was not popular with the Church of England, in which the High Church party distrusted him.

It is easy to trivialise William. He was short, thin and fragile in appearance. His manner was chill and repellent. Outside the camp and bottle his habits were unsociable. He had no English friends. His poor health made his temper uncertain and peevish. He disconcerted his ministers by listening to argument and making no response, to act later only after slow calculation. Yet in thirteen years of war, from which he had emerged with modest success, he had reigned with a workable constitution, had quietened religious strife in a country that had been torn apart, and by tact had restored peace with justice. His was not the character to inspire popularity, but then – he himself had not sought it.

ANNE

1702–1714

Anne was the second daughter of James II, and brought up a strict Protestant. As a child she formed a friendship with Sarah Jennings, later Duchess of Marlborough, who, with her husband, were to become the chief influences in her life. She was of little education, and without interest in art, music or literature. In 1683 she married Prince George of Denmark, a marriage which brought them both great domestic happiness, since they both preferred a retired life to mixing in the great world. A doggerel rhyme preserved at Longleat characterises them in the reign of William and Mary:

> King William thinks all,
> Queen Mary talks all,
> Prince George drinks all,
> And Princess Anne eats all.

In 1687 James II formed a project to exclude Mary from the throne if Anne would become a Catholic. Beyond sending her some books and papers his project never got under way. When a prince was born to James and Mary of Modena she persisted in the belief that he had been smuggled into the palace in a bedpan: 'I shall never now be satisfied,' she wrote to Mary, 'whether the child be true or false.' Later, however, she recognised the Old Pretender as her brother.

From the start she detested William III, for having undermined her father. She and the Duchess addressed each other as Mrs Freeman and Mrs Morley. In their letters William was Caliban or the 'Dutch Monster'. There were family quarrels about money, and jealousy between the childless Mary and the prolific Anne. In all she had eighteen pregnancies, of which twelve miscarried. Of the rest, one was stillborn, four died in infancy, and only one, the Duke of Gloucester, reached ten years. He died in 1700. It was this situation that caused Parliament to maintain the Protestant succession by enacting the Act of Settlement, 1701, by which, after Anne, the throne was to pass to her aunt Sophia, the daughter of Charles I's sister Elizabeth, and wife of the King of Hanover, whose son was to succeed in 1714 as George I.

When William died in 1702, Anne succeeded as Queen of England, Scotland and Ireland, but not to his Netherlands possessions. In some respects it was to be the most brilliant reign in the annals of England. The Act of Union united the English and Scottish thrones. Splendid victories crushed France, the hereditary enemy; at home architecture, art and literature blossomed. To all this the weakness of the monarch in a sense contributed, for it liberated the military genius of Marlborough and the skill of a succession of statesmen, whether Whig or Tory. The opposing parties had less defined political positions than were later to become evident, and much of the difference between them arose from personal animosities, friendships and intrigues. Until 1711 the queen was profoundly influenced by the Duchess of Marlborough, with whom she then quarrelled bitterly.

Anne's favourite preoccupation was religion. Early in her reign she issued a proclamation against vice. She feared greatly the Whigs, and, whenever things leaned towards them she observed: 'I shall think the church is beginning to be in danger.' In 1704 she announced that the tenths and first-fruits of livings, which the clergy had paid to the Pope up to 1534, and which were then annexed to the Crown, would be given to the increase of the stipends of poor livings, under the name of Queen Anne's Bounty. She was greatly concerned with appointments to bishoprics, and for long avoided or evaded the appointment of Whigs. The appointment of Cowper as Lord Chancellor in 1705, a Whig, gave her great pain and misgiving. It is mistaken to regard her as High Church in the sense that the nineteenth century Anglo-Catholics were to define it. It was rather that she stood for the constitutional position of the Anglican Church, with herself as Head.

Like Elizabeth I Anne had a horror of any discussion of her successor. She was furious in 1705 when the Tories in Parliament moved to invite the Electress Sophia to visit England, as heir presumptive. Pressure was put upon her in 1714, and she forbade the Hanoverian envoy, Baron Schutz, to proceed with the proposal that the Electoral Prince should take his seat in the House of Lords as Duke of Cambridge. It is said that Anne's angry letter to the

Electress caused the Electress's death on 8 June. This was not done out of any dislike for the Hanoverian family, for, on the contrary, it was Anne herself who in 1706 had made him a Knight of the Garter, and created him Duke of Cambridge. Nevertheless, her opinions were apt to waver. In 1708 she declared the Old Pretender 'a popish pretender bred up in the principles of the most arbitrary government'. Yet in 1714 it was reported in Holland that Anne had secretly determined to associate James with her in government. James wrote to her in this connection in 1714, but no reply was made. A proclamation was issued on 23 June for his arrest should he arrive in England.

All this was brought to an abrupt end. On 27 June the Queen sat in Council until two o'clock in the morning. She then collapsed with what turned out to be a fatal illness. She lingered on until 1 August. She was forty-nine years of age. She was buried in Westminster Abbey in the same tomb as her husband and all her children.

Anne was never fitted to rule. Ill-health, over-frequent pregnancies, and the incessant intrigues by which she was surrounded without the intelligence to counter them, filled her life with misery. She lacked ability, had a dull mind, and suffered from that obstinacy so often present in a weak character. She was homely, retiring and religious. Bishop Burnet said that she had diminished the splendour of the court too much, as if it were abandoned. It was Lord Chesterfield who regretted the strict morality of her court. Yet she served the state to the best of her ability, and it was Dean Swift, often the sharpest of critics, who named her in his Will as of 'ever glorious, immortal and truly pious memory, the real nursing-mother of her kingdoms'.

9   *The House of Hanover*

Continued from page 139

56. George I, b. 28 May 1660 (Georg Ludvig, Duke of Brunswick-Lüneberg), Elector of Hanover, s. 1 Aug. 1714, d. 11 June 1727, m. 21 Nov. 1682 (diss. 28 Dec. 1694) his first cousin Sophia Dorothea (b. 3 Feb. 1666, d. 13 Nov. 1726), d. of George William, Duke of Brunswick-Zell

57. George II Augustus, b. 30 Oct. 1683, s. 11 June 1727, d. 25 Oct. 1760, m. Caroline (b. 1 March 1682, d. 20 Nov. 1737), d. of John Frederick, Margrave of Brandenburg-Anspach

Frederick Lewis, Prince of Wales, b. 20 Jan. 1707, d. 20 March 1751, m. 27 Apr. 1736 Augusta (b. 30 Nov. 1719, d. 8 Feb. 1772), d. of Frederick II, Duke of Saxe-Gotha-Altenburg	George William, b. 3 Nov. 1717, d. 6 Feb. 1718	William Augustus, Duke of Cumberland, 'Butcher Cumberland', b. 15 Apr. 1721, d. unm. 31 Oct. 1765	Anne, Princess Royal, b. 2 Nov. 1709, d. 12 Jan. 1759, m. 25 March 1734 William IV, Prince of Orange-Nassau-Dietz (d. 22 Oct. 1751) issue

58. George III, b. 4 June 1738, s. 25 Oct. 1760, d. 29 Jan. 1820, m. 8 Sept. 1761 Sophia Charlotte, (b. 19 May 1744, d. 17 Nov. 1818), d. of Charles I, Duke of Mecklenburg-Strelitz	Edward Augustus, Duke of York and Albany, Earl of Ulster, b. 14 March 1739, d. unm. 7 Sept. 1767	William Henry, 1st Duke of Gloucester and Edinburgh, Earl of Connaught, b. 14 Nov. 1743, d. 25 Aug. 1805, m. 6 Sept. 1766 Maria (d. 22 Aug. 1807) widow of James, 2nd Earl Waldegrave, and illeg. d. of the Hon. Sir Edward Walpole issue	Henry Frederick, Duke of Cumberland and Stratheam, b. 27 Oct. 1745, d.s.p. 18 Sept. 1790, m. 2 Oct. 1771 Anne (d. 28 Dec. 1808), widow of Christopher Horton and d. of Simon Luttrell, 1st Earl of Carhampton

59. George IV, b. 12 Aug. 1762, Prince Regent from 5 Feb. 1811, s. 29 Jan. 1820, d. 26 June 1830, m. 8 Apr. 1795 Caroline Amelia Elizabeth (b. 1768, d. 7 Aug. 1821), d. of Charles William, Duke of Mecklenburg-Strelitz	Frederick Augustus, Duke of York and Albany, b. 16 Aug. 1793, d. s.p. 5 Jan. 1827, m. 1791 Frederica Charlotte Ulrica Catherine (d. 6 Aug. 1820), d. of Frederick William II, King of Prussia	**60. William IV** b. 21 Aug. 1765, s. 26 June 1830, d. 20 June 1837, m. 11 July 1818 Adelaide (b. 14 Aug. 1792, d. 2 Dec. 1849), d. of George I, Duke of Saxe-Meiningen 2d.—d. in infancy	Edward Augustus, Duke of Kent, b. 2 Nov. 1767, d. 23 Jan. 1820, m. 29 May 1818 Victoria Mary Louise (d. 16 March 1861), widow of Emich Charles, Prince of Leiningen, d. of Francis Frederick Antony, Duke of Saxe-Saalfeld-Coburg	Ernest Augustus, Duke of Brunswick-Lüneburg, King of Hanover, b. 5 June 1771, d. 18 Nov. 1851, m. 29 May 1815 Frederica (d. 29 June 1841) d. of Charles Louis Frederick, Grand Duke of Mecklenburg-Strelitz issue	Augustus Frederick, Duke of Sussex, b. 27 Jan. 1773, d.s.p. 21 Apr. 1843, m. 4 Apr. 1793 in violation of the Royal Marriage Act, 1772, Lady Augusta Murray (d. 5 March 1830); m. 2, May 1831, again violating the Royal Marriage Act, Lady Cecilia Letitia Buggin (later Underwood), created Duchess of Inverness 1840 (d. 1 Aug. 1873)

Charlotte Augusta, b. 7 Jan. 1796, d.s.p. 6 Nov. 1817, m. 2 May 1816 Prince Leopold of Saxe-Saalfeld-Coburg, elected Leopold I, King of the Belgians 4 June 1831 (d. 10 Dec. 1865)	**61. Victoria**, b. 24 May 1819, s. 20 June 1837, d. 22 Jan. 1901, m. 10 Feb. 1840 Prince Albert of Saxe-Coburg and Gotha (b. 26 Aug. 1819, d. 14 Dec. 1861), created Prince Consort 25 June 1857

Continued on page 170

Sophia Dorothea, b. 16 March 1685, d. 29 June 1757, m. 28 Nov. 1706 Frederick
William I, King of Prussia
|
issue

Amelia Sophia Eleanor, b. 10 June 1711, d. unm. 31 Oct. 1786	Caroline Elizabeth, b. 10 June 1713, d. unm. 28 Dec. 1757	Mary, b. 22 Feb. 1723, d. 14 Jan. 1772, m. as 1st wife 8 May 1740 Frederick II, Landgrave of Hesse-Cassel	Louisa, b. 7 Dec. 1724, d. 8 Dec. 1751, m. as 1st wife Frederick V, King of Denmark and Norway
		| issue	| issue

Frederick William, b. 13 May 1750, d. 29 Dec. 1765	Augusta, b. 31 July 1737, d. 23 March 1813, m. 17 Jan. 1764 Charles William Ferdinand, Duke of Brunswick-Wölfenbuttel	Elizabeth Caroline, b. 30 Dec. 1740, d. 4 Sept. 1759	Louisa Ann, b. 8 March 1748-9, d. unm. 13 May 1768	Caroline Matilda, b. 11 July 1751, d. 10 May 1775, m. 1 Oct. 1766 Christian VII, King of Denmark and Norway
	| issue			| issue

Adolphus Frederick, 1st Duke of Cambridge, b. 24 Feb. 1774, d. 8 July 1850, m. 7 May 1818 Augusta Wilhelmina Louise (d. 6 Apr. 1889), d. of Frederick, Landgrave of Hesse-Cassel, leaving issue (from whom descended Queen Mary, wife of King George V)	2s. d. young	Charlotte Augusta Matilda, Princess Royal, b. 29 Sept. 1766, d.s.p. 6 Oct. 1828, m. 18 May 1797 Frederick I, King of Württemberg (d. 30 Oct. 1816)	Augusta Sophia, b. 8 Nov. 1768, d. unm. 22 Sept. 1840	Elizabeth, b. 22 May 1770, d.s.p. 10 Jan. 1840, m. 7 Apr. 1818 Frederick, Landgrave of Hesse-Homburg (d. 2 Apr. 1829)	Mary, b. 25 Apr. 1776, d.s.p. 30 Apr. 1857, m. 22 July 1816 her first cousin, William Frederick, 2nd Duke of Gloucester (d. 30 Nov. 1834)	Sophia, b. 3 Nov. 1777, d. unm. 27 May 1848	Amelia, b. 7 Aug. 1783, d. unm. 2 Nov. 1810

continued from page 168

62. Edward VII, b. 9 Nov. 1841, s. 22 Jan. 1901, d. 6 May 1910, m. 10 March 1863 PrincessAlexandra, (b. 1 Dec. 1844, d. 20 Nov. 1925), d. of Christian IX, King of Denmark

Alfred Ernest Albert, Duke of Saxe-Coburg and Gotha, b. 6 Aug. 1844, d. 30 July 1900, m. 23 Jan. 1874 Grand Duchess Marie (d. 25 Oct. 1920), d. of Alexander II, Tsar of Russia

issue, including Royal Houses of Roumania, Russia and Yugoslavia

Arthur William Patrick Albert, 1st Duke of Connaught, b.1 May 1850, d. 16 Jan. 1942, m. 13 March 1879 Princess Louise (d. 14 March 1917), d. of Prince Frederick Charles of Prussia

issue, including the Royal House of Sweden

Leopold George Duncan Albert, 1st Duke of Albany, b. 7 Apr. 1853, d. 28 March 1884, m. 27 Apr. 1882 Princess Helen Frederica Augusta (d.1 Sept. 1922), d. of George Victor, Prince of Waldeck and Pyrmont

issue—
Dukes of Saxony

Albert Victor Christian Edward, Duke of Clarence and Avondale, b. 8 Jan. 1864, d. unm. 14 Jan. 1892

63. George V

Continued on page 204

Alexander John Charles Albert, b. 6 Apr. 1871, d. 7 Apr. 1871

Louise Victoria Alexandra Dagmar, Princess Royal, b. 20 Feb. 1867, d. 4 Jan. 1931, m. 27 July 1889 1st Duke of Fife (d. 29 Jan. 1912)

issue—Dukes of Fife

Victoria Adelaide Mary Louisa, Princess Royal, b. 21 Nov. 1840, d. 5 Aug. 1901, m. 25 Jan. 1858 Frederick, later King of Prussia and German Emperor (d. 1888)	Alice Maud Mary, b. 25 Apr. 1843, d. 14 Dec. 1878, m. 1 July 1862 Louis IV, Grand Duke of Hesse (d. 13 March 1892)	Helena Augusta Victoria, b. 25 May 1846, d. 9 June 1923, m. 5 July 1866, Prince Christian of Schleswig-Holstein (d. 28 Oct. 1917)	Louise Caroline Alberta, b. 18 March 1848, d.s.p. 3 Dec. 1939, m. 21 March 1871 9th Duke of Argyll (d. 2 May 1914)	Beatrice Mary Victoria Feodore, b. 14 May 1857, d. 26 Oct. 1944, m. 23 July 1885 Prince Henry of Battenberg (d. 20 Jan. 1896)
issue—Royal Houses of Hohenzollern and Greece	issue*— including the Imperial Family of Russia	issue		issue— including Royal House of Spain

Victoria Alexandra Olga Mary, b. 6 July 1868; d. unm. 3 Dec. 1935	Maud Charlotte Mary Victoria, b. 26 Nov. 1869, d. 20 Nov. 1938, m. 22 July 1896 her first cousin, later King Haakon VII of Norway (d. 21 Sept. 1957)
	issue— Royal House of Norway

* Their d. Princess Victoria m. Louis Alexander, Prince of Battenburg, later 1st Marquess of Milford Haven, by whom she had two s., George, 2nd Marquess of Milford Haven, and Louis, 1st Earl Mountbatten of Burma, and one d., Alice, m. Prince Andrew of Greece, whose son, Philip, Duke of Edinburgh m. H.M. Queen Elizabeth.

GEORGE I

1714–1727

George I's mother, Sophia, youngest daughter of Elizabeth, Queen of Bohemia, daughter of James I of England, was heir to the English throne by the Act of Settlement, 1701. She was the nearest Protestant heir after Queen Anne, although there were many persons who had better claims than she. She was already seventy-one when she was appointed, and took little interest in the matter, for at the time Anne was only thirty-six. Sophia's son George was only five years older than her. He had fought courageously in the wars of William III, and had succeeded his father as King of Hanover in 1698. He had sent reinforcements to support Marlborough at Blenheim, and had attached himself to Marlborough and the Whigs. It was more to be expected that George's son, George Ludvig, would eventually succeed, and for this reason he had already been created Duke of Cambridge. Sophia, however, died on 28 May 1714, and Anne followed her on 1 August.

The new king had already married his cousin Sophia Dorothea in 1682. It was not a happy marriage. Like Versailles, which they aped, the German courts made dynastic marriages when they could, and then took mistresses. It was a profligacy allowed only to princes, but Sophia Dorothea had the temerity to attract a lover, Count Königsmark. He was assassinated. Sophia Dorothea was divorced in 1694, and lived in seclusion until 1726. Asked if he would marry again, George Ludvig replied: *J'aurai des maîtresses*. As George I he brought two to England with him.

Aside from William III's stricter morals, George I bears certain comparisons with him. They were both foreigners. They had little knowledge of English politics or politicians, and little interest in English problems. Party spirit was running high between Whigs and Tories. The Whigs had won a victorious war. Some Tories were coquetting with James II's son, the Old Pretender. By contrast with the politicians, the new king had neither experience nor much intellect to guide him. Yet George I managed a balancing act which maintained and gave stability to the monarchy, even though he did not conceive it as a policy. The country gentry and country clergy supported the Tories; the Whigs had the support of the towns, the merchants and the higher aristocracy. The Old Pretender's bid for the throne, and his defeat, was in fact a benefit to George I: it demonstrated the existence of an effective government and an effective ruler, even if he contributed little to it.

George I was unable to speak English. His habitual languages were German or preferably French. They were not the language of ministers. When Walpole became the chief minister in 1722, he and the King communicated in Latin. The Whigs had the sense to borrow much of their policies from their opponents, leaving the opposition with very little to oppose. It was possible therefore for the cabinet to develop, particularly because the king was frequently absent in Germany, which he greatly preferred, or simply did not attend. Moreover, in Walpole as chief minister there emerged a politician who was particularly skilful in the management of Parliament, so that he became a king in all but name. George did not himself resign power altogether. At the beginning of his reign he both sacked and appointed ministers of his choice. It was rather he let power slip through his fingers. He did not understand his position as William III had done. His preoccupation was with Hanover, with enriching his German attendants and his German mistresses. In this state of mind he went off to Hanover in 1716, within two years of his accession. The clause in the Act of Settlement forbidding the sovereign to leave England without the consent of Parliament had been repealed unanimously.

The King, however, had refused to make the Prince of Wales regent. He had now reached thirty-three years of age. Like his father, he was stupid. A title was resurrected for him: Guardian and Lieutenant of the Realm. It had not been used since the days of the Black Prince. He was left almost powerless. He was forbidden to make any decision touching foreign affairs, the Royal Household, the Treasury or the Admiralty; he could not promote officers to command a garrison, or above the rank of colonel, nor appoint even a lieutenant in the Guards. All such matters had to be referred to the King. The slowness of communication caused friction on both sides; between the King and the Prince there was neither sympathy nor understanding. It was a pattern that was to be repeated in succeeding reigns. The King returned in 1717, only to have a squalid quarrel with the Prince over the naming of his newborn son, the short-lived George William. In London speculation was rife. Could it have been that the King had been responsible for the assassination of Königsmark? Would something of the sort happen again? The King had the Prince held in what was virtually house detention. He was forbidden to sit in the Cabinet, as he had been accustomed to do as heir to the throne. The King had relied upon him for his knowledge of English, and now he had denied this facility to himself. The King now ceased to attend the Cabinet altogether, only seeing the ministers in private. The Cabinet bored him. The Hanoverian propensity for quarrelling with their heirs had produced a constitutional change. Walpole had now reached the peak of his power. In June 1727 George I set out again for Hanover. In appearance he was hale and hearty. Near Osnabrück he had a stroke and died. His principal amusement, apart from the conversation of his mistresses, had been cutting paper out into pretty patterns.

GEORGE II

1727–1760

George II was thirty-one years of age at his accession. At twenty-three he had married Caroline of Brandenburg-Anspach, a lady of much stronger character than himself. Queen Anne had created him Duke of Cambridge in 1706. Two years later he had fought bravely under Marlborough at Oudenarde. He had long been on bad terms with his father, as has already been recounted. It was expected therefore that his first act on his accession would be to get rid of Walpole. His first act was to send to Sir Spencer Compton to draw up his accession speech. Within twenty-four hours his wife had circumvented him. Compton had no idea how to write the speech, and asked Walpole for aid. The Queen pointed out that this displayed Compton's incapacity, and Walpole was reinstated.

George II was not only stupid and easily bullied, by his wife, and later by his ministers. As a soldier he had the mentality of a drill-sergeant. He was over-precise. He had a very thorough knowledge of the genealogies of European nobility and of all the details of military uniforms and decorations. He kept accounts like a clerk and attended to the smallest minutiae of court etiquette. Nothing made him angrier than a mistake of protocol. He was for ever counting his money. He liked history, but chiefly for dates and data. He had no overall grasp. Obstinacy, a characteristic found in many weak men, prevented him from giving way gracefully; he made undignified scenes, and then gave way. Until her death in 1737 he was saved by his wife, and then, because they had learnt their business from her, his ministers.

Like all his contemporaries and family, he was greatly given to women. The Duchess of Kendal was long a favourite. So was Mrs Henrietta Howard. He nevertheless paid every attention to his wife, by whom he had three sons and five daughters. In 1735 he wrote constant letters to her, describing his infatuation for Countess von Walmoden, giving her a blow by blow account of the progress of her seduction. It was alleged that he had slept with Walpole's wife; Walpole himself was casual in his attitude to her. George II had many other short term relationships, but no other lasting liaisons. For all this, he greatly depended on his wife, and trusted her judgement.

Other than his Guards regiments, George II had no other interests than money and music. It was he who became the chief patron of Handel; the custom of standing during the Hallelujah chorus in the *Messiah* is said to have come about because he stood up in excitement at it. Handel's music was not at first well liked by the fashionable world. Nothing could exceed the pomp and dignity of Handel's coronation music or the *Music for the Royal Fireworks*. Inevitably he had a squalid quarrel with his eldest son; weak, rebellious and headstrong, he was banished from court.

The history of his years up to the 1740s is the history of Walpole, in which the King had little influence. When the war of the Austrian succession broke out in 1741 he sided with Maria Theresa of Austria against the rising power of Prussia. He had now become unpopular in England because he had greater regard for the safety of Hanover than the interests of England. His greatest feat was the defeat of the French armies at Dettingen in 1743; Handel wrote a *Te Deum* to celebrate the victory. England was in the hands of a succession of prime ministers, who organised the resistance to the Young Pretender in 1745, and who brought about the peace of Aix-la-Chapelle in 1748. The King could not resist the appointment of William Pitt at the end of the reign, although he hated Pitt because he had opposed the sacrifices imposed by assistance to Hanover. The execution of Admiral Byng is typical of his disregard for English opinion. Pitt had represented that it was the wish of the House of Commons that Byng should be pardoned. George II retorted: 'Sir, you have taught me to look for the sense of my subjects in another place than the House of Commons.'

The banishment from court of the Prince of Wales made his court at Leicester House a focus for the opposition. In 1751 he died unexpectedly, following a chill caught playing tennis. The King himself was now ageing, and his heir only thirteen. Pitt was now stronger than ever, and for his last three years of reign George II was the merest cipher. It was to Pitt that were ascribed the successes, in Canada, in the West Indies, at Dakar in West Africa, in India, with Clive in Bengal, and on the European continent at Fontenoy and Minden.

The reign ended in a blaze of glory for Pitt and the ministers, the fleet and the army. For the King it ended in farce. On 25 October 1760 he fell dead in his water-closet, brought about, it was said, by his exertions. His Will asked that his coffin be placed beside Queen Caroline's, and that one side of each be removed, so that their dust might mingle in death.

At no time had the monarchy been so marginalised.

GEORGE III

1760–1820

The King who now ascended the throne was only twenty-two years old. Since his father's death in 1751 he had been brought up in strict seclusion by his mother and her friend and counsellor, the 3rd Earl of Bute. He was taught to believe in Bolingbroke's Tory maxims of the *Patriot King*, and that it was his vocation to break the Whig aristocracy, and their power of patronage and corruption. In morals he was in sharp contrast to his two predecessors on the throne. Intellectually he was infatuated with Bute. As a boy he was a poor pupil, willing enough, but lacking concentration. He was fully conscious of his shortcomings, and clung to Bute for advice. He was grossly misinformed. He believed that his father had been the prisoner of a gang of unscrupulous politicians, greedy for the spoils of office and indifferent to the nation at large. This was the ministry of the elder Pitt and Newcastle, the founders of the wealth of nineteenth-century England. Bute, who had never had a central position at court or in politics, was in fact useless to him. Only time and experience could help him.

George had an almost frenetic desire for an heir as well as a full share of the strong passions of his forebears. In 1761 he hastily married Charlotte of Mecklenburg-Strelitz, whose plainness even he regretted. His high sense of morality kept him monogamous. His sensual nature kept her almost continually pregnant, from 1761 until 1783, during which time she had seven sons and eight daughters. After seven years of dependence on Bute, and extension of adolescence, he turned to the elder Pitt. By now George knew his routine duties and the ceremonial of monarchy. It was perhaps emotional strain that induced his first so-called fit of madness in 1765. Pitt and Newcastle, Hardwicke, George Grenville and others, were now in full cry in opposition. The King was not strong enough to contend with them, nor Bute. Four ministries followed Bute's resignation in 1763 up to 1767.

In opposition too was the City of London, merchants and bankers, who had grown rich in the succession of wars which had gone on since the turn of the century. Rich capitalists, they had behind them the professional classes and industrialists, now men of substance. All these and more had benefited from the wars. George wanted peace. When he rode to the City to be congratulated on his marriage, he was hissed; Pitt was received with loud cheering. Pitt collapsed in 1767; three years later Lord North became Prime Minister, remaining until 1782, the worst prime minister, it is said, that England ever had.

No one in England questioned the right of Parliament to tax the American colonies, least of all the King. Power was held to reside in the King in Parliament; if Parliament consented to tax on tea in London there was no apparent reason why it should not do so in Boston, Massachusetts. The theory that there should be no taxation without consent was irrelevant if the consent of Parliament was given. The King was at one with his English subjects; across the Atlantic they were unrepresented. Up to that time the question whether even the King's subjects at home were properly represented had not been fully raised. Only a small minority had a vote. The elder Pitt had called attention to the fact that representation was the true spirit of English government. No one had heeded.

The king was now called in question in a different way. John Wilkes was a protégé of Lord Temple. Temple's sister had been created Baroness Chatham while the elder Pitt was still a commoner. Wilkes was the son of a merchant, brash, bitter-tongued, and unrestrained. As a client of Temple, and therefore of Pitt, he attacked the king violently in his newspaper, the *North Briton*, for making peace. Halifax, the Secretary of State, issued a general warrant for his arrest for seditious libel against the king. He was taken to the Tower for trial. He brought countercharges against Halifax for wrongful arrest and damage to property when he was arrested. Mr Justice Pratt – a client of Pitt also – gave in favour of Wilkes.

The king was enraged. He had suffered insult; the criminal had escaped justice. Then among Wilkes' papers was found an obscene parody of Pope's *Essay on Woman*, an *Essay on Man*. For this he was expelled from the House of Commons. Wilkes escaped to France, but, a skilful publicist, had spread the word in his favour. Against

George III's 'that devil Wilkes' was the popular cry: 'Wilkes and Liberty'. The London mob became hysterical: they hated the king, his mother and Bute. Pitt was made Prime Minister, and created Earl of Chatham. He now suffered an acute clinical depression, that contemporaries called madness. He begged the king to release him from office. The king would have none of it. Chatham lay in a bedroom adjacent to the room where the Cabinet met. Lady Chatham conveyed his messages to it in his name. After two years Chatham gave way to the Duke of Grafton, and the farce was ended.

In 1775 the American colonies revolted. War lasted until 1783. In 1776, on 4 July, the Declaration of Independence, drawn up by Thomas Jefferson, was issued. In 1777 the Articles of Confederation, the United States' first constitution, was drawn up. They were confirmed in 1781. Already in 1778 Britain was at war with France, when the French ambassador in London announced that France had signed a treaty of friendship and commerce with the United States. In 1779 Britain was at war with Spain also. The king would neither provide money or troops to suppress the American rebellion, nor acknowledge what his ministers already knew, that he had lost the United Sates.

1780 witnessed agitation in England against the king's war policy. It took the form of the Gordon Riots in London against the Catholic Relief Act, demands for economic reform, the Sacheverell riots, attacks on the Excise Bill, and declamations by Wilkes' supporters. In March 1782 Lord North resigned, and short ministries followed, under Rockingham, then Shelburne, then Portland with a coalition. The final crisis arose over an India Bill. The King had authorised Lord Temple to declare in his name that he would count as his enemy any peer who voted for the Bill. On 17 December 1783 the Bill was thrown out. Next day William Pitt the younger became Prime Minister; a long and stable period began, which ended only with his resignation in 1801. He was only twenty-four, younger son of the great Chatham, and nephew of George Grenville. For the king, he had vindicated his right to dismiss and appoint ministers. He now was faced by a man of exceptional abilities, but of his own choice. He submitted to be managed by him. The success of the ministry brought him great credit, and he was satisfied with that.

Outside politics George III showed a lively interest in the voyages of discovery in the Pacific and in Canadian waters. The

Privy Purse made grants to the infant Royal Academy. A great collection of maps and of oil paintings was started. The King's overriding enthusiasm was for farming. He had already been ill in 1765, but the symptoms had been concealed. In 1788 his insanity became beyond all doubt, for he had become violent. In recent times it has been recognised that this was not simply a mental affliction. It was porphyria, a rare inherited disorder transmitted by females from a male ancestor. It had not hitherto been recorded in the royal family. The cause is a disturbance of the balance of the metabolism of porphyrine, the breakdown products of the red blood pigment. It can affect the liver or the bone marrow, or both. The urine becomes discoloured, the body oversensitive to sunlight, causing blistering skin rashes, bouts of abdominal pain, mental disturbance and neuritis. While in the House of Commons Pitt and Fox were arguing on what terms the Prince of Wales should be made Regent, the king was at the mercy of ignorant physicians, and the brutality of servants. Their rough treatment only exacerbated the case. Shortly, a Dr Willis, who had made a speciality of the treatment of the insane, was called in. He had made a name by prescribing gentleness in place of rigour. Although at times he found himself compelled to restrain the king, his gentleness and humane management was repaid. By February 1789 the king wrote to Pitt thanking him for all he had done during his illness. On St George's Day, 1789, he drove to St Paul's to give thanks for his recovery.

Already in 1788 the first rumblings of the French Revolution were heard. On 14 July 1789 the Paris mob stormed the Bastille; on 6 October it marched on Versailles, forcing Louis XVI to return to Paris. Clearly the end of the French monarchy was in sight. George III now became a symbol of resistance to France, just as Elizabeth I had been a symbol of resistance to Spain. The Whig landowners made their peace with the king, and shortly raised a militia. Pitt was allowed a free hand with raising taxes and equipping armies. His Foreign Secretary, William Wyndham, Lord Grenville, devised a system of subsidies to Prussia by which Prussia fought Britain's battles on land, while Britain recovered the costs by the export of manufactures. At sea Britain was soon to be paramount.

On 1 August 1800 Great Britain and Ireland were united in a single Parliament. The King then learnt from the Lord Chancellor, Lord Loughborough, that Pitt had it in mind to bring in a Bill to relieve Catholics of their disabilities. George III promptly took up the position that any concessions to Catholics, whether in Ireland or Britain, were contrary to his coronation oath. It was a decision from which he never swerved. He suffered a further attack of porphyria, but recovered rapidly. On 14 March 1801 Pitt resigned. George III thought Pitt should never have 'meddled'. He told his physician to inform Pitt of his recovery, 'but what has he not to answer for, who has been the cause of my having been ill at all'. Addington succeeded, a weaker man: the wags had it: 'Pitt is to Addington as London is to Paddington.'

In April 1803 Napoleon, now ruler of France, marched into Holland. It convinced George III and Parliament that war was again inevitable. In 1804 the King's mind was again affected. A ministerial crisis followed, and Pitt was recalled. Pitt died on 23 January 1806, and was succeeded by his Foreign Secretary, Lord Grenville. Long before, in 1788, he and Pitt and William Wilberforce had proposed to abolish the slave trade. It was to support this that Grenville was raised to the Lords in 1789. Now he was able to achieve one of his political ambitions, the abolition of the slave trade and with royal assent. The king and Grenville collided on the Catholic question, another of Grenville's ambitions. It was a Bill which would enable both Catholics and dissenters to serve in the army and navy without regard for religious disqualifications. The king now demanded a written undertaking that the ministry would never in any circumstances propose to him 'any measure of concession to the Catholics or even connected with the question'. The ministers very properly refused to be bound for the future, and were forced to resign. Grenville was not to get his wish until 1829, when he wrote to his brother: 'Thank God, I have lived to see this day.' Like the abolition of the slave trade, and then of slavery itself throughout British dominions, it was an act of profound constitutional consequence.

The collapse of the coalition 'Ministry of All the Talents' was the last phase of the effective reign of George III. The death of his favourite child Amelia in November 1810 drove him once again into madness. His remaining years were passed in increasing blindness and insanity; he did not die until 1820. He and his wife had married in 1761. After a decent married life that none of her predecessors had enjoyed since Queen Anne, she died at Kew in 1818. The remainder of George III's reign belongs, therefore, to that of his son, George IV, first as Prince Regent, and then as King.

 The long reign of sixty years was the longest Britain had ever seen. It was only to be surpassed by his granddaughter, Victoria, who shared his characteristics of rectitude and morality, but none of his hesitance. None of his family before her were blessed with any great intelligence, but he was not without a certain shrewdness. The chopping and changing of ministries did not make for stability, but it had now become apparent that where a Prime Minister had the unequivocal support of the Commons he could not easily become unseated. As often before, the King's own weakness had favoured, rather than hindered, constitutional growth.

GEORGE IV

Regent, 1811–1820; King, 1820–1830

George IV, first son of George III, was naturally gifted. He was well grounded in the classics, and spoke French, German and Italian fluently. As a young man he was notably handsome. He had a considerable interest in music and the arts. The exceedingly strict puritanical court of his father, the epitome of dullness caused the inevitable reaction in him and in his six brothers. In an aristocratic world which was already profligate, five of them and George himself were wholly without restraint. Of the royal dukes Cambridge was the only exception. York lived openly with a demi-mondaine while pursuing the elderly Duchess of Rutland; Clarence, later to be William IV, lived with an actress, the daughter of an Irish judge, by whom he had ten children. She left him for a time to earn on the stage the wherewithal to support them. Kent was a savage martinet, who lived with a French-Canadian; Sussex made ridiculous marriages; Cumberland concealed his vices: his family spoke of him with horror; Cambridge alone was mildly eccentric. It was his habit in church to answer loudly if the preacher asked a rhetorical question; to the request 'Let us pray' he answered 'By all means' with studious politeness. All but he gambled and wantoned without discrimination with a vulgarity that made the French court seem like a ladies' academy. All of them were heavily in debt, relying on Parliament and the taxpayer to rescue them to avoid too much scandal. No wonder critics and satirists abused and ridiculed them. Even though the king's life was exemplary, they dragged the monarchy to depths that were unexampled in England. If the monarchy survived in the period after 1811–1837, it was because the value of it as a political institution was patent to all, not because of the conduct of members of the royal family.

The Prince (and this is the most convenient style to call him) came of age in 1783. He was already on bad terms with his father.

He found the society of the Whigs, of Charles James Fox and Georgiana, Duchess of Devonshire, congenial politically and socially, but not least their opposition to his father.

Already by 1781 he had fallen in love with a widow, Mary Anne, or Maria, FitzHerbert. Daughter of a Catholic family, she had first married in 1775 Edward Weld, who died in the same year; and then Thomas FitzHerbert, who left her a considerable fortune in 1781. She was in the full bloom of her great beauty, and the Prince fell passionately in love. The Act of Settlement, 1689, provided that any member of the royal family who married a Catholic automatically forfeited the succession; while the Royal Marriage Act, 1772, forbade all George III's descendants to marry without his consent, and made such marriages illegal under the age of twenty-five. Mrs FitzHerbert was torn between the desire to return his love and her religion; she would not become his mistress, and was fully aware that reasons of state precluded marriage. She was likewise aware that as a Catholic she could not marry a Protestant without an episcopal dispensation. On 15 December 1785 they went through a ceremony of marriage according to the Anglican rite; if illegal, canonically the marriage oaths were undoubtedly valid. The Prince's friends treated it as a 'morganatic marriage'; rumour got out, and they firmly denied it. The Prince now lived in Carlton House in the most extravagant fashion; the King refused to bail him out, so he went off to Brighton with Mrs FitzHerbert. They had no children. The union lasted until 1794, when pressure was put on the Prince to marry a German princess and to produce an heir; none of the brothers showed any sign of doing so. He agreed to marry Caroline, Princess of Brunswick-Wölfenbutell.

Lord Malmesbury was sent to Brunswick to fetch the bride. Neither he nor anyone else gave the Prince any hint of her character. She was wildly eccentric. She was coarse, exhibitionist, flamboyant, dirty and highly sexed. She scarcely ever changed her linen and never washed. The Prince was overcome when he met her. To Malmesbury he said: 'I am not well, fetch me a glass of brandy.' The marriage took place on 8 April 1795. The Prince was drugged with drink; she behaved immodestly, the marriage was consummated that night; a daughter, Charlotte, was born precisely nine months after. It was the only occasion.

The Prince now fell in love with Lady Jersey, whom he appointed as a Lady-in-Waiting to his wife. This only lasted a short while; the Prince hankered after Mrs FitzHerbert, who now with papal sanction, so it is said, returned to his bed. Princess Caroline paraded herself as a wronged woman; the London populace received her with rapture, and blackguarded the Prince. Princess Caroline was now alleged to be pregnant with an illegitimate child. This was disproved. In 1814 she went abroad, and lived with an Italian adventurer, Pergami, who affected the dress of King Murat. Doubtless Caroline was vulgar and silly, but there was no attempt to treat her with kindness. More was to come in 1821.

In 1788 George III had his first serious attack of porphyria. Fox maintained that the Prince of Wales, as heir to the throne, had an automatic right to become Regent; Pitt denied that he could do this without a Parliamentary vote. The King recovered in the spring of 1789, but fell ill again in 1811. It was assumed that the Whigs would now come into office, and the Prince asked Lord Grenville to form a ministry again. After some differences of opinion, Grenville recommended that the existing ministry under Perceval should continue.

The ministry foundered later in the year, and the Prince proposed a coalition. The Whigs declined on the ground that Catholic disabilities were too important a matter to be shelved, and that their difference with Perceval could not be ignored. Then Perceval was assassinated by a madman; Lord Liverpool succeeded, but again the Whigs declined to serve with him. Liverpool served until his death in 1827

In 1820 George III died. Almost immediately Queen Caroline returned to England. She had been warned that if she did so, proceedings would be taken against her for adultery. An attempt to divorce her by Act of Parliament failed. Public opinion was on her side, outraged that an adulterous husband should charge his wife with adultery. George IV's popularity was at its lowest ebb. In 1821 Caroline attempted to force her way into Westminster Abbey for the coronation. In this she had no popular support. Then in August she died.

The King almost at once set sail for Ireland. His effusive temperament charmed the Irish, whose only memory of a king would have been of William III. He had an uproarious reception in Dublin. This success encouraged him to visit Edinburgh in August 1822. He delighted in splendid clothes, and wore the full dress Stuart tartan, with, somewhat bizarrely, tights underneath the kilt. No king had set foot on Scottish soil since Charles II. Sir Walter Scott organised the reception, which equalled, if not outdid, the enthusiasm with which he had been received in Dublin.

He returned to London to the crisis caused by the suicide of the Foreign Secretary, Castlereagh (Lord Londonderry). At first he resisted the appointment of George Canning, but Liverpool insisted. It was a battle which George III had fought earlier with success, but now the office of prime minister had grown in power. It was a constitutional change of the first importance, that no longer could the sovereign choose his own ministers. Lord Liverpool's ministry had otherwise been highly conservative, and the country was ripe and eager for reform. There was dissatisfaction with the rotten boroughs and the landowners who controlled them, the burning question of the emancipation of Catholics and Protestant dissenters, only partially solved in 1829; the abolition of slavery throughout British dominions and the fundamental reform of Parliament was yet to come. Liverpool died in 1827; Canning followed him and then himself died later in 1827. Goderich lasted no more than a few months, until the Duke of Wellington took office in January 1828. He was well able to cope with royal hysteria, for Ireland was already on the brink of war.

Whatever George IV lacked in statesmanship and character he left his country a splendid heritage in buildings. Carlton House Terrace, the enlargement of Buckingham Palace, which he virtually rebuilt, the Nash Terraces, Regent's Park, are all his creations. Carlton House no longer exists, but its façade adorns the front of the National Gallery. At Windsor the Castle was splendidly restored, and the Royal Lodge also; but the King's favourite was the exotic Pavilion at Brighton, where oriental fantasies ran mad. Of it Sydney Smith said: 'It was as if St Paul's had gone down to the sea for a day for a bathe, and had had pups.' Here the King spent the last of his days, in riotous luxury and gluttony. His chef Carême, in spite of his name, contrived dinners which on one occasion ran to 900 dishes. Oriental decoration, however, was not the only royal pleasure. The walls of the palaces were enhanced by the finest oil paintings, the basis of the royal collection which is unsurpassed in all Europe. Here at Brighton George IV had the comforting companionship of Mrs FitzHerbert. He was grossly obese, and lay on a bed to receive ministers, clad in exotic dressing-gowns in brilliant peacock colours. In spite of his oddities, he was perhaps more sophisticated than all his predecessors.

WILLIAM IV

1830–1837

With two elder brothers William IV had no early expectation of ascending the throne. George IV's only child, Charlotte, died in childbirth in 1817; only his childless brother Frederick, Duke of York and Albany, stood between him and George IV. He died in 1827, thus clearing the way. William was in sharp contrast to all who had gone before him. Eccentric, explosive, and neither highly intelligent nor highly educated, often hesitant, there was a fundamental steadiness that carried him through times that would have tried the most able monarchs. There is a touch of modernity about him which was instinctive rather than cultivated; there was also what today is called the 'common touch'. He was intensely self-disciplined, and apt to be capricious in dealing with politicians.

George III had no intention that his third son should pass his life in gilded idleness. At thirteen years old he was sent to the Royal Navy. Although he was entered on the ship's books as HRH Prince William Henry, he immediately made it known that he wished to be called William Guelph (the surname of the House of Hanover). He added: 'I am nothing more than a sailor like yourselves.'

It was no pleasure cruise in the wooden ships. In 1780 he served at the relief of Gibraltar; in 1781 he sailed in the *Prince George* for America, the first – and the last – British prince to see the Flag of Union flying over New York. George Washington ordered him to be captured, but said he should be treated kindly. Fortunately the plan did not succeed. He came home in 1783, and toured central Europe, visiting the Emperor in Vienna and Frederick the Great at Sans-Souci. In 1789 his father created him Duke of Clarence, reviving the title of the brother of Edward IV who was allegedly drowned in a butt of Malmsey. In 1786 he was commanding a frigate on the West Indies Station, where he formed a close friendship with a virtually unknown Captain Nelson. He had a life-long admiration for him. He was in tears at Nelson's funeral; he kept part of the *Victory*'s main mast in his dining-room. It is not clear why he was withdrawn from the Navy; he seemed destined for the life of idleness which his father had wished to avoid for him.

Any thoughts that Prince William might have for the future were precluded by the Royal Marriages Act, which has already been described. It was inevitable that he should seek a wife; if she were not to be German princess, whom could he seek? His eyes fell on Mrs Jordan, an actress, the daughter of an Irish judge, of exquisite beauty by all accounts. William was Ranger of Bushey Park; he retired there, where she gave him ten beautiful children. They were known as FitzClarences, or *les bâtards*. Their happiness was clouded over only when she left him from time to time for the stage, for much needed money, for he was for ever in debt. This lasted twenty years, until 1811, when the King broke down, and there began to be anxiety about the ultimate course of the succession. In the next six years various *démarches* were made to find William a bride: the situation became more acute in 1817, when Princess Charlotte died: it spelt that, when his two elder brothers died, William would be King of both Great Britain and Hanover. William was so heavily in debt that he was no attractive proposition.

At this moment William fell helplessly in love with a Miss Wykeham. In 1818 a bride was found for him, Princess Adelaide of Saxe-Meiningen. He sacrificed Miss Wykeham with sobs and tears; Princess Adelaide, however, made him an admirable wife, an exemplary Queen Consort, and a kindly stepmother to the ten children. Her sole failure was that she only produced two daughters who died in infancy. It was in this way that when he became king, the future Queen Victoria became his heir presumptive.

The Duke of York died in 1827, making William heir apparent. It was thought to give him an honorific position, and he was made Lord High Admiral. The office was an anachronism; its last occupant had been Queen Anne's husband more than a century before. William took himself seriously, visiting dockyards, and generally making a nuisance of himself. He got across the Board of Admiralty, most of them in any case civilians. He even took a squadron to sea, without notifying either the king or the Board. No one knew where they were. Eventually the government told the king that unless the duke resigned, they would themselves demit office. William had had fifteen glorious months. He accepted defeat, and went to bed for a week to recover from his exertions.

Finally, in 1830, George IV died. The new king drove up from Bushey. Far from showing any sign of grief, he bowed and smiled to the people as he went. At Windsor he followed George IV's immense coffin up the nave of St George's Chapel, shaking hands with friends whom he recognised as he went. He never cared for court etiquette, and at first refused coronation. He regarded it as a waste of money. He was only finally persuaded when it was agreed to simplify its style. The splendid Coronation Banquet was cancelled. The gorgeous dishes were no longer brought in preceded on horseback by the Great Officers of State; the ceremony of the challenge by the King's Champion, on horseback, and 'in a complete suit of bright armour', with a shield bearing the arms of the family of Dymoke, was omitted. Observers noted that after what was called the 'half-crownation' the King and Royal Family were greeted and cheered by the crowds more loudly than had been heard for some time.

George IV had died on 26 June; on 27 July a fresh revolution against the Bourbons broke out in France, and the rebels seized the Arsenal, the Hôtel de Ville and the palaces. On 2 August Charles X abdicated, to be replaced by Louis-Philippe on 9 August. Later in the month there was a rising in Belgium. In England in November the bad harvest provoked the 'Labourers' Revolt'. In such circumstances it was a difficult beginning for an untried monarch who had no experience of politics and whose character inclined him to caution.

England was now to suffer an agitation more violent than any undergone since 1689. Throughout the country there was an immediate demand for reform. William had called himself 'an old Whig', but his hesitancy, if not timidity, brought the country to the edge of revolution.

At that time the death of the sovereign required a general election. The Tories lost fifty seats, leaving the Duke of Wellington with a slender majority. A fortnight later it was beaten, and Wellington was replaced by the Whig Earl Grey. He introduced the first Reform Bill on 1 March 1831; the second reading was carried by a majority of only one. Very shortly the government was beaten in committee, and Grey offered to resign. The King refused him, and refused a dissolution, although it was obvious that a government pledged to parliamentary reform could not hold office. The opposition then moved a resolution against dissolution; William regarded this as an attack on the royal prerogative, and promptly dissolved Parliament.

The general election gave the Whigs an overwhelming majority. In June a second Reform Bill was introduced; the third reading in the Commons had a majority of 109. Nevertheless, the Lords threw the Bill out by a majority of forty-one, and a prolonged crisis began. Riots and disturbances started, and the King's carriage was stoned by the London mob. A stone passed through the carriage window as he returned from the theatre, and landed in the lap of Prince George of Cumberland, later King of Hanover. The king hesitated in his support for the government. The stumbling block was now the House of Lords, and, after further hesitation, William agreed to create sufficient peers to enable the Bill to pass. The Lords defeated the Bill, and Grey then asked for an unlimited creation of peers, saying he would resign if it were not agreed. The king accepted the resignation with tears.

The Duke of Wellington was now Prime Minister for one week, after which Grey returned to office. The king now gave way and the Royal Assent to the Reform Bill was given on 7 June 1832. The 'regal authority', said the diarist Charles Greville, had fallen into contempt. The peers, nevertheless, were as much to blame as the king for not understanding the feeling of the country.

Grey resigned in 1834, and was succeeded by Lord Melbourne. In August slavery was abolished throughout all English possessions. The leader of the House of Commons now succeeded to a peerage, and Melbourne proposed to the king to appoint Lord John Russell in his place. The king detested Russell, and turned on Melbourne, using his prerogative to dismiss the government. It was a great act of folly that has never been repeated by any of William's successors. A provisional government under Wellington followed; Sir Robert Peel then became Prime Minister, but resigned in 1835, when Melbourne returned. Finally the king had to accept Russell as Leader in the Commons.

By now he had lost all patience with the Whigs. He suspected that they were trying to subvert the Church. William was not a particularly religious man, but, like others, he had been influenced by John Keble's Assize sermon which claimed that the Whigs were a threat to the Church. For William the Church was part of the dignified aspect of the constitution, the foundation of the Hanoverian right to the throne. In May 1834 he was sixty-eight, and spoke to the bishops of having to pay the debt of nature. He slowly slipped into debility, mercifully with no more crises to overwhelm him. He died, murmuring, 'The Church, the Church.'

VICTORIA

1837–1901

When William IV was dying his thoughts turned again and again to his niece and successor. He was sure she would be:

> 'a good woman and a good queen. It will touch every sailor's heart to have a girl queen to fight for. They'll be tattooing her face on their arms, and I'll be bound they'll all think she was christened after Nelson's ship.'

She was destined to be much more than that. She was just eighteen years old; H. E. Dawe's drawing of her in 1841 shows her as a little rosebud. She was the youngest monarch to succeed in England since Edward VI; but far outpaced in Scotland by James VI (and I), who was only thirteen months old at his accession. Her reign of sixty-four years goes through several distinct phases: the secluded and downtrodden child; the gay young Queen, deeply attached to Lord Melbourne; the happy bride, wife and mother with the Prince Consort, Albert; the sad widow, secluded in Windsor, Osborne or Balmoral; and finally the triumphant symbol of British Imperial power at its greatest.

Her father had died five days before George IV's accession. Her mother, the Duchess of Kent, a Princess of Leiningen, had brought her to England to be born; nevertheless, she was surrounded by Germans: Prince Leopold, later King of the Belgians, her mother's brother; Baroness Lehzen, her governess; her mother's secretary, Baron Stockmar, a man of stupendous erudition. She had tutors in Latin, music, history and writing; until she was twelve years old it was kept from her that one day she would be Queen.

Parliament had appointed the Duchess as her guardian, and Regent should she succeed to the throne. The Duchess was not liked by the English royal family. The child was scarcely allowed to know anybody. Sir Walter Scott came to dinner, remarking later that the

Duchess and the governess watched her closely. Archbishop Howley and Lord Conyngham came to her at five o'clock in the morning to announce her accession to her; her Coronation showed immediately a swing in favour of the monarchy such had not been seen under any of the Hanoverians. William IV had been right.

She was fortunate in her first Prime Minister, Melbourne. His majority in the Commons hung by a shoestring. He became a father to her; her journal, which she kept throughout her reign, save for a few weeks after Prince Albert's death, displays a relationship which went far beyond politics. She was enchanting, and he enchanted her. Adroit and diplomatic, he taught her the Court and the ways and personalities of society in general. The Queen was noticeable for her self-reliance and composure; the Duchess was not to give up quite so easily.

At first the Queen Mother lived with her. Their two courts were not on happy terms. The Duchess's lady-in-waiting was Lady Flora Hastings, her principal adviser Sir John Conroy, an Irish soldier of fortune who had served under the Duke of Kent. They, and the Duchess of Kent, had already conspired to bring about a regency even after the Princess Victoria had reached full age; they spread rumours that she was stupid and ignorant, incapable of learning, still adolescent. The Duchess, indeed, did not want to give up. Conroy was known for familiarity with ladies. In late 1838 he and Lady Flora travelled together from Scotland in a chaise. Rumour at once spread at court, and then Lady Flora was noticed to have a swelling, adding fuel to the flames. Eventually Lady Flora was pressed to have a medical examination, for other symptoms had given ladies at court reasonable expectations that she was with child. She denied it, and the matter reached the press, blown out of all proportions. The medical examination revealed the truth; it was no pregnancy, but a malignant tumour of the liver, from which Lady Flora shortly died. The sordid tale was now to have political repercussions, know as the Bedchamber Question.

In 1839 Peel succeeded Lord Melbourne, of whom the Duke of Wellington said he had 'taught the Queen to preside over the destinies of this great country'. The relationship had been virtually as father and daughter. Peel found her surrounded by Whig ladies, and not unnaturally the Queen was loath to give her first friends up. Peel, by no means remarkable for his tact, insisted that her ladies should be replaced by Tories; the Queen wept, refusing flatly. Peel then resigned, and Melbourne returned to office until 1841. By then the Queen had married, and a new relationship had begun. Nevertheless, the Queen had shown spirit and determination, that she was a force to be reckoned with. Said Creevey: 'The Queen is a resolute little tit.'

The Duchess of Kent would have been very remiss if she had not long considered her daughter's marriage. She and Prince Leopold had the ambition that she should marry Albert, the younger of the son's of their brother, the Duke of Saxe-Coburg. He was exceptionally clever and good-looking. Prince Albert had already visited London in 1836, when the Queen was seventeen. She had been pleased by him, but the excitement of the accession and the press of public business had set aside his image. He wrote, she did not reply. The Prince's father did not wish his son to be kept dangling, and Prince Leopold began to press the matter. The Queen at first insisted that there had been no understanding between them, and that no question of marriage could be entertained for two or three years.

Nevertheless in October 1839 the Prince arrived in England; the Queen recorded in her diary: 'Seeing Albert has changed all this.' At the end of the twentieth century such arranged marriages are virtually unknown. Yet they often in times past turned out to be more fortunate than those where the parties exercised free choice. This was in October; the wedding took place in the Chapel Royal in St James's Palace on 10 February 1840.

Prince Albert now *de facto* took the place of the Queen's private secretary, but not without some opposition to himself. An annuity of £50,000 was proposed, but a Colonel Sibthorp, MP, got it reduced to £30,000. When the Queen had announced her betrothal to the Privy Council she had not raised the question of religion; Lord Palmerston, who numbered among his ancestors two of Cromwell's regicides, questioned whether the Prince belonged to any Protestant sect that would preclude him from receiving the Sacrament according to the Anglican rite. He was answered that the Prince was of the House of Saxony, to which in some measure Protestantism owed its existence. High Churchmen (the term Anglo-Catholic had been coined in 1838) claimed that Lutherans were dissenters, and that the Prince should be required to subscribe to the Thirty-nine Articles. There were also certain legal difficulties, which the Queen smoothed away by the use of her prerogative to create him Prince Consort. The wedding passed off unclouded. It became known that the Queen was dressed entirely in articles of British manufacture.

The originals of the *Letters of Queen Victoria* at Windsor consist of some five or six hundred bound volumes up to the Prince's death in 1861. They are perhaps the most detailed archive of any reign in the past. They owe their original and systematic filing to the Prince's initiative. The Prince had given organisation to the monarchy, and a depth of memory in the archive. He was careful, however, not to intrude, and had gained such respect in the first five months of the marriage that an Act of Parliament, unsolicited by the Court, appointed him as sole Regent should the Queen die in giving birth to an heir, or die before the son or daughter came of age. The Regency Bill was brought forward after a mad boy had fired on the Queen and Prince Albert. He was apparently a member of a society called 'Young England'; whether it was Chartist or, as the Irish pretended, of Orangemen who wished to set the Duke of Cumberland on the throne, is unknown. There were several other attempts up to 1882, none of them with serious results.

Between 1840 and 1857 the Queen and the Prince had four sons and five daughters. They and their issue came to relate the Queen to the royal houses of Roumania, and Yugoslavia, Sweden and Denmark, Imperial Germany and Russia, Spain and later Norway. Belgium would shortly be ruled by the Queen's uncle and confidant. Dynastically the Queen became the central figure in a galaxy of monarchs related to one another by family ties, and corresponding with one another. Apart from the politics of power and the growth of the Empire, it was a system that never before had been seen.

The Queen had been a late riser, breakfasting usually at ten o'clock. On their wedding morning she and the Prince were seen out walking early in the morning. The diarist Greville remarked: 'That's not the way to provide us with a Prince of Wales.' Their record belies this. Albert, on the other hand, had always risen early, and disliked evening parties to the point that he could hardly keep awake after nine o'clock. He was already weaning the Queen away from town life, and towards the pleasures of domestic seclusion that became so marked in her life. She at least had what she had not had before, a companion. In 1841 Melbourne withdrew from public life, and Peel was glad to recognise the Prince's capacity and charm. In 1842 the Queen's first journey by train produced a curious incident; the master of the horse insisted on his right to inspect the engine, which he did among much amusement; and then the royal coachman claimed it as a right to travel on, if not to drive, the engine. His livery was so dirtied that the experiment was not repeated.

The Queen now took to travel by way of relaxation. Brighton was inconvenient, for she could not avoid being mobbed. It was for this reason that Osborne on the Isle of Wight was acquired, and the house built to meet the needs of a growing family. Balmoral was first leased in 1848, and the castle rebuilt in 1852. These were refuges, where they could live the quiet lives of ordinary country gentlepeople. There were also visits to country houses, such as the visit to Stowe in 1845, when the Duke of Buckingham and Chandos entertained with such liberality that he was brought to bankruptcy. In Scotland the Queen visited cottages also, and was delighted by a crofter's wife who called out: 'Come in, Queen Victoria.'

1848 was a year of revolutions, in Berlin and Budapest, Dresden, Madrid, Paris, Rome, Venice and Vienna. It was a time of anxiety; Louis-Philippe of France took refuge in England, and so did Prince William of Prussia, later German Emperor. In 1849 the Queen and Prince made a successful visit to Ireland, amid scenes of jubilation. The peak, perhaps, of Prince Albert's career was in 1851, when the great International Exhibition took place under his chairmanship, and the South Kensington Museum of Science and Art founded. The cultural events papered over the hard labour of monarchy, not eased by the cavalier temperament of Lord Palmerston, both as Foreign Secretary, and then as Prime Minister. It was a relief when he finally resigned in 1851. By the end of the 1840s the Palace had become wholly established as a source of government which imparted stability to the chances and changes of ministers.

Then in 1861 the Queen suffered the most distressful year in her life, first the death of her mother, and then of her husband. She was at his bedside, but it has been shown to be untrue that she was hysterical, The Queen now lived in solitude. She could not bring herself to appear in public; at the marriage of the Prince of Wales in St George's Chapel, Windsor, she watched from a private box. She did not open Parliament in state until 1865. Disraeli's two premierships, 1868, 1874–80, were turning points. It was his view that the monarchy should be a power in politics, to be informed, to counsel and advise, and sometimes to warn; it was the opposite of Gladstone, who considered it was the duty of all to agree with himself. The Queen did not care for him; it is said that she once remarked that he addressed her as if she were a public meeting. Disraeli's approach was loyal and chivalrous; he knew better how to charm and please.

After the troubles of the Indian Mutiny in 1857 much ground needed to be recovered in India in respect for Britain. In 1876 a bill was introduced to give the Queen the title of Empress of India, its object to conciliate the Indian princes. It was with the same object that the Prince of Wales was sent to tour India in 1875–6. The new title met with opposition in England, but had its effect – as intended – abroad.

The Queen had now reached her half century, and until 1880 lived almost in retirement. The Prince and Princess of Wales took much of the Queen's part in public life; it was noticed that the Queen had a particular attachment to her Highlander servant John Brown. *Punch* even published a *Court Circular* making fun of him. It was inevitable that there were republican murmurings, and these were not discouraged by movements in Ireland, both political and religious.

1887, however, was the fiftieth anniversary of the Queen's accession. A solemn service took place in Westminster Abbey amid scenes of hitherto unprecedented magnificence. There were celebrations in every town and village, and the Queen paid a visit to the East End, the poorest part of London. On 14 May she opened the People's Palace there, amid scenes of enthusiasm. On 4 July she laid the foundation stone of the Imperial Institute, which she opened later in 1893. On 9 July she reviewed 60,000 men at Aldershot, and then, on 23 July, the fleet at Spithead. Thereafter the Queen's public appearances became more frequent, with a consequent increase in popularity. The spectre of republicanism, if not laid to rest, was at least mitigated. Visits abroad were to follow, to Italy and Germany, to Grasse and Costebelle, chiefly by way of relaxation, but with some public appearances. Even in remote villages in the 1920s there was hardly a cottage which did not have a lithograph of her.

By September 1896 the Queen's reign had been longer than any other British sovereign. It was at her own request that its celebration, the Diamond Jubilee, should be delayed until the summer of 1897. All the prime ministers of the British colonies were invited to the celebration, together with their families. Drafts of local troops from every colony and dependency were brought to take part in the state review. The Queen attended a service outside St Paul's seated in her carriage. At the review she sat for four hours as the troops passed her, no small feat for a woman who was now seventy-eight. It was a sight of unparalleled magnificence, the Sikhs and Rajputs from India, Hausas, Zaptiehs from Cyprus, to mention only a few. She sent a simple message: 'From my heart I thank my beloved people.

May God bless them.' These were the words of a woman whose *Pax Britannica* ruled a quarter of the inhabited globe.

The next two years were uneventful. The red boxes of state papers came and went; the Prince of Wales had no access to them. In May 1899 the Queen's last public appearance was to open the museum at South Kensington, now called the Victoria and Albert Museum. Not many hundred yards away was the memorial to the Prince Consort. 1899 also brought anxiety, for war had broken out in South Africa. Paradoxically, the war played a part in welding together the Empire, for troops were sent from all quarters to take part, the Queen encouraging them with frequent messages. The Federation of the Australian colonies into a single Dominion gave her great satisfaction, but, in the words of the *Court Circular*, she had 'suffered great strain'. Nevertheless in 1900, she paid a quiet visit to Ireland. Until a week before her death she took her daily drive. Then, on 22 January 1901, she died, surrounded by her children and grandchildren.

She had reigned. She was a ruler of a new type. She never hesitated to speak the truth, as John Bright remarked; but instinctively she had learnt to trim her sails to the wind and not to be carried away with it. She had adapted herself over a long period to a complete change in society; she had not resisted it. Liberal in the best sense by instinct, she had known how to draw out the best in others.

EDWARD VII

1901–1910

Only two monarchs had passed their meridian at their accession since the Norman Conquest; William IV had been sixty-five: Edward VII was now sixty. The majority had been far younger. Neither William or Edward had had any previous acquaintance with state papers. Edward had expressly been denied this by his mother, although he had been born her heir.

In character, even as a child, he had been wholly different from his parents. He was lively, chatty, affectionate, and responsive; the Queen and Albert both terrified him, even though he loved them. Their object was that he should grow up in such a way as 'to make him the most perfect man.' Albert was preoccupied with intellectual occupations, the Queen terrified lest Edward should be spoilt by the obsequious trappings of court life. The Victorian school-room was a harsh place; the Prince was subject to a daily report to his parents on his conduct and progress under four male tutors, two of them clergy. Later he was sent, without any experience of school, to Oxford, then to Cambridge, and finally to Edinburgh, where he studied chemistry in its industrial application. He was not allowed even the freedom of college life, but hedged about with tutors and equerries. He was given a colonel's commission in the army and sent to the Curragh in Ireland, only shortly to be reprimanded for an amorous adventure, which, the Queen believed was responsible for Albert's fatal illness. Then he was sent on tour to the Holy Land under the Dean of Westminster; he had already visited Canada and the United States.

It was remarkable that he emerged with such good nature and affability; at Oxford he had charmed the wives of dons; in America he immediately adapted himself to a still formal archaic society. The British Minister at Washington reported that all had been much struck by his tact and instinctive judgement.

In 1863 he married Princess Alexandra, 'the sea-king's daughter' – the daughter of the King of Denmark. Among the royal portraits in the Palace of Westminster hers is outstanding for her beauty. She was not yet twenty. Shortly there were six children, all born between 1864 and 1871, three sons and three daughters. The Princess's temperament was essentially domestic, and she delighted in her young family. Edward had no intellectual interests. His were social: cards, dancing, a party, a good dinner, racing and sport. He read newspapers, but no books. In 1867 the Princess had a severe illness after the birth of her first daughter; it left her lame and deaf. She had no taste for ceremonial or for his amusements. She maddened him by her lack of punctuality. The Prince enjoyed rounds of country-house visits, often without her. She particularly disliked his love of horse-racing.

In 1874 the Prince went to Russia for the wedding of his brother, the Duke of Edinburgh, to the Grand-Duchess Marie. It was the beginning of a series of public appearances that was to last for nearly half a century, and which now was to become the hallmark of royalty. In 1875–6 he visited India, supposedly as heir-apparent; it became a political event of first importance. He spent seventeen weeks in India, visiting the princes, the Queen's feudatories, travelling 8,000 miles by land and 2,500 by sea. On Sundays the royal train stopped so that he might attend church; he had long made it a practice to read a chapter of the Bible every day. He probably saw more of India than any individual Englishman had ever done. It was after this that the Queen assumed the title of Empress of India.

Visits to Ireland, to Paris, to Germany, to members of the family and to take the waters at Baden-Baden, to Wales, two more visits to Russia, to Denmark, to cities at home, followed. The list is endless. In 1887 and in 1897 he bore responsibility for the celebrations of his mother's Jubilees, riding at her right hand as she drove to St Paul's; then, as Admiral of the Fleet, he presided over the naval review at Spithead. He lost no popularity when an anarchist fired on him in Brussels when he was on his way to Russia in 1899. No harm was done. He twice won the Derby with his racehorses, Persimmon in 1896, Diamond Jubilee in 1900; his third victory, in 1909, with Minoru, was the first time that the Derby had been won by a reigning sovereign. With horses went diversion in the company of spirited and witty women, of whom Mrs George Keppel stands out as favourite. Among others were Consuelo, Duchess of Marlborough,

Lily Langtry, Lady Londonderry, Lady Lonsdale, Mrs Willie James and Mrs Cornwallis West; these he met as he made the rounds in country houses, or who were courteously entertained at Sandringham by a tolerant Alexandra.

Queen Victoria died on 22 January 1901, and he immediately set out to meet the Privy Council in London. The first question to be answered was that of his throne name. Queen Victoria had wished it to be Albert, and he had been baptised Albert Edward. He thought otherwise, and announced that he would be called Edward the Seventh. An Act of Parliament now enlarged the royal title to include the colonial empire, which had grown in the 'scramble for Africa' in the last fifteen years of the nineteenth century. The King would now be called Edward VII, by the grace of God, of the United Kingdom of Great Britain and Ireland, and of all the British Dominions beyond the Seas, King, Defender of the Faith, Emperor of India.

A coronation with great pomp had been planned for 24 June 1902. Two days earlier it was announced that the King was suffering from appendicitis, and that an immediate operation was necessary. The King made a surprisingly rapid recovery, and the coronation was fixed for 9 August. It was shorn of much of its magnificence, for many of the foreign royalties and visitors had gone home. The King convalesced by making a yachting trip round the coast, sailing as far as Stornaway. New Year's Day 1903 was marked by a splendid Durbar in Delhi.

In 1903 the King sailed to Lisbon to make a state visit to the King of Portugal. He went to Gibraltar and to Malta, and then to Rome, and thence to Naples, where he was received by the King of Italy. Two days later he visited Pope Leo XIII in the Vatican. When Prince of Wales he had already visited Pope Pius IX three times. In the following year President Loubet of France and also the King and Queen of Italy paid state visits to London. In May the King held a court at Holyrood on his first formal visit to Scotland, and then went on to Ireland. September found him taking the 'cure' at Marienbad, and then on to visit Vienna, where the Emperor of Austria received him. He visited Ireland again in 1904, attended the yacht races at Kiel with the German Emperor, and visited Hamburg. In November the King and Queen of Portugal were entertained at Windsor, both the king's cousins by blood as descendants of John of Gaunt.

It was in all these ways that Edward gained his title as Edward the

Peacemaker; in 1904 treaties of arbitration were concluded with France, Germany, Italy, Portugal and Spain. The King's work in foreign affairs was visible to all, but perhaps most remarkable was his success in France. On the last evening of his visit the President gave a state banquet. There had for some time been strain between France and Britain. He had had a cool reception. French historical memories are long: the Hundred Years War; the burning of Joan of Arc; the long struggle against Napoleon, and his final humiliation. His body had only been brought to the Invalides in the year the King was born. More recently French and British interests had clashed at Fashoda, to the French disadvantage. Cries were heard of *Vivent les Boers*, *Vive Fashoda*, and even *Vive Jeanne d'Arc*. The President was unnerved, and made a speech already written for him by his officials, which he read with it propped up against a candlestick. Few could hear him. The King then got up and spoke from the heart in irreproachable French. He spoke without note or paper in his hand. All could hear, even at the end of the table. The King had never been at a loss for words. His speech had its effect. He spoke of old and happy associations with the city that time could never efface. His audience had expected a speech as dull as the President's. Edward VII was received enthusiastically, the past forgotten. This was the triumph of the *entente cordiale*.

In home affairs the King was not troubled by the social legislation of Liberal governments. There was never the kind of enmity that existed between Queen Victoria and Gladstone, nor, for that matter, the cordial relation between her and Disraeli. In 1909 a constitutional crisis was developing, which could involve the Crown in difficulties. Lloyd George's budget convulsed the country, and was rejected by the House of Lords. The Liberals now put in the forefront of their policies the abolition of the Lords' 'veto', and murmuring was heard, as in the reign of William IV, of the creation of pro-government peers. The King's health was visibly upset, as later the doctors were to point out. The reduction of the powers of the Lords was yet to come.

Certainly the King had not been prejudiced against the Liberals. Perhaps in certain ways, with broad acquaintance with men, with statesmen and other countries, he was more experienced and far-sighted than they. He was little inclined to intervene in domestic matters, but one occasion stands out above all others. It was in 1905, when Haldane was Secretary of State for War. He reformed the army drastically and created what became called the Territorial

Army. The King put his weight enthusiastically behind him. He summoned to Buckingham Palace all the Lord Lieutenants, and made a powerful speech to urge them to make the Territorials effective in their own counties. The King was very well aware of the situation in Germany, and had in fact travelled there with Haldane in his company. In the event the King's action was one of those that enabled the British army to stand and win against the German military machine in the First World War.

Edward VII left no diary, nor was he a letter writer, save out of necessity. We know little or nothing of his inmost thoughts or policies. In the spring of 1910 he had gone to Biarritz, 'that dreadful Biarritz' as Queen Alexandra called it. There he developed a bronchial infection. He returned to England, and on 5 May it was announced that he had bronchitis. In the palace his death was expected, and the Archbishop of Canterbury sent for. He was politely waved away. The King sent for the parish priest from the little Catholic church not far from Buckingham Palace to receive him into the Catholic faith. The Court kept silence, and the funeral took place with the customary Anglican rite in Westminster Abbey. The coffin was followed by his son, now George V, the German Emperor, the Kings of Belgium, Bulgaria, Denmark, Greece, Norway, Portugal and Spain, the heir to the throne of Austria, the Prince Consort of the Netherlands, and a host of ambassadors, and Mr Theodore Roosevelt representing the United States. It was a superb tribute to a man who, in spite of the disadvantages of his restricted upbringing, had overcome them to make himself a force for good in the world at large.

10   The House of Windsor

Continued from page 170

63. George V (George Frederick Ernest Albert), b. 3 June 1865, Duke of York 1892, Prince of Wales 1901, s. 6 May 1910, d. 20 Jan. 1936, m. Princess Mary, only d. of the Duke of Teck (b. 26 May 1867, d. 24 March 1953)

64. Edward VIII, b. 23 June 1894, s. 20 Jan. 1936, abdicated 10 Dec. 1936, created Duke of Windsor 8 March 1937, d. 28 May 1972, m. 3 June 1937 Wallis (formerly Simpson), d. of Teakle Wallis Warfield

65. George VI, b. 14 Dec. 1895, s. 10 Dec. 1936, d. 6 Feb. 1952, m. 26 Apr. 1923. Lady Elizabeth Angela Marguerite Bowes-Lyon (b. 4 Aug. 1900). d. of 14th Earl of Strathmore & Kinghorne (H.M. QUEEN ELIZABETH THE QUEEN MOTHER)

66. HER MAJESTY QUEEN ELIZABETH II (**Elizabeth Alexandra Mary**), s. 6 Feb. 1952, b. 21 Apr. 1926, m. 20 Nov. 1947 H.R.H. Prince Philip, Duke of Edinburgh (see Table 9) (b. 10 June 1921)

Princess Margaret (Rose) b. 21 Aug. 1930, m. 6 May 1960 Anthony Armstrong Jones, cr. 1st Earl of Snowdon 1961

David Albert Charles, Viscount Linley, b. 3 Nov. 1961

Sarah Frances Elizabeth, b. 1 May 1964

H.R.H. Prince Charles, Prince of Wales, b. 14 Nov. 1948

H.R.H. Prince Andrew, b. 19 Feb. 1960

H.R.H. Prince Edward, b. 10 March 1964

H.R.H. Princess Anne, b. 15 Aug. 1950, m., 14 Nov. 1973, Captain Mark Anthony Peter Phillips (b. 22 Sept. 1948), son of P. W. G. Phillips

Henry William Frederick Albert, Duke of Gloucester, b. 31 March 1900, d. 10 June 1974, m. 6 Nov. 1935 Lady Alice Christabel Montagu-Douglas-Scott, d. of 7th Duke of Buccleuch

George Edward Alexander Edmund, Duke of Kent, b. 20 Dec. 1902, k. in an aircraft accident while on active service 25 Aug. 1942, m. 29 Nov. 1934. H.R.H. Princess Marina, (d. 27 Aug. 1968) d. of Prince Nicholas of Greece

John Charles Francis, b. 12 July 1905; d. 18 Jan. 1919

Victoria Alexandra Alice Mary, Princess Royal, b. 25 Apr. 1897, d. 28 March 1965, m. 28 Feb. 1922 6th Earl of Harewood (d. 24 May 1947)

issue

William Henry Andrew Frederick, b. 18 Aug. 1941, d. in an aircraft accident 28 Aug. 1972

Richard Alexander Walter George, 2nd Duke of Gloucester, b. 26 Aug. 1944, m. 8 July 1972 Birgette Eva, d. of Asger Proben Wissing Henriksen, and his first wife Vivian, d. of Waldemar Oswald van Deurs

Alexander Patrick Gregers Richard, Earl of Ulster, b. 24 Oct. 1974

Edward George Nicholas Paul Patrick, 2nd Duke of Kent, b. 9 Oct. 1935, m. 8 June 1961 Katharine Lucy Mary, d. of Sir William Worsley

issue

Michael George Charles Franklin, b. 4 July 1942

issue

Alexandra Helen Elizabeth Olga Christabel, b. 25 Dec. 1936, m. Angus James Bruce Ogilvy, 2nd son of (12th) Earl of Airlie

issue

GEORGE V

1910–1936

At birth George V had no expectation of succeeding to the throne. It was not until his elder brother Albert Victor (known as Prince Eddy) died in 1892 that he found himself in the direct line of succession to his father. In Queen Alexandra he, his brother and three sisters had a most affectionate mother, who was happiest in the nursery. Neither she nor his father had any intellectual or artistic interests. Life centred, whether at Osborne, Abergeldie near Balmoral or at Sandringham, round the pursuits of a country gentleman. At the age of twelve he was sent to Dartmouth, the youngest naval cadet ever admitted, together with his brother. By 1880 he had already served in the West Indies, and then voyaged round the Horn to Vancouver, Australia, Fiji, Singapore, Japan and China. They returned via Ceylon and Suez, and then spent six weeks in the Holy Land, followed by a visit to Greece. Prince George was now seventeen, and had travelled more than 45,000 miles, much of it under sail. After a year ashore he was posted to the Canadian station, and then sent on a senior course at the Royal Naval College at Greenwich. Thus at twenty he had earned his promotion to lieutenant. In July 1889 he was given command of a torpedo boat, in 1890 of a gunboat, and in 1892 of a cruiser. In no case was his promotion due to his rank or birth.

His naval career was now ended, his royal career begun. He was created Duke of York; in 1893 he married Princess Mary, daughter of the Duke of Teck, who had long been resident in England. It was a marriage which exemplified all the virtues of family life, in contrast to some other aspects of the age. In 1894 they visited Russia, where Nicholas II had now become Tsar. The cousins bore such a strong resemblance to each other that could have been mistaken for one another. In 1899 there was a visit to Ireland. These more official state occasions were interspersed by a continuous round of smaller engagements, but which left time to the Duke to indulge in his favourite sports of yachting and shooting.

With the death of Queen Victoria in 1901 the Duke's public duties were increased. Unlike Queen Victoria's treatment of King Edward when Prince of Wales, King Edward and his son had a close and affectionate relationship, and at the same time discussing public affairs almost every day. It could not have been a better preparation for kingship. The Duke also acquired Queen Victoria's private secretary, Sir Arthur Bigge, later Lord Stamfordham, and thus the wealth of knowledge and experience of a devoted royal servant. In March 1901 the Duke and Duchess embarked for Australia, via Gibraltar, Malta, Aden and Colombo, and opened the first Commonwealth Parliament. They went next to New Zealand, and then across the Indian Ocean to Mauritius and South Africa, and thence to Canada, which they crossed and recrossed on the Canadian Pacific Railway. Everywhere they received ovations, the Princess in particular impressive by her dignity and practical interest in all they were shown. On King Edward's sixtieth birthday, 9 November 1901, he wrote to his son to create him Prince of Wales and Earl of Chester, in a touching letter of appreciation for all he had done for the Colonies. State Papers were now put at the Prince's disposal, and more tours followed. Of these the most important was to India in the winter of 1905-6.

The death of King Edward in May 1910 fell like a blow in spite of all the long and careful preparation. The gorgeous solemnity of the coronation was followed by state visits to Ireland and Wales, and then one of incomparable splendour to India, at which the King wore his coronation robes at the durbar. Some relief was found in tiger shooting, 'the best sport,' he said, 'in the world'.

The King returned to a constitutional crisis, of head-on collision between the Lords and the Commons. The Lords had thrown out the whole budget legislation, and the quarrel that followed would have tried even the most skilful of statesmen. Pressure was now coming to a head in Ireland for home rule, and disorder was expected to lead to a rising. A conference was summoned to Buckingham Palace of all the parties concerned, at which the King implored them to 'a spirit of generous compromise'. The conference broke down, but Asquith, the Prime Minister, did not fail to write to the King of his admiration of the tact and patience that his efforts to bring about a solution had displayed.

Yet worse was to befall. Already in 1912 Prince Henry of Prussia had asked the King whether Britain would support France and Russia in the event that Germany and Austria went to war with them. He was told that it was undoubtedly to be expected in certain circumstances. There was nothing the King could do; Luxembourg and France were invaded on 2 August 1914, and Belgium on 3 August. Britain declared war on 4 August. Within little less than a week the King, as had many of his fellow-countrymen, had lost a number of his friends.

The King now shared in the austerity of the people. No wine, no beer or spirits were permitted in the royal household. The King rarely left London. When he went to Sandringham for a few days shooting, the game was sent to hospitals. By necessity the King's movements during the war were cloaked in secrecy. He visited 300 hospitals, and personally distributed 58,000 decorations for valour. Some 300 naval and military establishments were visited, and as many factories. There were five visits to the Grand Fleet, and seven to the forces in France and Belgium. In 1915 a restive horse, frightened by all the cheering, reared, and fell backwards on the King, whose pelvis was fractured. The visits greatly heartened all ranks, and particularly his visit in 1918, a week after the Germans had begun their final attack, which was made at his personal request. Little of this reached the public eye, but on Armistice Day and the peace celebrations in 1919 crowds turned out to demonstrate their affection with ecstatic emotion.

The ending of the war brought renewed trouble in Ireland. The Home Rule Act of 1920 was repudiated in the South, but accepted in the North. There was an immediate demand that the first Ulster Parliament should be opened by the Sovereign in person. There were strong misgivings about the possible danger to the King, but it would have been wholly contrary to his nature to shirk the issue. At the last moment the Ulster government asked that the Queen should go too, and she accepted with equal alacrity. The King seized the occasion to make a personal appeal for peace and conciliation. Later in the year, when Lloyd George was proposing to send an aggressive message to Sinn Fein, the King intervened to persuade him to be more conciliatory, with the result that delegates came to London. In December an agreement inaugurating the Irish Free State was signed, a personal triumph for the King.

There were other outstanding issues on which his gentle guidance was brought to bear: the suffragettes and votes for women, the disestablishment of the Welsh Church, the Parliament Bill amongst others. In 1922, when the Prime Minister, Bonar Law, was seized by throat cancer, it was expected that the King would send for Lord Curzon, the most eminent statesman of the time, who had been Viceroy of India and Foreign Secretary. The King thought otherwise: the Labour party was now the Official Opposition in the Commons, and the King considered that it was better that the Prime Minister should face the Opposition in the Commons than sit in the Lords where the Labour Party was scarcely represented. Curzon, who had come to London, expecting the summons to the Palace, was mortified. When shortly he died, it is said that it was of grief. It was the beginning of the long tenure of Stanley Baldwin.

In January 1924 the Labour Party came to office for the first time. In spite of widespread fears the King, with his naval background and experience from meeting all walks of men in many different parts of the world, got on very well with the new ministers. The Chancellor of the Exchequer J. H. Thomas's rich vocabulary was easily matched by the King's quarterdeck language: the two men saw eye to eye very well. This first Labour government lasted no more than nine months; it was superseded by Baldwin, who now held office for four years. It was during this time that Lord Balfour gave a new definition to the idea of the Commonwealth, which became embodied in the Statute of Westminster in 1931: it was to be seen as an association of free peoples, in which the King was the sole bond of union, a concept which binds even today an association which contains states that still have the Queen as sovereign, and others which are republics.

In 1926 the General Strike was to some extent defused by the attitude of the King. He declined to hold a Buckingham Palace Conference except, he said, on the advice of his Prime Minister. Hitherto he had enjoyed good health. In 1925 he cruised on the royal yacht for a month in the Mediterranean following an attack of influenza. In November 1928 he fell ill with a streptococcal chest infection, which necessitated drainage of the lungs. Counsellors of State were appointed: the Queen, his eldest sons, the Archbishop of Canterbury, the Lord Chancellor and the Prime Minister. Any three were empowered to exercise the royal prerogative, except to dissolve Parliament or create peerages. The Privy Council assembled in an anteroom to the royal bedroom, and the King signed the documents with his own hand.

There was great fear for the King's life, and even schoolboys of the time felt the gloom that descended on the nation. It was not until the following July that he was wholly recovered, although he was cautioned to take things more easily. He now had to face the gravest crisis of his reign. The problem was not of the Labour Party's making, but as a result of the international financial situation. Foreign depositors took alarm, and withdrew deposits of gold from the Bank of England, bringing the nation almost to bankruptcy. The King went for his annual holiday to Balmoral, but turned round at once when he learnt of the crisis in London. In the palace he at once summoned the party leaders. The Labour Cabinet was in disarray, and the Liberals advocated an all-party Government. For the Conservatives Baldwin at once offered to serve under MacDonald. By the following day MacDonald, Sir Herbert Samuel and Baldwin had agreed upon a government. A general retrenchment was necessary. The King himself surrendered part of the Civil List, but at Invergordon the Fleet mutinied, causing a further run on the Bank. A general election followed, in which the King's solution was endorsed by an overwhelming majority.

The climax of the reign was reached in the Jubilee of 1935. On 6 May, the twenty-fifth anniversary of his accession, he and the Queen drove to St Paul's to a Service of Thanksgiving. Vast crowds assembled to cheer them as they drove in state. The celebrations, services, bells, fêtes, street parties, and bonfires as night fell, embraced the whole nation. The King was heard to say: 'I did not know they loved me so much.' The celebrations concluded, the King was now patently showing the weight of his years. He went to Sandringham, and then, after a short illness, died peacefully. There were many moving tributes, and great crowds filed past the catafalque, on which the Crown gleamed, in Westminster Hall. For those who came to pay their last respects, perhaps the most moving sight of all was the night when four of his sons, splendid in the full dress uniform of his four regiments of foot Guards, could be seen mounting guard over the coffin.

EDWARD VIII

January–December 1936

Edward VIII, King of Great Britain, Ireland, and the British Dominions beyond the Seas, Emperor of India, was the only British Sovereign to abdicate the Throne of his own free will. He was the eldest of the five sons and one daughter born to the Duke and Duchess of York, who, when Queen Victoria died in 1901, became Prince and Princess of Wales, and then, in 1910, King George V and Queen Mary. He was thus always in the direct line of succession to the throne.

Sovereigns and their heirs apparent or presumptive are most frequently at loggerheads, and this was enhanced in this case by the martinet, albeit kindly, character of his father, and the chill, frigid character of his mother, whom many regarded as lacking normal maternal instincts. With his brothers, he shared a not less aloof tutor. So in later life he sought the affection lacking to him in childhood, in a succession of women, and finally with one for whom he abandoned the throne.

He was not lacking in intelligence, but his tutors failed to attract his attention to books or knowledge. He learnt French and German in childhood, and later Spanish, but never their culture and sophistication. His principal characteristic was his charm, what today is called charisma, in an extraordinary quality.

He was schooled at Osborne, and then two years at Dartmouth, before two years at Magdalen College, Oxford. There he did little or no work, and left behind a reputation for dissipation. In 1914 war broke out, and he was immediately commissioned in the Grenadier Guards. He begged to be sent to fight along with his comrades, but this was refused lest he should be taken prisoner and used as a hostage. He was posted to various headquarters in France, and used to raise morale. He preferred to travel round on a green army bicycle rather than in the official Daimler allotted to him. In this way he got into the front lines at Loos and had a narrow escape. He served later in the Middle East, and got to know Australians and New Zealanders as well as other Allied troops. His army experiences were truly formative, and he learnt to get on with all sorts and conditions of men, and to raise their morale.

Lloyd George recognised his excellent qualities, and sent him to Newfoundland, Canada and the United States in 1919, the first of many overseas tours. In the following year he went to New Zealand and Australia, and then home via Fiji, Hawaii and the Panama Canal, and then in 1921–2 to India. Congress boycotted his visit, but huge crowds turned out to greet him. A British observer reported that one Indian had said: 'If only all Europeans were like you.' He then visited Nepal, Burma, Malaya, Hong Kong, Japan, the Philippines, Borneo, Ceylon and Egypt.

In the following years up to 1936 he was constantly abroad on visits, in all but three years. Visits to South America in 1925 and 1931 were particularly successful. His work in spreading British interests abroad led to the creation of the British Council in 1935. It was not all work. Golf now became fashionable, and much of his time was given to sport, and to dancing to all hours of the night. Strange it seemed to all that, while his brothers all married, he remained single, the world's most eligible bachelor.

He found consolation with a succession of affairs with married women, among whom Mrs Dudley Ward seems to had the chief place in his affections. It was through Lady (Thelma) Furness that he became acquainted with her fellow American, a Mrs Wallis Simpson. She was of a Maryland family that was richer in pride of ancestry then in worldly goods. Her first husband, Lieutenant Earl Winfield Spencer, US Navy, enabled her to enjoy the pleasures of life on the China Station. He became an alcoholic. Divorce followed, and she then married Ernest Simpson, an Anglo-American with a shipping business in England. They settled in London, and thus she became friends with the Prince. He was enchanted by her, and, while the British press maintained a courteous silence, the French press was full of what now became a new liaison. Edward realised that she was unfitted for the context of the court of King George V and Queen Mary. It was only after his death on 20 January 1936 that the news of Edward's determination to marry her began to leak.

It can, of course, be said that it was already time for a less formal royal set-up, but he was not the man to carry this out. His unpunctuality, and casualness, which extended even to carelessness with State Papers, offended not only courtiers but the whole official class. A monarch who paid assiduous attention to the business of state might have been successful. He had been tried, too, by too much success and adulation without the solid comfort of a well-ordered domestic life. The public at large knew nothing of his way of life: he was altogether a popular king. In July 1936 a loaded revolver was thrown at his horse as he rode down Constitution Hill. Its only effect was to increase his popularity, for he came to no harm. When the Hunger Marchers, unemployed coal-miners from Jarrow in County Durham, reached London later in the year, they cheered him in the Mall.

In the summer he cruised in the Mediterranean with Mrs Simpson in the yacht *Nahlin*. It was fully reported by the world press, and especially in the United States. In October the divorce suit of the Simpsons was set down for hearing in a provincial court. On 20 October the Prime Minister, Stanley Baldwin, saw the king by special request. He tried to persuade the King to get Mrs Simpson to withdraw her petition. He met with no success, and the decree *nisi* was granted.

On 3 November the King drove to open Parliament in a closed car rather than in the traditional Irish coach, and then inspected the fleet at Portsmouth. On 16 November he met Baldwin again, and stated his intention to marry Mrs Simpson, in spite of the advice that the marriage would not be acceptable to the country. It was not, as many Americans thought, that this was because she was an American. At this time in England divorce was not commonplace as it was later to become, and divorced women, even if 'innocent' parties, were regarded with suspicion. For Cosmo Gordon Lang, Archbishop of Canterbury, the marriage of the Head of the Church of England to a divorced woman was unthinkable. Baldwin's reply to the King was, 'Sire, this is most distressful news.'

On 18–19 November the King toured distressed areas in the coal-mining villages of South Wales, where he made the much quoted remark: 'Something must be done to find them work.'

A further meeting with Baldwin took place on 25 November. Esmond Harmsworth, later Lord Rothermere, had suggested that the King might marry Mrs Simpson morganatically – much as George IV had done with Mrs FitzHerbert. It was a political error of the first magnitude: it implied that Mrs Simpson was unfit to be Queen. Among the privileged classes there were objections to Mrs Simpson on social grounds, and ladies stated quite openly that they would not curtsy to her. This kind of argument counted for nothing with the people at large, but no more would they have understood a morganatic marriage. This was made quite clear by Clement Attlee (later Earl Attlee), the Labour leader, and in any case legislation would have been needed to enable it. Less emphatic views were expressed by Commonwealth Prime Ministers. Although it cannot be proved, it seems likely that the Empire as a whole would not have approved of it.

The King then wished to make a broadcast, to explain his position to the nation. Baldwin told him this would be unconstitutional, since it would be divisive. Winston Churchill begged the King to stand and fight on, but with no effect. On 10 December the King signed an instrument of abdication, which came into effect on the following day when he gave his consent to the necessary Bill. That night Edward broadcast a final message to the nation. It came from Windsor Castle, and contained these words: 'I have found it impossible to carry the heavy burden of responsibility and to discharge my duties as King as I would wish to do, without the help and support of the woman I love.'

That night Edward left Windsor for France under cover of darkness. Mrs Simpson's decree was not made absolute until 1937. In June she and Edward married according to Anglican rites in a château, but without a licence. Edward was created Duke of Windsor, but the title of Royal Highness was expressly denied to the Duchess. It was a studied insult that brought friction and bitterness within the family, and not helped by an indecent quarrel over money. On October 1937 the Windsors visited Germany as guests of the Nazi government, Edward even signing as Herzog von Windsor. He said nothing that could be interpreted as approval or sympathy with the Nazi government, but nevertheless his visit was widely interpreted as pro-Nazi.

When war broke out the Duke was attached to the French army as a liaison officer, his rank of Field-Marshal reduced to Major-General. He and his wife escaped to England in 1940, and then was posted as governor to the Bahamas. While he had no wish to see his country a German puppet, it was known that he favoured a negotiated settlement with Germany. He had not reckoned with the indomitable spirit of Winston Churchill.

When his term of office ended, he went back to France. George VI, his brother, discouraged him from returning to England: there was no room for two kings. He spent the rest of his life in somewhat futile socialising, dying in 1972. In a post-war world in which republicanism was rife, in a paradoxical way he had, by handing over to his brother and loyally demonstrating his allegiance to him, strengthened rather than weakened the monarchy. Now there was to be a new and remarkable reign in the hands of a king who, at the moment of his accession, had never seen a state paper.

GEORGE VI

1936–1952

George VI, King of Great Britain, Ireland, and the British Dominions beyond the Seas, and, until 1950, Emperor of India, was the second of the five sons of King George V and Queen Mary. Born on the anniversary of the death of the Prince Consort, the first of his names was Albert. At his christening Queen Victoria gave the infant a bust of the Prince. The family knew him as Bertie.

Shy and sensitive as a child his father's bluff manner and teasing did not help him, and, by his seventh or eighth year, he had developed a serious stammer. He was apt to withdraw into himself, to suffer wild outbursts of sobbing, alternating with high spirits. He shared a tutor with his brothers Edward and Henry; the tutor failed to inspire any of them with any love of learning. It was feared that Bertie's mathematics was not good enough for him to pass to Osborne, but he responded to a warning, and faced up to the difficulty.

He was posted to HMS *Collingwood* in 1913 and saw active service in her at the battle of Jutland, 31 May 1916. He suffered greatly from seasickness, and in 1917 was operated on for a duodenal ulcer. He was transferred into the Royal Naval Air Service, and to the Royal Air Force in April 1918. He did not care for flying, but nevertheless qualified as a pilot in 1919. He and Prince Henry were then sent for a year at Trinity College, Cambridge, but were not allowed to live in College. He read history, civics and economics, and with particular attention to the Constitution. He now began to take more part in royal duties, and became President of the Industrial Society. This gave him a special interest in industrial areas, and in relations between employers and workers. From this evolved the Duke of York's camps, which brought together boys from public schools and from industry. He had been created Duke of York in the Birthday Honours in 1920.

In 1923 he was the first of the royal brothers to marry. The bride was Lady Elizabeth Angela Marguerite Bowes-Lyon, daughter of the fourteenth Earl of Strathmore and Kinghorne, now (1997) the greatly loved Queen Elizabeth the Queen Mother. Together they shared a devotion to duty and to a dignified married life which was to earn them not only the respect but also the love of the nation.

As a younger prince with no prospect of ascending the Throne they left to him the more humdrum duties of royalty, less exciting or spectacular than those that fell to the Prince of Wales. In 1923 they visited the Balkans, in 1924 Northern Ireland, and a tour of East Africa and the Sudan in 1924–5. The Duke then presided over the second year of the British Empire Exhibition at Wembley, which brought him into contact with all the Empire. In 1927 they visited Australia and New Zealand, opening Parliament at Canberra on 9 May. The simple sincerity of the Duke, and the graceful charm of the Duchess aroused enormous enthusiasm. The King and Queen went to Victoria Station to congratulate them on their return.

It was shortly before this journey that the Duke became in touch with the speech therapist Lionel Logue. The Duke was able to overcome his stammer, which became more of a slight hesitancy. In 1928–29, when the King was seriously ill with pneumonia, the Duke was appointed one of the Council of State. Otherwise the Duke and Duchess lived quietly, little in the public eye. Two princesses had been born to them, the present Queen in 1926, and Princess Margaret in 1930. In their domesticity there was no presage of what was to come.

The Duke and Edward VIII had always been on good terms, but now the Duke found himself more and more excluded from his company. Mrs Simpson was not welcomed within the royal family. On 17 November the King informed the Duke of his intention to marry Mrs Simpson, and then on 7 December of his decision to abdicate. On 9 December the two brothers talked. The Duke attempted to persuade the King to alter his decision, but to no avail. Later in the day the Duke told his mother that he 'broke down and sobbed like a child'. On 12 December, to the sound of trumpets, George VI was proclaimed King, with the style he had chosen for himself. A coronation had been planned for 12 May 1937, and was broadcast to the nation by royal command, but now with both a King and Queen. The King was anointed with oil with words of a prayer used for so many of his predecessors:

as Solomon was anointed king by Zadok the priest and Nathan the prophet, so be thou anointed, blessed and consecrated King over the Peoples, whom the Lord thy God hath given to rule and govern.

Now the shouts of 'Long Live the King' that had so alarmed the Norman soldiery at the coronation of William the Conqueror could be heard by sound radio all over the Empire, the Commonwealth and the world.

The shadows of war were already lengthening. In 1936 the Nazi German government had occupied the Rhineland, while Italy had occupied Ethiopia. Germany and Italy were rattling their swords in their scabbards. Then in 1938 Germany seized Austria, and a crisis arose over Czechoslovakia. In September the Sudetenland, the western border of the Czech state, was transferred to Germany, and an agreement was reached between the United Kingdom, France, Italy and Germany, which Neville Chamberlain, as Prime Minister, hailed as 'peace in our time.' Its hollowness was revealed on the following March, when Hitler seized Czechoslovakia.

The King was not idle. A State Visit to France took place in July 1938, and was returned by the President of France in March 1939. France and Britain now guaranteed the independence of Poland if the Germans should attack. In May the King opened Parliament in Canada, and then went on to the United States, the first British monarch to do so. At the Roosevelt home in Hyde Park the King and Queen were entertained, the King in the massive library, the Queen in the curiously small drawing room. Their signed photographs are now on the grand piano. The King and President had long talks, discussing what help the United States might offer in the event of a European war.

War was inevitable, and on 3 September the King broadcast to the nation, calling them to fight for freedom of the world. He never doubted or lost confidence in the outcome, even though Britain, as compared with Germany, was weak and ill-prepared, and France weaker still. In October he visited the fleet, and in December the British Expeditionary Force in France. He followed his father's custom of broadcasting to the Empire on Christmas Day. In the spring France collapsed, and the British Expeditionary Force was evacuated from Dunkirk; Chamberlain, shortly to die of cancer, gave way to Winston Churchill, with whom the King and Queen formed a genuine friendship.

Throughout the war the King and Queen remained in London, but sleeping at Windsor during the Battle of Britain. Buckingham Palace was bombed twice within three days. Both King and Queen constantly visited the bombed areas, in London and in the provinces, heartening the people. They had in common with them that their homes had been bombed. In 1942 the Duke of Kent was killed in a bomber while flying on active service; later in the war some more remote members of the royal family were taken prisoner in Italy.

In 1943 the Germans and Italians in North Africa surrendered, and the King went there and to Malta to congratulate the troops. In May 1940 he had created a new decoration, the George Cross, for civilian bravery, and this he presented to the island for its conspicuous courage. In May 1944 the King attended the conference in St Paul's School that completed the preparation for the invasion of France. By the day of the invasion he had visited every unit in the Army that was to fight in Normandy. Both he and Churchill wished to take part in the invasion, but it was only common sense that they did not. Ten days later he visited Field-Marshal Montgomery's HQ in Normandy and later the armies in Italy.

When the war ended on 8 May 1945 huge crowds massed round Buckingham Palace to rejoice with the King and Queen and their family. In the evening he broadcast, calling for thanksgiving to Almighty God and for work for a better world.

The first general election of the King's reign was held in July. A Labour government took office in August, with many inexperienced ministers. The debts of the cost of war had to be paid, and a new welfare state was being evolved. While the King was not out of sympathy with the new policies, there were times when these were being pressed too hard and too fast; and on occasion the King found it necessary to advise and to warn. By 1947 things were more settled, but food rationing continued into the 1950s. In 1947 the King and Queen, with the princesses, paid a long visit to South Africa and Rhodesia, now Zimbabwe. The King always regretted that he had had no opportunity to visit India before it and Pakistan became independent, and then republics.

The marriage of Princess Elizabeth to Lieutenant Philip Mountbatten gave the King and Queen great joy. In the following year they drove in state to St Paul's to celebrate their silver wedding. By then the King's health was visibly deteriorating. An Australian tour had to be cancelled when it was feared that his right leg might have to be amputated. In 1949 a lumbar sympathectomy was performed, and in 1951 his left lung was removed when it was found to have a malignant growth. At the end of January 1952 the King went to London Airport to see Princess Elizabeth and the Duke of Edinburgh off on a visit which was intended to East Africa, Australia and New Zealand. They had only reached Kenya when, after a happy day shooting, the King was found dead in bed on 6 February 1952.

It had been a remarkable life. He had filled the role of constitutional monarch to the satisfaction of all. He made no claims to brilliance or learning. Modest, he was practical; he was the perfect foil to the ebullient war leader, Churchill, and set the example of a man who lived a decent life. Innumerable tributes were paid to him from all over the world. Not least was that of an African peasant, who, when told of the King's death, said simply, in Swahili: *Alimpenda Mungu* – God loved him.

IRISH KINGS

While Scotland had only four kingdoms and England no more than seven and occasionally eight, Ireland in Roman times had some eighty to one hundred petty kingdoms, and sometimes more. Irish traditional historians divide them into three classes: *ri tuaithe*, petty kings; *ruiri*, great kings; and finally *ri ruirech*, kings or overkings. They are represented as war leaders, not as supreme judges or lawgivers. The temptation to compare them with some of the Beduin tribes of Arabia is irresistible, for the Beduin *shaykh's* function is rather to declare tribal custom and to lead in raids and war. We find among them even bishops and abbots leading in battle regardless of their holy office.

The concept of the king as holy is underlined by references to I Samuel 10, of the anointing of Saul by Samuel: 'God made him a different person', and again: 'the man whom God has chosen'. The earliest mention of religious coronation occurs in Abbot Adomnan's *Life of Columba*, written c. 700, with reference to two kings of the Ui Neill and to Oswald of Northumbria (632–42), a century before the Pontifical of Archbishop Egbert of York (732–66), the oldest surviving record of the rite. There are many examples of its observance in different parts of Ireland from the eighth to tenth centuries. Later the *ri tuaite*, petty kings, are referred to in Latin as *dux*. The translation duke is misleading; rather it derives from the Latin *ducere*, and simply means leader. Next are provincial kings, and above all is the great king, the High King, claimed by the great family of Ui Neill and others. In point of fact no king ever ruled, so far as the record goes, 'through the kingdoms of Ireland from sea to sea', regardless of royal pretensions. The seat of this kingdom was situated at Tara, but some of the legends connected with it are clearly fictitious. Other families made similar claims in all parts of the country, groups of dynasties rising and falling, marrying and cross–marrying. So in the seventh to tenth centuries, when the kings of Munster claimed a supremacy, angels, it was said, pointed out Cashel for the seat of their founding ancestor Oengus, who was baptised and blessed by St Patrick. For sure the line was authentic, but the limits of its power, its succession, and its chronology are as uncertain as its history. What seems to be certain is that Feidlimid mac Crimthainn, who died in 847, was a scribe, an anchorite, a bishop, and finally king of Munster. For all this he was a ruthless politician who did not scruple to plunder monasteries and abbeys, and to make war on the Ui Neill. In Connacht people looked back to Guaire Aidni, who died in 663, as a model of goodness and generosity. There were doubtless all sorts of this widespread royalty. We must beware of regarding these as rough, uncultivated people. On the contrary, the wealth and learning of their monasteries as well as that of the rulers betokens a broad sophistication with its art and its knowledge of the church fathers and the classical writers. Numerous examples of its minor arts remain, attesting a high degree of appreciation.

In the ninth century Ireland shared with England the raids of the Vikings and the Northmen, first on the eastern coasts, and then on the western coast and up the rivers which flow into the Atlantic. Dublin became a Viking capital, but in the interior the old order was already in decay. Endless power struggles took place between the kings, and only the monasteries preserved some semblance of order. The incomers became merchants, seamen and traders, gradually transforming the political scene. By the beginning of the twelfth century a writer describes the wealth of Limerick, in jewels, gold and silver, beautiful foreign saddles, and silks and satins. Dublin was a great trading city.

Two families quarrelled for Munster, the Eoganacht and the Dal Cais. These last were helped by the attacks of the Ui Neill on the Eoganacht; the Ui Neill were divided amongst themselves; both kingdoms, north and south, dominate all Ireland. By the end of the tenth century Mael Sechaill II, the southern king based at Tara, was in possession of both kingdoms. Their chief enemies were the Dal Cais, whose king Mathgambain, or Mahon, was king of both Munster and Thomond. In 976 he was murdered, and his brother Brian Boru, or Boruma, determined to avenge him. By 978 he had seized all Munster and Limerick, and campaigned into Connacht and Leinster. In 999 he faced a revolt. He seized and plundered Dublin, and then set himself to control the whole island. He had the blessing of the church; the *Book of Armagh* describes him as Emperor of the Irish. He was now the greatest king in Ireland. His reputation has grown as memory of his violence and ruthlessness has diminished.

In 1012 his relations with Leinster became strained; a seige of Dublin followed. A force of Vikings came from the Hebrides and the Isle of Man to assist the rebels, and a great battle eventually took place at Clontarf in 1014. Brian won, but died after the battle. Again things fell apart; the dream of Irish unity was shattered. It was a victory for no one. While Mael Sechnaill II remained High King of Ireland until he died in 1022, it was an empty honour. The future lay with numerous provincial kings and semi-independent lords, wicked and arrogant as a twelfth century poem portrays them.

Between 1089 and 1114 the most powerful king in Ireland was Muirchertach O'Brien. His relations extended to Norway and the Norman court in England. He was to some extent checked by the Ui Neill, until the energetic Turlough O'Connor, of Connacht (1106–56) rose to power. He bridged the Shannon, erected numerous castles, and destroyed the power of Munster with a large army and navy. When he died in 1156 power passed to the Ui Neill, who allied with the king of Leinster. The king of Connacht, Rory O'Connor, was his main opponent. O'Connor and his allies succeeded in driving him out of Dublin. He then made a mistake which for ever has proved fatal to Ireland: he appealed to Henry II of England for help. In 1166 O'Connor was installed in Dublin as High King, but shortly what was little less than a Norman invasion made the title meaningless.

The Norman leader, Richard FitzGilbert de Clare, Earl of Pembroke, commonly known as Strongbow, gradually established himself. By 1171 all Leinster and the surrounding area was conquered. For Henry II there could be no question of another Anglo-Norman kingdom; Irish appeals for help against Strongbow were also heard. Henry landed near Waterford on 17 October 1171. Strongbow swore fealty, and was granted Leinster. The kings of Cork, Limerick, Breifne, Airgialla and Ulaid, and the chiefs of Leinster all did homage, promising hostages and tribute in Dublin. The city was now granted by charter to Bristol, and Hugh de Lacy appointed Justiciar of Dublin, as royal representative. Garrisons were installed in the seaports. On 17 April 1172 Henry departed. The sub-kings remained, now to be absorbed into the Norman feudal system. Henry had already been recognised as Lord of

Ireland by the Pope. The process of the alienation of the Irish had already begun when the young prince John, later to succeed to the English throne after the death of his brother Richard, visited Ireland in 1185. It was symbolic of Anglo-Norman contempt for the Irish that some clean-shaven English courtiers pulled the beards of Irish chieftains as they landed in Waterford. John was not less rude. Colonisation had truly begun.

Irish women have a charm all of their own, and it was not long before we learn of marriages between the ancient royal houses and the incoming Norman knights. The area of royal control at the same time pushed westwards and northwards; by 1205 there was a Count Palatine of Ulster. In 1210 there was a rebellion in defiance of the justiciar, punished by King John with an army in the same year. Twenty Irish kings were said to have done homage to him in Dublin; before he left John exacted consent to a decree that all the laws and customs of England should be observed likewise in Ireland. It was a matter of time for the process of colonisation to become complete.

For King Lists of Ireland before 1198, see F. J. Byrne, *Irish Kings and High Kings*, paperback edn, 1987, pp. 275–301, in which Appendix I lists (1) 50 High Kings from the mid fifth century to 1198; (2) 29 Kings of Tara, without dates; (3) 47 Kings of Cashel and Munster, from the fifth century to 1194; with 21 genealogical tables. The author states that the lists, tables and dates are not wholly reliable.

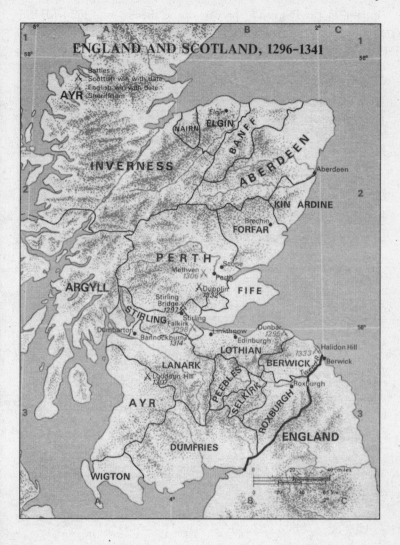

ENGLAND AND SCOTLAND, 1296–1341

11 Kings of Scotland

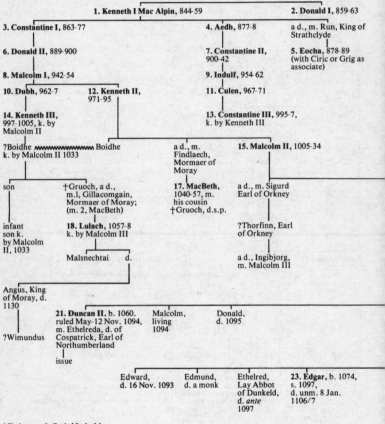

1. **Kenneth I Mac Alpin,** 844-59

2. **Donald I,** 859-63

3. **Constantine I,** 863-77

4. **Aedh,** 877-8

a d., m. Run, King of Strathclyde

5. **Eocha,** 878-89 (with Ciric or Grig as associate)

6. **Donald II,** 889-900

7. **Constantine II,** 900-42

8. **Malcolm I,** 942-54

9. **Indulf,** 954-62

10. **Dubh,** 962-7

11. **Culen,** 967-71

12. **Kenneth II,** 971-95

13. **Constantine III,** 995-7, k. by Kenneth III

14. **Kenneth III,** 997-1005, k. by Malcolm II

15. **Malcolm II,** 1005-34

?Boidhe k. by Malcolm II 1033 〰〰〰〰〰〰 Boidhe

a d., m. Findlaech, Mormaer of Moray

son

†Gruoch, a d., m.1, Gillacomgain, Mormaer of Moray; (m. 2, MacBeth)

17. **MacBeth,** 1040-57, m. his cousin †Gruoch, d.s.p.

a d., m. Sigurd Earl of Orkney

infant son k. by Malcolm II, 1033

18. **Lulach,** 1057-8 k. by Malcolm III

?Thorfinn, Earl of Orkney

Malsnechtai   d.

a d., Ingibjorg, m. Malcolm III

Angus, King of Moray, d. 1130

21. **Duncan II.** b. 1060. ruled May-12 Nov. 1094, m. Ethelreda, d. of Cospatrick, Earl of Northumberland

Malcolm, living 1094

Donald, d. 1095

?Wimundus

issue

Edward, d. 16 Nov. 1093

Edmund, d. a monk

Ethelred, Lay Abbot of Dunkeld, d. *ante* 1097

23. **Edgar,** b. 1074, s. 1097, d. unm. 8 Jan. 1106/7

†Shakespeare's 'Lady Macbeth'.

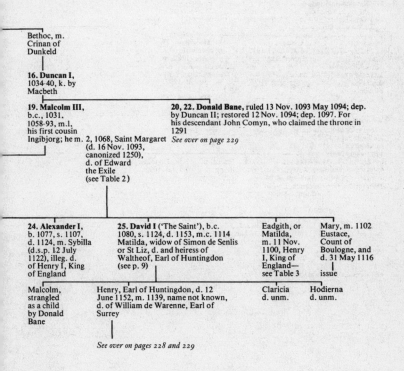

Bethoc, m.
Crinan of
Dunkeld

16. Duncan I,
1034-40, k. by
Macbeth

19. Malcolm III,
b.c., 1031,
1058-93, m.1,
his first cousin
Ingibjorg; he m. 2, 1068, Saint Margaret
(d. 16 Nov. 1093,
canonized 1250),
d. of Edward
the Exile
(see Table 2)

20, 22. Donald Bane, ruled 13 Nov. 1093 May 1094; dep.
by Duncan II; restored 12 Nov. 1094; dep. 1097. For
his descendant John Comyn, who claimed the throne in
1291
See over on page 229

24. Alexander I,
b. 1077, s. 1107,
d. 1124, m. Sybilla
(d.s.p. 12 July
1122), illeg. d.
of Henry I, King
of England

25. David I ('The Saint'), b.c.
1080, s. 1124, d. 1153, m.c. 1114
Matilda, widow of Simon de Senlis
or St Liz, d. and heiress of
Waltheof, Earl of Huntingdon
(see p. 9)

Eadgith, or
Matilda,
m. 11 Nov.
1100, Henry
I, King of
England—
see Table 3

Mary, m. 1102
Eustace,
Count of
Boulogne, and
d. 31 May 1116
issue

Malcolm,
strangled
as a child
by Donald
Bane

Henry, Earl of Huntingdon, d. 12
June 1152, m. 1139, name not known,
d. of William de Warenne, Earl of
Surrey

Claricia
d. unm.

Hodierna
d. unm.

See over on pages 228 and 229

Continued from previous page

26. Malcolm IV ('The Maiden'), b. 20 March 1141-2, s. 1153, d. unm. 9 Dec. 1165

27. William ('The Lion'), b.c. 1143, s. 9 Dec. 1165, d. 4 Dec. 1214, m. 5 Sept. 1186 Ermengarde (d. 11 Feb. 1233-4), d. of Richard, Viscount of Bellemont; he had illegitimately

28. Alexander II, b. 24 Aug. 1198, s. 4 Dec. 1214, d. 8 July 1249, m.l, Joan (d.s.p. 4 March 1237-8), d. of John, King of England; m. 2, 15 May 1239, Mary, d. of Enguerand, Seigneur de Couci

Margaret, d.s.p. 1295, m. 1221 Hubert de Burgh, Earl of Kent

Isabella, m. 1225 Roger Bigod, Earl of Norfolk (d.s.p. 4 July 1270)

Marjory, d.s.p. 17 Nov. 1244, m. 1 Aug. 1235 Gilbert, Earl of Pembroke (d. *post* 27 June 1241)

Isabella m. William Ros (1) | Robert Ros | †William Ros (2)

Ada, m. 5th Earl of Dunbar | Patric, 6th Earl | Patric, 7th Earl | †Patric, 8th Earl, 1st Earl of March

Margaret m. William de Vesci (1) | †William de Vesci (2)

29. Alexander III, b. 4 Sept. 1241, s. 8 July 1249, d. 19 March 1285-6, m.l, Margaret (d. 26 Feb. 1274-5), d. of Henry III, King of England; he m. 2, Yolande, d. of Robert IV, Count of Dreux

········ he had illeg. Marjory, m. Alan Durward the Justiciary | Ermengarde | †Nicholas Soules

Alexander, b. 21 Jan. 1263-4, d.s.p. 28 Jan. 1283-4, m. 15 Nov. 1282, Margaret, d. of Guy of Flanders

David, b. 20 March 1272-3, d. unm. June 1281

30, Margaret 'The b. 28 Feb. 1260-1, d. 9 Apr. 1283, m. 31 Aug. 1281, Eric Magnusson,† King of Norway (d. 1299)

30, Margaret 'The Maid of Norway', b. *ante* 9 Apr. 1283, d. unm. 26 Sept. 1290

†The twelve competitors for the throne in 1290-2 as submitted to the arbitration of King Edward I of England. These included claimants of illegitimate descent, in accordance with Scottish law.

David, Earl of Huntingdon, d. 17
June 1219, m. 26 Aug. 1190 Maud, d. of
Hugh de Kevilloc, Earl of Chester

. . . .
Aufrica   Henry
| Galithly
William |
| †Patrick
Aufrica   Galithly
|
Agatha
|
†Roger
de
Mandeville

Ada, m. 1161   Margaret, m.1,   Matilda,
Florent III,   Conan, Duke   d. young
Count of   of Brittany,   1152
Holland   Earl of Rich-
| mond (d. 20
William I   Feb. 1170-1)
|
Florent IV   Constance, m.
| Geoffrey, s. of
William II   Henry II, King of
| England; she m.2
†Florent V,   Humphrey de Bohun,
Count of   Earl of Hereford
Holland

DESCENDANTS
OF DONALD
BANE
|
Bethoc (2)
|
Hextilda
|
William Comyn
|
Richard Comyn
|
John Comyn of
Badenoch (1)
|
†John Comyn
(2), m.
sister of
John Baliol
|
John Comyn
(3) ('Red
Comyn'), k.
by Robert
the Bruce

2s. 1d.   John ('The Scot'),   Margaret,
unm.   Earl of Chester   m. 1209
           and Huntingdon,   Alan, Lord
           d.s.p. 5 June 1237   of Galloway
                                 (d. 1234)

Isabella, m.   Matilda   Ada
Robert Bruce,   d. unm.   m. Henry
Lord of Allan-   de
dale (d. 1245)   Hastings
| |
†Robert, d. ante   Beatrice,   Sir Henry
3 May 1294, m.   m. Hugo   de Hastings
Isabel, d. of   de Neville |
Gilbert de Clare,   †John, 1st
Earl of Glouces-   Lord
ter and Hereford   Hastings

Helen, m.   Christian   Dervorguilla
Roger de   d.s.p. 1245-   d. 28 Jan.
Quincey,   6, m. 1236   1289-90,
Earl of   William,   m. 1233
Winches-   Earl of   John Baliol
ter, (d.   Albemarle   (d. 1269)
1264)
|
issue

Robert Bruce, Earl   3s
of Carrick jure
uxoris, m. 1271
Margaret, d. of 2nd
Earl of Carrick

3s.   †31. John Baliol, b.c. 1250,   2d.
       d.c. Apr. 1313, crowned,
       following award of Edward I
       of England, 30 Nov. 1292, dep.
       10 July 1296, m. ante 7 Feb.
       1280-1 Isabel, d. of John de
       Warenne, Earl of Surrey

Edward, crowned   Henry,
by the English   k. 16 Dec.
at Scone 24 Sept.   1332
1332; fled Scot-
land 1332; d.s.p.
1363

32. Robert I 'The Bruce',   Edward, Earl of   3s, 5d
b. 11 July 1274, d. 7   Carrick, King of
June 1329, crowned   Ireland 2 May 1316,
King of Scotland 27   k. at battle of
March 1306, re-estab-   Dundalk 14 Oct. 1318
lished independence of   s.p.
Scotland following Edward
I's subjugation (1296-1314)
at the battle of Bannockburn,
m.1, Isabel, d. of Donald,
6th Earl of Mar; he m.2, 1302, Elizabeth de Burgh
                       (d. 26 Oct. 1327), d. of Richard,
                       Earl of Ulster

Marjorie, d. 2 March 1315-16,
m. 1315 Walter the Stewart,
6th High Stewart of Scotland

34. Robert II (first King of
the House of Stewart), b. 2
March 1315-16, s. 22 Feb. 1370-1,
d. 19 Apr. 1390, m.1, Elizabeth (d.
ante 1355), d. of Sir Adam Mure;
he m.2, 1355, Euphemia
      (d. 1387), widow of John
      Randolph, Earl of Moray,
      d. of Hugh, Earl of Ross

33. David II, b. 5 March   John,   Matilda,   Margaret,
1323-4, s. 7 June 1329.   d. young   d. 20   d. 1358,
d.s.p. 22 Feb. 1370-1, m.1,   July   m. ante
Joan (d.s.p. 7 Sept. 1362),   1353,   10 Nov.
d. of Edward II, King of   m.   1345
England; m. 2, 20 Feb. 1363-4,   Thomas   5th Earl o
Margaret (div. 20 March   Isaac   Sutherlan
1369-70, d.c. 31 Jan. 1374-5),
widow of Sir John Logie and
d. of Sir Malcolm Drummond

See page 231

See page 231

| **35. Robert III,** b. 1337, s. 19 Apr. 1390, d. 4 Apr. 1406, m. Annabella, (d. 1401), d. of John Drummond of Stobhall | Walter d.s.p. *post* 14 Aug. 1362, m. Isabel, Countess of Fife | Robert, 1st Duke of Albany, b.c. 1340, d. 3 Sept. 1420, m.1, 9 Sept. 1361, Margaret, Countess of Menteith (d. 1380) and had issue; m. 2. Muriella (d. 1449), d. of Sir William Keith and had issue | Alexander, Earl of Buchan ('The Wolf of Badenoch'), d.s.p. 24 July 1394, m. Euphaemia, Countess of Ross | Margaret, m. 14 June 1350 John Macdonald, Lord of the Isles (d. 1387)
 issue | Marjorie, m.1, c. 11 July 1371, John Dunbar, Earl of Moray (d.c. 1390, leaving issue); m. 2, c. 1403, Sir Alexander Keith |

| David, Earl of Carrick, Duke of Rothesay, b. 24 Oct. 1378, d.s.p. 26 March 1402, m. Feb. 1399–1400 Marjorie, d. of Archibald, 3rd Earl of Douglas | Robert, d. young | **36. James I,** b. Dec. 1394, s. 4 Apr. 1406, assassinated 21 Feb. 1436-7, m. 2 Feb. 1423-4, Lady Joan Beaufort (d. 15 July 1445), d. of 1st Earl of Somerset | Margaret, m. Archibald, 4th Earl of Douglas, Duke of Touraine <br> issue | Mary, d. 1458, m.1, 1397, George, Earl of Angus; m. 2, 1404, Sir James Kennedy of Dunmure; m.3, 1413, William, 1st Lord Graham; m. 4, 1425, Sir William Edmonstone of Duntreath, and had issue by all four | Egidia |

| Alexander, b. 16 Oct. 1430, d. an infant | **37. James II,** b. 16 Oct. 1430, s. 21 Feb. 1436-7, k. by a piece of ordnance bursting at Roxburgh Castle 3 Aug. 1460, m. 3 July 1449 Mary (d. 1 Dec. 1463), d. of Arnold, Duke of Gueldres | Margaret, d.s.p. 16 Aug. 1444, m. 24 June 1436 Louis, Dauphin of France, later King Louis XI | Isabella, d. 1494, m. 30 Oct. 1442 Francis, Duke of Brittany <br> issue |

38. James III, b. 10 July 1451, s. 3 Aug. 1460, d. 11 June 1488, m. 13 July 1469 Margaret (d. 14 July 1486), d. of Christian I, King of Denmark — Alexander, Duke of Albany, d. 1485, m.1, (diss. 1478) Lady Katharine Sinclair, d. of William, Earl of Caithness; m.2, 19 Jan. 1479-80, Anne, d. of Bertrand de la Tour, Count of Auvergne | issue

39. James IV, b. 17 March 1472-3, s. 11 June 1488, k. at battle of Flodden Field 9 Sept. 1513, m. Margaret, d. of Henry VII of England (see Table 7) — James, b. March 1475-6 d. unm. Jan. 1502-3 — John, created Earl of Mar, b. 2 March 1486-7, d. unm. 11 March 1502-3

James, b. 21 Feb. 1506-7, d. 27 Feb. 1507-8 — Arthur, b. 20 Oct. 1509, d. 14 July 1510 — **40. James V,** b. 10 Apr. 1512, s. 9 Sept. 1513, d. 14 Dec. 1542, m.1, 1 Jan. 1536-7, Madeline de Valois (d.s.p. 7 July 1537), d. of Francis I, King of France; m. 2, June 1538, Marie de Lorraine (d. 10 June 1560), d. of Claude de Guise Lorraine, Duke of Aumale, Regent of Scotland during her d.'s minority

41. Mary, Queen of Scots, b. 7 or 8 Dec. 1542, s. 14 Dec. 1542, compelled to abdicate 24 July 1567, executed 8 Feb. 1586-7, m.1, 24 Apr. 1558, Francis, Dauphin of France, later King Francis II (d.s.p. 5 Dec. 1560); m.2, 29 July 1565, her cousin Henry, Lord Darnley, created Duke of Albany, Earl of Ross (murdered 10 Feb. 1566-7) m. 3, 15 May 1567, 4th Earl of Bothwell, created Duke of Orkney (d.s.p. 14 Apr. 1578)

42. James VI, b. 19 June 1566, s. 24 July 1567, and s. his cousin Elizabeth as King of England, 24 March 1603 – Table 8 – House of Stewart

Continued from previous page *Continued from previous page*

Jean, m.1, Sir John Keith; m. 2, 1379, Sir John Lyon, ancestor of the Earls of Strathmore; m. 3, Sir James Sandilands of Calder, ancestor of the Lords Torphichen	Isabella, m.1, c. 1371, 2nd Earl of Douglas (d.s.p. 19 Aug. 1388); m.2, *ante* 1390, Sir John Edmonstone	Elizabeth, m. *ante* 7 Nov. 1372 Sir Thomas Hay, Lord the Hay, Constable of Scotland, from whom descend the Earls of Erroll	David, Earl Palatine of Strathearn, Earl of Caithness, b.c. 1356, d. *ante* 1389	Walter, Earl of Caithness, m. *ante* 19 Oct. 1378 Margaret, d. and heiress of Sir David de Barclay, Lord of Brechin, and was executed and attainted 26 March 1437	Egidia, m. 1387 Sir William Douglas of Nithsdale, illeg. s. of Archibald, 3rd Earl of Douglas	Katherine (or Jean, or Elizabeth), m. 1380 Sir David Lindsay, 1st Earl of Crawford, from whom descend the Earls of Crawford and Balcarres
	issue		issue	issue	issue	

Elizabeth, m. 1387
James, Lord of
Dalkeith, grand-
father of 1st Earl
of Moreton

Joanna (both deaf and dumb), m. *ante* 15 May 1459 1st Earl of Morton, from whom descend the Earls of Morton	Eleanor, d.s.p. 4 March 1496, m. 12 Feb. 1449 Sigismund, Duke of Austria	Mary, m. 1444 Wolfaert von Borselen, Count of Grandpré	Annabella, m.1, 14 Dec. 1447 (div.) Louis, Count of Geneva, s. of Duke of Savoy; m. 2, *ante* 10 March 1459 (div. 24 July 1471), George, Earl of Huntly

David, d. an infant *ante* 18 July 1457	John, Earl of Mar, b. 1459, d. unm. 1479	Mary, d. May 1488, m.1, *ante* 26 Apr. 1467, Thomas Boyd, Earl of Arran (d. c. 1474), leaving issue; m.2, *ante* Apr. 1474, James, 1st Lord Hamilton, from whom descend the Dukes of Abercorn	Margaret, d. unm.

KINGS AND QUEENS REGNANT
OF SCOTLAND
from Kenneth MacAlpin to James VI

As in the rest of Britain, the Scots are an amalgam of the different peoples who settled there. Ice retreated from there some 8000 years ago; by 4000BC the first settlers would seem to have been established. In about 500 BC the great wave of Celtic peoples would have reached Scottish shores; they had passed already and peopled much of Europe, from Austria into Germany, into France and finally Britain and Ireland. These were the Brythonic Celts or P group, since they substituted P for B, saying Pretani, whence Picts, as opposed to the Britanni to the south. These Picts were those on whom Agricola imposed Roman rule in AD80, against whom Hadrian's Wall was built in 120, and the Antonine Wall farther north in 142–3. We know nothing of their political organisation.

The Roman forces withdrew in 176, and shortly after Scoti from Ireland crossed into western Scotland, to found the kingdom of Dalriada, pushing the Picts to the north and east. Later Norwegians had penetrated and peopled the western isles in the south west; followed by Angles, Saxons and Jutes for the Kingdom of Strathclyde. It seems it was a Pictish king, Kenneth MacAlpin, who first succeeded in amalgamating the three kingdoms, which later were enlarged to include Lothian, peoples from English Northumberland.

It is a tradition which cannot be verified that among the Picts the kingship did not pass from the father to the son of the deceased king, but to the son of his sister, or of his mother, that is, a nephew or a brother. The sense of this is that a royal descent through women is certain irrespective of whether the father is royal or not: his identity cannot be taken on trust. This practice is found in other parts of the world, and is not unique. It explains why Malcolm II killed his cousin as a potential usurper; why Macbeth killed his cousin Duncan I; and why Lulach was killed by Malcolm III. Shakespeare's *Macbeth* wholly misunderstood the dynastic custom and confused the issue. It was a law of inheritance, not of simple feud and jealousy.

Christianity had entered Scotland with St Ninian *c.*400, but a century and a half later, with St Columba's foundation of Iona, there was still missionary work to do. Royal families understandably cling to custom and convention; it is only with the long reign of Malcolm III and his marriage to the Saxon Princess St Margaret that we begin to see other principles in operation.

Many years later the Scots were able to jeer at England in that they had coalesced into a single kingdom when England was still divided into seven kingdoms. While this was not altogether historically justified, it is true that from 1013 to 1066 England was subject to the Danes, only finally to be united by the Norman Conquest. This enabled William the Conqueror to assert his right to be the sole owner of all the land, an assertion the Scottish kings were never able to make. Like so many of his predecessors, Malcolm III had reached the throne by force, with the assistance of an army supplied by Earl Siward of Northumberland. He had married Ingibord, widow of the great Earl Thorfinn of Orkney, his first cousin. In 1066 he gave refuge at his court to Edgar Atheling, the male heir to the Saxon kings, and his sisters, Margaret and Christina. Ingibord died – perhaps somewhat opportunely – so that in 1068 he was able to marry Margaret. She gave him six sons, three of whom ascended the throne, and two daughters.

One might have expected that Malcolm would have sought peace with England. Nevertheless he was killed, together with his eldest son by Margaret, in a raid on England; she died also within a few days. Malcolm's brother, Donald Bane, succeeded, but reigned only for some six months; he was deposed by Duncan II, Malcolm's son by his first wife, only in turn to be murdered in the following November. Donald Bane now returned, but was deposed by Edgar, Malcolm's eldest surviving son by Margaret. He died childless at the beginning of 1106.

There now followed two long reigns, Alexander I, 1107–24, and David I, 1124–53, his brother. Their mother had been a woman of remarkable personality and gifts. She is remembered today chiefly for her concern for religion and the church, and for her charity to the poor. Accustomed to the disciplined church of England, she was instrumental in reconciling Scottish practices to Rome. The Benedictine monastery which she founded at Dumfermline became the centre from which new order, discipline and austerity spread. She was nevertheless not unworldly. The strengthening of religious contacts with Europe had the effect of improving commercial contacts. The court now became more luxurious and cultured, and the rising merchant class followed suit. The once-great abbey of Iona was restored and revived; building activity was to increase, especially under her sons.

Of these, David I is perhaps the greatest king ever to rule over Scotland. He attracted Norman knights to his court, giving them land. First among them was Robert de Brus from Cotentin, his descendants to be the founders of a dynasty, and from Brittany, Walter FitzAlan, whom he appointed his Steward, giving him the name Stewart to a dynasty that would rule Scotland and later in England. Others were the Balliols, Comyns, Grahams and Lindsays.

These strengthened his council, as did members of religious orders brought from abroad, Augustinians, Cistercians, Premonstratensians, Tironensians. Great new abbeys were built, Jedburgh, Kinloss, Holyrood, Melrose, Dryburgh, Dundrennan, Sweetheart, not to mention daughter houses. All these encouraged industry and commerce, markets and trade.

At the same time there was a reorganisation of the secular government. Counties were now instituted, with sheriffs answerable to the King's Justiciar in charge. Royal castles were built from which control and administration could flow. David's elder brother Alexander had married an illegitimate daughter of Henry I of England; he himself married the heiress of Waltheof, Earl of Huntingdon; their second son Henry married a daughter of William de Warenne, Earl of Surrey, thus forging further links with Norman England. It led to trouble for Scotland.

In due course David succeeded to the lands of the Earl of Huntingdon and accordingly did homage to Henry I and Stephen of England for them. There were precedents. Malcolm III had done homage to William I for lands held in England in 1072, and again to William II in 1091. These in fact were submissions to military defeat; they were never held to imply that the Scottish throne was subject to England. Yet the sight of the King of Scotland kneeling in homage before the King of England looked very like subjection in the eyes of the English noblemen, who had themselves have done homage. Scottish eyes saw it differently.

For all this, David's achievements was very real, and even the ruins of his abbeys proclaim this today. Scotland was now part of the medieval European comity of Europe; it had been the work of Malcolm III, Margaret and Alexander, crowned by David.

David's son predeceased him. Two grandsons succeeded. Malcolm IV the Maiden was only eleven, but the monarchy was now strong enough not to be upset by a minority. His brother, William the Lion, succeeded at twenty-two, and was to have the longest reign in Scottish history, dying in 1214 aged seventy-one after fifty-nine years on the throne. Reckless and a man of action, he was fool enough to fall into the hands of Henry II of England. In 1174 at Falaise he was forced to do homage for Scotland. In 1189, when Richard Coeur-de-Lion was raising funds to go the on Crusade, he purported to buy his consent to homage back. Certainly he paid his acquittance, but in England the possibility of release from oath simply for money was never accepted, Therefore William wisely stayed at home, creating new burghs, or self-governing cities. New religious houses were founded, the most notable the abbey of Arbroath. William left a legitimate son and three daughters, together with five illegitimate daughters and one son. He also left a brother who was ancestor of King John Balliol, and of the Bruce and Stewart dynasties. Of these more anon.

William's immediate successor, Alexander II, married a daughter of John of England, and had a turbulent reign with many troubles. At one time it looked as if the barons might call on John to succeed him. Apart from other troubles with local factions, in the Hebrides the Kings of Norway were interfering to regain power. An expedition brought mainland Argyll under control, but Alexander died near Oban before establishing authority over the islands.

Alexander II succeeded at the age of eight, and, like his father, married an English Princess, a daughter of Henry III. Committees of guardianship took control until he was twenty, but the stability of the monarchy was remarkable, given the factious nature of Scottish nobility. In December 1251 he travelled to York for his marriage, and was knighted by Henry III, doing homage for his English lands. Henry III invited him to do homage for Scotland also, whereupon Alexander retorted that he came to be married, not to discuss serious matters of state policy which he had not discussed with his Council. Politically he showed himself adroit and skilful, advancing economic growth in trade and agriculture. The port of Berwick-on-Tweed was soon handling trade twenty-five per cent greater than that of England, and the standard of living was improving. He made a point of travelling round the country, supervising the work of the sheriffs.

When Alexander II died the only external threat was from Norway. Alexander III attempted to buy out the Norwegian-held islands. Haakon of Norway assembled an immense fleet in 1263, to compel Alexander's submission. Shortly he was gathering supporters in Skye and the Firth of Lorne. He sailed into the Clyde, and then took Arran and Bute. Protracted peace talks took place at Ayr, and then the Scottish weather took a hand. On 30 September the Norwegian galleys were driven ashore at Largs; on 1 and 2 October their personnel were attacked by the Scots under Alexander the Steward. Haakon was forced to retreat with such vessels as remained. It was the last of the Norwegian domination of the western isles. Haakon then himself died in the bishop's palace at Kirkwall. Finally in 1266 the Treaty of Perth gave Alexander all the Norwegian territories on the islands and mainland. Friendship was now achieved, and in 1281 his daughter Margaret was married to the new King of Norway, Eric Magnusson.

Alexander's troubles were not yet over. His father-in-law Henry III was now dead, and had been succeeded by his son, Edward I, who had his own ideas. It was with some trepidation that Alexander and his court travelled to England to do homage for his English lands. The English and Scottish versions of his oath do not agree. For the Scots Alexander swore 'to bear faith to Edward . . . and will faithfully perform the services for the lands I hold of him, reserving my kingdom'. The English version denies that the last three words were used. The Bishop of Norwich intervened, suggesting that Edward might claim that Alexander should do homage for Scotland. Alexander replied: 'No one has the right to homage for my kingdom, for I hold it from God alone.' Edward had clearly determined to force Alexander, and had failed. It looked as if stability was restored on all fronts. Disaster now struck.

David, Alexander's second son, died in 1281. Then in 1283 his daughter, the Queen of Norway died shortly after childbirth, leaving a baby daughter, also Margaret. In the following January the elder brother, also Alexander, died, leaving little Margaret, 'The Maid of Norway', heir to the Scottish throne. Finally, in March 1286, Alexander III himself died, his granddaughter Queen of Scotland. Guardians of the Kingdom were appointed as before, and it testified to the stability of the kingdom that it held steady. They thought fit to consult Edward I, who suggested that his son Edward, born only in 1284, and Margaret should marry, thus uniting the two countries. In July 1290 representatives from Scotland, England and Norway agreed to a marriage treaty at Birgham-on-Tweed, and to bring Margaret from Norway. In October Margaret died in the Orkney Islands on her way to Scotland. The circumstances of her death are a mystery.

The intricacies of Scottish law now produced a contentious situation. It has to be remembered that in Scottish law an illegitimate person, provided that that person is born in Scotland, may equally be heir in default of a legitimate one; and that a question arises concerning daughters, who do not necessarily have precedence in order of birth. In this way no less than twelve competitors claimed the throne, an illegitimate descendant of Alexander II, illegitimate descendants of William the Lion, legitimate descendants of William's brother David and his sister Ada, and a member of the Comyn family, descended legitimately from Donald Bane.

The Guardians and others determined on Edward I as arbitrator, but had not reckoned that first he would require from them a statement that he was invited as their overlord. He gave them three weeks to accept. The claimants hurried to seize the advantage, the Guardians and others more slowly. Edward had pointed out that as overlord he was prepared to settle the matter by force of arms. Eventually all agreed.

Edward accordingly awarded the throne to John Balliol, great-grandson of David, Earl of Huntingdon, William the Lion's brother. He was not the strong man that the times needed, and Edward made the mistake of bullying him. In 1295, when Edward was preparing war against France, he summoned Balliol, as a feudal inferior, to take part. For all that he was known as 'Toom Tabard', or 'Stuffed Shirt', he refused, and renounced his allegiance that Edward had extorted from him. Instead he entered into an alliance with France, known as the 'Auld Alliance', which was to be the basis of Scottish foreign policy even into the sixteenth century. Edward turned on Balliol, destroyed Berwick and massacred its people, and then routed Balliol's army at Dunbar. On 2 July he made an unconditional surrender, and was deposed. Scotland was now put in charge of the Earl of Surrey, Balliol's father-in-law, together with Hugh de Cressingham as administrator.

It was now that a heroic resistance fighter arose, William Wallace. To the English he was an outlaw. In 1297 he defeated an English army at Stirling, and declared himself Guardian of Scotland. Edward retaliated in 1298 with a huge army; on 22 July he defeated Wallace at Falkirk, and retired to England. Wallace continued guerrilla operations, but on no great scale. On 5 August 1305 he was betrayed, and sent to Westminster. Edward had him executed as an outlaw, without further to-do. Wallace remains the most heroic figure in Scottish annals. It was never likely that his challenge would not be taken up.

After much intrigue Robert the Bruce, a great-grandson of David, Earl of Huntingdon, William I's brother, emerged as leader. Bishop Wishart of Glasgow had him crowned at Scone on 27 March 1306-7, but the struggle was not over. Later in the year he was defeated at Methven, but then Edward I died. Under Edward II the war rumbled irresolutely on so far as the English were concerned, while Bruce occupied himself with small actions against the castles from which the English ruled. These were picked off one by one, for Bruce wisely avoided any frontal assault. By 1314 only Stirling and Bothwell castles remained. Edward II had no choice but to send a large army. He reached Edinburgh on 21 June. Bruce waited for him at Stirling, where he was attacked on 23 June. It had been a stroke of great tactical wisdom, and Bruce had prepared the ground with great care. Edward hastened to attack, and Sir Humphrey de Bohun charged at Bruce in person. Coolly Bruce turned his horse aside, and, as Bohun passed, brought his axe down on his head. Next day he attacked a demoralised army, using the ground to paralyse the English. By nightfall they were surrendering, while Edward and his staff escaped. Scottish independence, and the authority of Robert I the Bruce, were now beyond question, but war dragged on. Only in 1328 was peace finally made at Northampton. Robert I died in the following year, his task complete. His heir, David II, was five years old, and married to Joan, daughter of Edward II, but what bode fair for a union of the crowns was frustrated in the event; there were no children.

The Crown thus passed to Robert II, the first King of the House of Stewart, by the marriage of Robert I's daughter to Walter the Stewart. By two marriages Robert II fathered twenty-one children, for whom, as he himself had done, wives or husbands were found from the Scottish nobility. This practice continued for the next two reigns, bringing about a large brood of semi-royals to intrigue with one another. It is a period up to the reign of James IV of shadowy kings and ineffectual government, of war with England, intermittently to embarrass her in the Hundred Years War against the French, in the event to court Scottish defeats.

It is only with James IV that a leader of real merit emerges, of dignity and with a realistic policy. Between 1488 and 1506 he brought back all the islands under royal control, establishing a navy, based on the provision of one twenty-ton ship from each coastal burgh. His Shipping Act had the effect not only of policing the seas but of encouraging and enabling trade. A chief pride was the giant *St Michael*, of which it was said that all the oaks in Fife had been felled to provide her timbers. Law and order were enforced in the Highlands, Islands and Borders; freemen from the shires and burgers now selected representatives to the Parliament, in which, if elected, service was compulsory. The legal system was overhauled, together with the currency. James's marriage to Henry VII's daughter, Margaret, drew the countries together, at least until the accession in England of Henry VIII. Relations then deteriorated rapidly. There were border skirmishes and incidents at sea. In 1512 Henry, as a member of the Holy League, attacked France. The Queen sent James IV a ring, asking him to 'break a lance for her sake'. James assembled a vast Scottish army, encountering the Earl of Surrey at Flodden Field. Surrey was an experienced commander; James lost his life, surrounded by twelve earls, his son the Archbishop of St Andrews, and other lords, clan chiefs and several thousand men. Flodden was the most disastrous defeat Scotland had ever suffered.

James V came to the throne at sixteen months old. He continued the policy of the 'Auld Alliance', even travelling to France uninvited, so it is said, to marry Marguerite de Valois. She died within the year, and in 1538 he married Mary of Guise, as she is commonly known. He was at war with England again in 1542, and died after his disastrous defeat at Solway Moss, only in time to hear that his Queen had given birth to a babe and heir, now Mary, Queen of Scots. James, second Earl of Arran, was now the next heir to the throne, a great-grandson of James II by his daughter Mary.

In 1543 Arran made the Treaty of Greenwich with Henry VIII of England by which the Queen of Scots would marry Henry's heir, the future Edward VI. The Scots repudiated the agreement; they had no desire for any sort of union with England. Similarly they had no wish for dependence on France, and for this reason Mary of Guise, now Queen Mother, had been passed over as Regent in favour of Arran. Nevertheless in 1548, following Arran's disastrous defeat at the battle of Pinkie, when she decided that the child should go to France for her safety, Arran ceded the Regency to her. She now allowed the execution of a Protestant martyr, provoking the 'Congregation' and what eventuated in civil war. French professionals supported the Queen Mother; the 'Congregation' appealed to Elizabeth of England, who sent a fleet. The Queen Regent died in June 1560, and peace ensued.

Mary, Queen of Scots, had been in France since 1548, and had married the Dauphin in 1558. She was wholly French by culture and religion, with all the sophistication of the debauched and murderous court of Queen Catherine de' Medici. The Dauphin died in 1559, and Mary returned to Scotland after her Mother's death. Elizabeth I was *de facto* Queen of England, unless it was that, by English law, she had been conceived before Henry VIII was free to marry her mother. In any case, Elizabeth was unmarried; and Mary, former Queen of France, Queen of Scots, was the heir presumptive to England as granddaughter of Henry VII's elder daughter Margaret. It was a unique position, the source of Elizabeth's fears.

Mary was only eighteen, plainly marriageable. Various suitors were suggested from among the nobility. Her choice was her cousin Darnley, whose mother was a granddaughter of Henry VII, by his daughter Margaret. It was love at first sight which speedily turned to bitterness. Mary had already had one lover executed, Pierre de Boscosel de Chastelard; he had been seen leaving her bedroom. Darnley was no better, weak and whining; and soon Mary turned to Rizzio, her secretary, for friendship. Darnley suspected more, and had him murdered in Mary's presence. She was with child, and was convinced that it was done to make her miscarry. Shortly she went her full term, and gave birth to the future James VI and I. In 1567 she seems to have become reconciled to Darnley, but on 9 February she left her sick husband at Kirk o'Field House to attend a ball in Holyrood Palace. Kirk o'Field blew up; and Darnley's body was found in the garden, propped up against a tree; he had been strangled.

James Hepburn, Earl of Bothwell, was the prime suspect. In April he abducted the Queen, whom he married on 15 May. It is difficult not to convict her of Darnley's murder, nor of protecting Bothwell. The Darnley marriage had cost her support, and particularly of John Knox and the Presbyterians; the Bothwell marriage cost her more, her throne. Eventually she gained asylum in England, virtually a prisoner.

Twenty years later, in 1586, she was found to have been in contact with authors of the Babington Plot against Elizabeth's life. Elizabeth was reluctant to have her executed, but her gaoler declined to murder a former sovereign. Eventually Elizabeth gave her consent; Mary died on the scaffold with great dignity in Fotheringhay Castle on 8 February 1587. She had a curious and complex character, but it cannot be said that she had done much good for Scotland.

James VI succeeded at little more than one year old. He took power nominally in 1580, and effectively in 1582–3. His upbringing and career in England has already been described. In his twenty years of rule in Scotland he was cautiously conservative, greatly to Scottish advantage. He concentrated on national prosperity, on peace in the Highlands and not less in the Church. It was with the Presbyterians that he had the greatest difficulties, under the leader Andrew Melville, who informed him: 'King James the Saxt, in the kingdom of Christ, is nocht a king, nor a Lord, nor a heid, but a member.' It was this that convinced him that monarchy and Presbyterianism could not co-exist.

With James's departure for England the story of kings in Scotland effectively comes to an end. The crowns of Scotland and England were not united, but the Scottish king ruled from London through a Privy Council in Scotland. James himself remarked that he found this an advantage; he was freed from local pressures and simply passed on his instructions to officials. At the same time it had the effect of strengthening the Scottish Parliament. The finale came in 1707 with the Act of Union, by which Scotland was to send sixteen representative peers and forty-five members of Parliament to Westminster into a new unitary state, Great Britain.

WELSH RULERS

When the Romans invaded Britain in 55 BC there were four distinct tribes west of the Severn: the Decangi in Anglesey and Snowdonia; the Ordovices in central Wales; the Dimetae in the southwest; and the Silures in the east. Under Caractacus (Caradog) the Silures put up a serious resistance against Ostorius; the Roman conquest was not complete until AD 78 under Frontinus. Evidence is lacking to enable the construction of any consecutive history of Welsh rulers in any normal sense. Oral tradition, written down later, is more the history, obscure as it is, of some 500 Celtic saints and missionaries. While the peoples of Wales shared a common origin with the Celts of Scotland, Ireland and Cornwall and the European mainland, they do not appear to have developed any stable political institutions.

As elsewhere in Britain, when the Romans withdrew in 410, there was chaos. No political structure remained. A Celtic leader, Cunedda, with the title Gwledig, assumed the title of the Roman *Dux Britanniarum*, but it did not imply sovereignty over Wales. He held court at Deganwy, near Llandudno. In the sixth century refugees from what is now England were pushing westwards, into Cumbria, Wales and Cornwall, as Angles, Saxons and Jutes pressed forwards into their lands. At the battle of Deorham in 577 the West Saxons cut the Welsh off from their cousins in Cornwall. In 613 at Chester King Ethelfrith cut Cunedda's descendants off from the northern Celtic territory of Stathclyde, which fell finally in 676. All Wales was now isolated in the valleys and mountains. In *c.*784 Offa the Great of Mercia (757–96) built his great Dyke to demarcate his territory from the Welsh, apparently with local agreement; it ran from Chepstow, near the mouth of the Wye, to the sea near Prestatyn.

Between 400 and 500 kingships emerged in Ceredigion (Cardigan), Gwynedd, Powys, Dyfed, and in Gwent and Glamorgan. Up to 800 they are shadowy rulers. In the ninth century attacks by Norse and Danish pirates provoked the emergence of a leader. Rhodri Mawr (Roderick the Great) built a fleet to protect Anglesey. He succeeded his father as ruler of Gwynedd in 844, an uncle as ruler of Powys in 855, and a brother-in-law as ruler of Seisyllweg in 871. When he died in 877 he ruled Wales from Anglesey to Gower. Nevertheless, since Welsh customary law divided inheritance in shares between brothers, his kingdom was once again subdivided. There was not that urge towards national unity that was apparent east of Offa's Dyke or in Scotland. It was restored by strong rulers in the tenth to eleventh centuries: Hywel Dda (the Good) c.900–50, from Seisyllweg; Maredudd ap Owain c. 986–99, from Deheubarth; and Gruffudd ap Llywelyn 1039–63, from Gwynedd and Powys. There is a certain similarity with the Bretwaldas in England, which stopped short at the fissiparous mode of succession. It was Hywel Dda, son of Cadell, who is credited with framing or codifying the traditional laws of the people. By contast with the development of law in England, the laws were aimed more at conciliation than at penalties and punishment. The rulers, and no less the chieftains subject to them, were quarrelsome and turbulent among themselves. Hywel, however, was a frequent visitor to the English courts and, in 928, even made the pilgrimage to Rome, whither, it was claimed in later centuries, he took the laws to have them blessed by the Pope. It has been shown recently that they contained elements of mercy, common sense and respect for the rights of women and children which were lacking in the law of England until quite recently.

Gruffudd ap Llywelyn fought for many years against Harold, Earl of Wessex. When he was killed by treachery in 1063, Harold replaced him by his uncles, Bleddyn and Rhiwallon, and himself married Gruffudd's widow, Ealdgyth, who thus was Queen both of Wales and of England after Harold's election in 1066. After the Conquest William the Conqueror paid no immediate attention to Wales, until tribal squabbling and raids forced it. In 1081 he visited Wales in person, carrying out a reconnaissance which reached as far as St David's. He realised that he must secure his frontier. By 1088 three palatine counties had been erected between the Earldom of Mercia and the Welsh, at Chester, Montgomery and Hereford. The counts palatine and the marcher barons were awarded such lands as they were able to conquer. By the end of the eleventh century no less than 500 motte-and-bailey castles had been built, of timber and earth, being replaced by stone castles after 1110.

William II's expedition into Wales was a failure, for the heavily armoured Normans could not keep pace with the nimble Welsh in their mountains. Henry I planted Flemish colonists in Dyfed; in 1136 the Welsh repelled them, killing thousands in battle near Cardigan. In 1137 Gruffudd ap Cynan of Gwynedd died, 'sovereign and protector and peacemaker of all Wales', and was succeeded by his son Owen. He reigned for thirty-three years until 1169. In Deheubath Rhys ap Gruffudd did homage to Henry II of England in 1171. In 1176 he held a historic bardic entertainment in Cardigan Castle, at which the poets and harpists of Gwynedd and Deheubath competed in friendly rivalry. With his death his principality ceased to have any importance, and Wales was united under the Princes of Gwynedd. They considered themselves sovereign and independent, owing only personal allegiance to the English king. In 1206 Llywelyn ap Iorwerth of Gwynedd strengthened his position by marrying Joan, the illegitimate daughter of King John of England, reigning for forty-four years from 1194–1240. It was her blood which was of account, not her illegitimacy. His heir, Dafydd, was solemnly presented to all his vassals at an assembly held at the Cistercian Abbey of Strata Florida in 1238.

Dafydd died in 1244, and the succession passed to the three sons of his uncle Gruffudd, Owen, Llywelyn and David: Dafydd. Of these, Llywelyn was the most popular, celebrated extravagantly by the bards. Like many of his forebears, he was turbulent and rash, and imprudent enough to be hostile to the Prince Edward, the future Edward I. He had been created Earl of Chester. In 1273 he proposed a marriage with Eleanor de Montfort, Simon de Montfort's daughter, and in the following year declined to attend Edward I's coronation as a vassal. It was not customary for independent sovereigns to attend the coronation of others. For all that, in 1276 Edward I entered Wales, and made Llywelyn submit to the treaty of Conway. By now he had learnt prudence, and his marriage to Eleanor de Montfort was agreed. Nevertheless it was distasteful to Edward I. The wedding was celebrated in Worcester Cathedral with great pomp in 1278.

It was a time of discontent in Wales, and in 1281 Prince David turned against his brother Llywelyn. In 1282 David attacked and burnt Hawarden Castle without warning, and had all Wales up in arms. Edward was furious, and came to Wales with an army. While Edward was campaigning, Llywelyn was killed in a skirmish on 11 December. His head was brought to Edward, who had it exhibited wreathed in ivy. He was mocking a bardic prediction that one day a Welsh prince would be crowned in London. David III now carried on the princely line, fighting in the mountains of Snowdonia. Eventually he was captured, but died at Shrewsbury in 1283. In 1293 Llywelyn's natural son attempted to raise the Welsh again, but was soon captured, ending his life in the Tower of London.

Edward now reorganised Wales on the English model. It was to be wholly Anglicised, and obedient to English law. In 1284 Queen Eleanor gave birth to a son, later Edward II, in Caernarvon Castle. The story that Edward I presented his infant son to the Welsh as their future prince is without foundation. He was not created Prince of Wales and Earl of Chester until 7 February 1301. Although Welsh national feeling was to emerge again from time to time, and Welsh families, claiming princely descent, took pride from their ancestry, there is little to show for it.